COMPREHENSIVE EDUCATION: EVOLUTION, ACHIEVEMENT AND NEW DIRECTIONS

Comprehensive education was and is designed to provide the highest standards of education for **every** young person, not just for a privileged sector of society.

'We can't afford to write off children after six years of schooling. The worst start any child can have in life is to be branded a failure.'

Tony Blair, 2000

First published February 2006
by The University of Northampton
Northampton NN2 7AH

Typeset in Frutiger
by Stanley L. Hunt (Printers) Ltd
Printed and bound by Stanley L. Hunt (Printers) Ltd

Copies of the book are available from
CSCS (Centre for the Study of Comprehensive Schools)
Moulton College
Moulton
Northampton NN3 7RR
Tel: 01604 492337

ISBN 1900 868 490

COMPREHENSIVE EDUCATION: EVOLUTION, ACHIEVEMENT AND NEW DIRECTIONS

The search for high quality education for all

INTRODUCTION

This book is a timely contribution to the debate on the evolving nature of post-war English education now focusing on the White Paper of October 2005 which reflects significant changes in nine years of New Labour Government. The debate – inside and outside Parliament – which will run through until Spring 2006, is about the nature of comprehensive education. In speaking about the White Paper, Secretary of State for Education, Ruth Kelly (18 November 2005), rejected any return to selection. 'There will be fair admissions. There will be no free-for-all. And there will not be a return to selection by ability – by the front door, back door, or any other door.' The Prime Minister writes in his introduction to the White Paper of, 'energising comprehensive education' and retaining the comprehensive principle of non-selection and harks back to impetus for reform coming from middle-class parents dissatisfied with standards in secondary schools and fearful of the stigma of secondary modern schools (the inevitable corollary of having grammar schools).

The White Paper endorses comprehensive principles, of which overall effectiveness, fairness, equal opportunity and social justice are central. At the same time it seeks to take forward preceding New Labour reforms which have emphasised choice, diversity, specialisation and greater independence for schools which it is assumed will further energise the school system. But the White Paper according to former Secretary of State Estelle Morris, 'is very confusing'. There is apparent uncertainty about the best way forward to achieve the 'equity and excellence' central to the political rhetoric, the unexceptionable aims of which are to provide the widest opportunities and highest standards for all learners – of every ability and social class. But policies in many cases seem to run counter to the rhetoric. Greater independence for schools in regard to their internal management, curriculum and pedagogy is widely welcomed but there is serious concern, as expressed for example by the 'Compass Group' of MPs, that freedom over admissions will lead to greater disparity between schools and further disadvantage the already disadvantaged. However idealistic schools may be they are generally disinclined to make life difficult for themselves and to harm their reputation by going out of their way to recruit difficult and low achieving students. The Compass Group (January 2006) recommends adoption of a Code of Practice which schools are statutorily required to follow to ensure a fair, efficient, non-selective admissions policy.

This book, required reading for all seriously concerned with the future of English education, sheds light on hotly debated issues. For example, do variety and choice enlarge and equalise opportunity or promote disparity, giving relative advantage to parents who are aware of opportunities and have the wherewithal to exercise choice? Will increased parent influence advocated in the White Paper exacerbate inequality and injustice? Are faith schools compatible with the term 'comprehensive'? Are all sections of the population, especially the disadvantaged, given a fair deal? These are questions of relevance to people of all political persuasions, left, centre and right. While we are currently focusing on the debate surrounding the Government's White Paper, we are aware of the likelihood of education having a higher profile following the election of David Cameron as Conservative leader: on his first day in office he talked about social justice. He said he wanted no return to grammar schools. But what about existing secondary modern and grammar schools? What about the extensive overt and covert selection within the comprehensive system? As the Conservative Party repositions itself and embarks on a period of intensive thought he will hopefully want his team to have intelligent, informed views on all the issues discussed in this book which provides comment and evidence on vitally important questions.

The emphasis is on evidence. The book originated in papers delivered at a seminar series held in 2003 at the University of Oxford Department for Educational Studies under the aegis of Professor Richard Pring and supported by CSCS (Centre for the Study of Comprehensive Schools) and CASE (Campaign for State Education). The many who attended the series, mainly academics and senior staff in schools, did not travel from afar to listen to political rhetoric. The series sought to provide clarifying light not obfuscating heat. Speakers were not invited because of their known predilection for comprehensive education. A pro-comprehensive political rally it most certainly was not, though some contributors put their case with a degree of feeling – where, for example, it was perceived that political expedience had interfered with rational process.

The expectation was that speakers would give their considered views, to present evidence whether or not it supported the comprehensive case; to present it fairly and to recognise and acknowledge where there may be awkward questions which need honest answers to the extent, in at least one case, of challenging the audience as to whether they fully appreciated what comprehensive really means. Having said this, it would be idle to deny that the overall balance of the chapters is in favour of comprehensive education. But that would be deemed a result of the weight of evidence presented, the clarity and common sense of the a priori reasoning and the absence of any adequately argued rationale for selective education.

Lest any reader thinks that the arguments have been presented, wrapped and parcelled, what emerges from the chapters is a questioning spirit – a desire to get at the essence of the issues, to weigh evidence, to provide ideas to take education forward, reflecting a recognition that our educational system does not at present provide excellence and equity and leaves many young people deprived of what all contributors would feel should be their entitlement.

The book, a rich resource of research and ideas covers considerations ranging from philosophy, rationale and political theory to discussion of practical problems. Though we have grouped the chapters into four general themes, they are not entirely discrete; inevitably our contributors touch on a range of issues, most obviously the rationale of comprehensive education in providing the context of their arguments. In regard for example to defining comprehensive education, though there is one chapter with that title, almost all contributors shed light on what they feel are the essential characteristics of comprehensive education.

Philosophical, Political and Historical Context

David Miliband in Chapter 1, 'A Social Democratic Education Settlement', argues against 'a determinism that says education is doomed to perpetrate social and economic disadvantage and against the voluntarism that says Government should withdraw and allow market forces to drive change... Government intervention can make a difference; it can make most difference to those who need it most'. The paper is of interest not just for its thoughtful context but for the very fact that it represents an attempt to set out a rationale for policy – something relatively rare at government level. Miliband refers to a vision of educational purpose and practice incorporating a drive to equalise life chances so that all may have an opportunity to lead a full life as democratic citizens.

Referring to the ineffectuality of post-war reform, reflecting complacent acceptance of social assumptions, producing a policy which was loaded against the working classes, he notes that through the 1950s the comprehensive case gathered strength driven as much by inequities of the selective system as by any compelling inclusive vision.

The decline of selection and the progressive introduction of comprehensive education has seen standards rise across the board and Miliband notes that there has been no support from parents for a return to selection. He quotes Ernest Bevin in the 1940s, 'the greatest poverty is poverty of aspiration', which leads the disadvantaged to assume that things can't change. Arguably such assumptions remain endemic in English society manifest in social immobility which may be measured by the fact that a child born into Social Class 1 is thirty-two times more likely than a child in Social Class 7 to end up as an adult in Social Class 1.

In Chapter 2 **Roy Hattersley** asks, 'Does New Labour believe in Comprehensive?' Inevitably there is a gap between theoretical aspiration and reality. (New Labour has introduced an impressive range of policies directed towards improving the quality of education in England, especially for the disadvantaged: for example SureStart, Excellence in Cities, Education Action Zones, Every Child Matters.) But there is a lack of clarity about the purpose and function of reform ostensibly designed to vitalise and reform comprehensive education by offering choice, variety and differentiation but in reality designed to woo the floating Conservative voter. The effects of these reforms - specialist schools, which allow some selection of students, faith schools, increased parental choice and a failure to grasp the nettle of selection in authorities which retain grammar and secondary modern schools - have been to emphasise division, exacerbate differences bringing about a hierarchy of schools whose quality of intake, and thus success, differ markedly. These differences become embedded in the public mind through league tables which add to the practical problems of disadvantaged schools by burdening them with the stigma of failure. All this while cynically denigrating comprehensive schools, for example, through the notorious 'bog standard' jibe. Hattersley addressed these problems in his lecture. It offers fascinating insights into sad realities of the political process.

In Chapter 3, 'A Brief History of Comprehensive Education in England and Wales', the progress and the problems of comprehensive education are traced by **Ken Fogelman** who provides a substantial, indeed masterly, contribution to the book by mapping the origins, development and recent evolution of the comprehensive movement in England and Wales.

In Chapter 4, 'The Road Not Taken: Deconstructing the 1960s, the Formative Decade', **Harry Judge** argues that the development of comprehensive education in the 1960s was not born out of egalitarian, romantic idealism as has subsequently been misrepresented, but out of deep rooted public disillusionment with the selective system. There were hard-fought political battles which endeavoured (not wholly successfully) to reconcile conflicting aims of parity of esteem between the independent and state sectors. Many argued that comprehensive schools would create greater disparity of esteem vis-à-vis the independent sector. It proved difficult, arguably impossible, to reconcile the 'unhappy bedfellows' of equality, diversity and choice, bedfellows still jostling each other fifty years later in 2006.

Arguments about comprehensive education did not split along obvious party lines: many on the left argued for grammar schools as the route out of disadvantage (especially in Wales now perceived as possessing the soul of the comprehensive movement). No wonder there was a fudge as Crosland issued the celebrated circular 10/65 which 'requested' rather than 'required' local authorities to submit plans for (comprehensive) secondary education. We are heirs to a decision (which in 2006 leaves 15% of the population in selective systems) in hindsight arguably too cautious. But we must perhaps not judge the past too harshly.

In Chapter 5, 'Comprehensive Schools: Continuing the Success Story', **John Dunford**, reflecting on twenty-eight years in comprehensive education in different roles, emphasises the imperative of celebrating the success of comprehensive education. As evidenced by other contributors to this book, comprehensive systems perform better than selective systems, even taking examination results as the measure, and of course the value of comprehensive education is far more than examination results.

Observing that the comprehensive idea has been adopted more fully and with greater commitment in Wales and Scotland, Dunford regrets that in England we seem bedevilled by a predilection to **divide**: into better and worse, selective and state, O level and CSE, now GCSE, with tiers, academic and vocational. Moreover there has been acceptance by Government of judgments (for example by league tables and Ofsted inspectors) which militate against schools in disadvantaged circumstances and which then misinform public debate and parents who make consequent choices which further damage disadvantaged schools. We need accountability but it must be intelligent and not suffocating or misleading. We need to recognise that once abolished, no selective system has been reintroduced – because parents do not want it and for good reason. But, despite evidence that shows that comprehensive systems are more successful than selective, one sixth of students in England are educated in selective systems; and more students are attending grammar schools than in 1997. We must beware covert selection through competition and parental choice, and specialist schooling; there has been at various times talk of ladders - and more bizarrely escalators - of schools, beacon schools, advanced schools/leading-edge schools. We all want progress and development, eg through federations and collegiates (see Hewlett and Brighouse) towards the twin goals of excellence and equity but at government level there is little sense of clear vision.

And we need to think more carefully – more comprehensively - about the curriculum (linked to an appropriate assessment system) which has languished for want of a coherent model – an issue taken up in the last two chapters. Why was Tomlinson set aside? Political fudge? There are times when the educational, social and economic needs of young people must take precedence over party political advantage.

Research into Comprehensive and Selective Systems and Their Effects

In Chapter 6, 'Achievement and Inclusion in Comprehensive Education', **Geoff Whitty** starts by referring to findings published in *Education and the Middle Class,* Open University Press 2003, which tracks academically able populations at elite independent, grammar and comprehensive schools. The average A level subject grades were 7.7, 7.2 and 6.5 respectively (findings confirmed by Jesson 05). 'At first sight these findings might not seem a great advertisement for comprehensive education but if you analyse the context and resources available what is notable is how small the differences are.' The results of research (Crook, Power, Whitty, Jesson, and NFER) together constitutes a remarkable testament to the academic success of comprehensive schools.   In many cases comprehensive schools outperformed grammar and independent schools academically, ie quite apart from the immeasurable social and cultural benefits of comprehensive education. Whitty discusses growing disparities between different types of schools (grant maintained, specialist schools, etc) and consequent growing social polarisation. Does the Government recognise what a huge task it will be to increase the absolute and relative achievement of disadvantaged groups? He discusses a range of problems embedded in our education system. Referring to the importance of the need for a 'critical mass of able students' and associated parental support and aspiration he comments on the damage done to the state comprehensive sector by parents opting out, either to private schools, grammar schools or elite comprehensives.

Noting that advocates of comprehensive education have never denied the importance of diversity to cater for learners of different abilities and interests, there is concern that diversity appears to be creating a divisive hierarchy of schools. To avoid this, collaboration – for example through Brighouse's collegiates backed by the necessary funding required to compensate disadvantages - will have to be promoted and supported.

Stephen Gorard in Chapter 7, 'The Impact of School Diversity', addresses the effects of school diversity. He challenges advocates of diversification of secondary schools who erroneously claim that:

- increased diversification does not lead to increased segregation of students between schools;

- the new school types, including academies, specialist schools etc, driving diversification produce higher levels of student attainment (with equivalent intakes) than their predecessors.

He demonstrates that neither claim can be shown to be true. Evidence shows that diversification tends to lead to increased student segregation without producing overall improvement in results. Diversification is not only pointless but harmful (ref the importance to schools of having a critical mass of able students). Gorard concludes by noting that examination results are an inadequate measure of school achievement; the value of a comprehensive school education is to foster wider societal understanding and responsible citizenship.

In Chapter 8, 'Secondary School Admissions: Exploring the Extent of Overt and Covert Selection', **Ann West, Audrey Hind** and **Hazel Pennell** examine secondary school admission criteria. They reveal that a variety of criteria are used to select certain groups of students and exclude others. These criteria range from schools which exercise responsible 'social justice' criteria to a small but not insignificant minority, notably those with greater freedom to take responsibility for their own admissions, who use opaque and questionable selection criteria.

The degree of selection by schools is almost certainly to be greater than emerges from the research findings presented here. Inferences may be drawn from the fact that 11.4% of children at Church of England schools, 6.2% for Jewish and 6.5% for Sikh schools were eligible for free school meals compared with a national level of 16.1% for all the maintained secondary schools. The author concludes that 'Legislation now requires co-ordinated admissions arrangements, both within and between LEAs. This calls into question the whole issue of schools retaining the role as their own admissions authorities' (House of Commons 2003 p 35). More radical steps may well be needed to deliver an admissions system to parents that is fair and equitable, contributing to overall benefit.

In Chapter 9, 'Using National Value-added Datasets to Explore the Effects of School Diversity', **Ian Schagen** and **Sandie Schagen** describe the use of value added data sets to explore the effects of school diversity. They note the value of the mass of data now available (for 380,000 pupils in 3044 schools in 149 LEAs) at key stage 2, key stage 3 and key stage 4 to consider a range of variables which could affect the results. After describing their methodology they present findings which include the following:

- overall differences at GCSE level between selective and comprehensive LEAs in value added terms are very small;
- specialist schools performed above the norm;
- Jewish schools performed significantly well on six out of seven outcomes;
- borderline pupils who narrowly obtained a grammar school place obtain better GCSE results than pupils of equal prior attainment at comprehensive schools;
- pupils of higher prior attainment (eg key stage 2 level greater than 5) may perform better in comprehensive schools.

The researchers observed that they had not looked at the possible reasons for these results, eg the higher funding and selective nature of specialist schools and the low proportion of children with English as an additional language in church schools.

In their talk they also acknowledged that though the existence of rich data was valuable, comprehensive education was more than test and examination results.

David Jesson, in Chapter 10, examines 'Performance of Pupils and Schools in Selective and Non-selective Local Authorities'. There are fifteen LEAs considered by Ofsted to be fully selective. Jesson's starting point was the 2001 White Paper, *Schools Achieving Success.* 'The selection system clearly failed to meet the needs of all children and the talents of many were not recognised. Comprehensive schools overcame the ill effects of rigid selection and have done a great deal to improve opportunity.'

In April 2000 the DfEE 'showed that as far as the most able pupils were concerned those in comprehensive schools did at least as well, if not better, than those in grammar schools' undermining superficial conclusions reached by those who perceive grammar schools heading the annual league tables (as they inevitably do).

Jesson observes, 'Worrying signs are emerging suggesting that all may not be well in schooling in selective areas:

- selective areas have proportionately more failing schools;
- 'schools facing challenging circumstances' are represented at double the level in selective areas despite the selective areas serving socio-economically advantaged areas;
- rates of improvement are in general slower in selective areas;
- evidence suggests that the performance of secondary modern schools – which perforce exist alongside grammar schools - lags behind that of students of similar prior attainment in comprehensive schools. Jesson notes the misnomer of 'comprehensive' for secondary schools in areas with grammar schools (as Rhodes Boyson observed as far back as 1980).

Quoting Gorard, Jesson says, 'The future for selective systems of secondary school organisation must now be seriously in doubt' and if education is to continue to play its historic role in breaking down divisions between different sectors of society, retaining selective systems does not appear to be a constructive choice.

In Chapter 11, 'Selection, Diversity and Inequality in Secondary Education', **Tony Edwards** and **Sally Tomlinson** take issue with current pressures to increase selection overtly or covertly. The evidence they review indicates that:
- the private sector is the main source of selective unequal opportunity;
- grammar schools do not provide better for able children;
- selective systems depress standards overall;
- parental choice has intensified resource differences between schools;
- government policies promoting differentiation produce inequality.

They criticise Labour's retention of complex balloting procedures (which de facto support selection despite rhetoric to the contrary - see also Tulloch, Chapter

13). They note a 20% increase in admissions to grammar schools and comment that leaving grammar schools to survive encourages the view that comprehensives are inherently second best.

They draw attention to comparative international PISA data which show that the most successful systems are the most comprehensive. They tackle the issue of covert selection which occurs as a result of parents availing themselves of access to favoured schools where the 'critical mass' of able children and supportive parents is achieved. They particularly noted covert selection by church schools. Increased selection exacerbates problems of disadvantaged schools.

They end with a set of policy alternatives to enable achievement of a fairer and more effective system. Everyone claims to want 'equity and excellence'. Government policy is arguably slowing if not reversing progress to these ends.

In Chapter 12, ' Are children being set up to fail? Discrimination Against Racial Minorities', **David Gillborn** describes how black children are condemned to a second-rate education in a two tier system which sees teachers contributing (passively not deliberately) to a self-fulfilling prophecy of low achievement which reflects low aspirations and cultural deprivation. The Government's strategy has nothing to say about racism. He argues that a 'colour-blind' policy can have racist effects and that schools are inactive on race equality; at best they are too busy, at worst complacent. We have a comprehensive system which provides neither equity nor excellence.

Obstacles to Ending Selection

In Chapter 13, 'Grammar Schools: Can Parents Decide? How the (Labour) Government is protecting selective education', **Margaret Tulloch** dissects policies which block the stated aims of New Labour's First Term Election manifesto published in *Diversity and Excellence* 1995. Many had assumed that a Labour Government would finally abolish selection in the authorities where secondary modern and grammar schools (166 in 1997) existed. 'We are implacably opposed to a return to selection by eleven plus. Labour's commitment to comprehensive education means ensuring that every child in every school has available the highest possible education thus avoiding the division which segregation inevitably brings. Our opposition to segregation is clear. But while we have never supported grammar schools... change can only come through local agreement... following a clear demonstration of support for parents affected by such decisions.'

But the policy had shifted by 1997 to, 'Any change in the character of a particular (grammar) school should only be agreed by a ballot of all parents affected by such a decision'. The Government's position on existing grammar schools/secondary moderns had become at best neutral.

Tulloch describes the Ripon Grammar School case study where, for example, 25% of the voters were parents of children in private schools, many were parents in a school ten miles away while some Ripon parents could not vote. De jure there was a neutral if complex procedure; de facto, because of the confused and unfair balloting procedure which makes it virtually impossible to get rid of secondary moderns and grammar schools, government policy protected selective education.

In Chapter 14, 'Northern Ireland: How Comprehensive Education has been Opposed', **Niall McCafferty** disposes of the notion promulgated in the right-wing press that Northern Ireland exemplifies the academic success of selective systems. He starkly portrays the socio-economic divide between the favoured intake of the grammar schools (80% from professional background) and the secondary moderns. Only 8% of grammar places go to pupils in the Register General's scale bottom categories (4 and 5); only 2% of children in Greater Shankhill are selected for grammar school. The existing system protects an ossified social structure in which the poor are denied opportunity.

What is Comprehensive Education: Broadening the Perspective

Comprehensive education is more than comprehensive schools. **Mark Hewlett**'s paper, 'Defining Comprehensive Education', Chapter 15, arose from a CSCS consultation with Andrew Adonis about how to reconcile comprehensive education with specialisation. The answer lies in looking beyond the boundary of the individual comprehensive school to the wider community and mobilising all the resources available in a locality, for example the resources of three or four secondary schools and their feeder school families, further education, higher education, local clubs, societies, businesses, faith groups in what he describes as a comprehensive learning community – a model now being taken up in some leading-edge federations with highly developed extended schooling through which it is possible to enrich provision available to all young people. Hewlett argues that we need a more comprehensive vision of what education is and where it takes place. We place limits on what we can achieve by restricting our educational efforts to the small amount of time that students spend in school. (Only15% of the waking hours of a student in 'full-time' education).

In Chapter 16, 'Collegiality: the Way Forward', **Tim Brighouse** whose experience as CEA runs across a range of environments from rural in Oxfordshire to inner city in Birmingham and London, goes as far as to say, 'I argued that the comprehensive ideal had... except in a few environments... not been realised.... The time had come to stop chasing a comprehensive school mirage but to think again what we mean by secondary education. It was clear that no secondary school alone could meet all educational needs of all their people'. A strong supporter of comprehensive ideas, Brighouse articulates a set of conditions that should be met to provide pupils with a quality comprehensive experience. He proposes the Collegiate Academy, a co-ordinated group of schools of varied type including faith schools and further and higher education providers. 'Diversity, equality and choice can co-exist.'

In Chapter 17, on multi-faith schools, **Richard Pring** addresses the increasingly contentious issue of whether faith schools have a place in a comprehensive system. The teaching and ethos in faith schools can enrich moral, aesthetic and political understanding; they can protect independent views, help maintain distinctive perspectives which enrich our culture, and there are important legislative and human rights issues involved. Faith schools' existence should depend on the extent to which they eschew indoctrination, prevent social and cultural fragmentation and guard against selection which protects social privilege. The practical answer lies in looking at the idea of a comprehensive system rather than individual comprehensive schools.

In Chapter 5 Dunford drew attention to Government failure to give proper attention to curriculum. In Chapter 18, 'A Comprehensive Curriculum', **Mark Hewlett** argues that the term comprehensive should apply to the curriculum in the sense that a curriculum should be a full, complete, balanced reflection of aims – as stated by schools and by Government. We are heirs to a legacy of a curriculum deemed suitable for a highly selective group of pupils in the nineteenth and earlier centuries which is inappropriate to meeting the (comprehensive) needs of all young people in a fast developing and challenging world. Starting from first principles he presents a curriculum which derives from aims and suggests a comprehensive rethink of what we are offering young people, both the gifted and talented, currently offered an undemanding, fragmented 'two dimensional' curriculum and equally unsuitable for those from disadvantaged backgrounds who are further disadvantaged by a curriculum largely irrelevant to their economic, social and moral needs.

Richard Pring, currently directing the Nuffield Review of 14-19 education and training in England and Wales, in Chapter 19, ' Education and Training 14-19: Comprehensive Provision', further develops this theme: 'For many the experience of education has meant little more than failure and deselection.'

The Nuffield Review exposes the absence of serious fundamental thinking about educational aims and consequences. Politicians and officials are trapped in an impoverished language of debate exemplified by the continued use of the spurious and damaging distinction between academic and vocational. The key question is, 'What counts as an educated nineteen year old in this day and age?' A simple mechanistic answer won't do. Training for a vocation is important but the fuller answer must reflect the kinds and qualities of achievements which constitute the kind of life worth living: what knowledge and understanding, what qualities and virtues, what social competences are needed for all young people, but especially for the not inconsiderable proportion who fail in school and reject learning which in many cases means rejecting the society they live in. We do not have an inclusive system of education in our country: we should return to those values which created the comprehensive ideal.

We hope that in presenting a multi-dimensional set of perspectives on comprehensive education, we can through this book enrich the quality of debate about education and thus improve the quality of education offered to all young people – of all abilities, aptitudes, interests and talents. We are travelling along a road hopefully to a better world, perhaps to a holy grail. Taking Harry Judge's metaphor from Robert Frost, faced with choosing different roads, we hope that this contribution will provide a map to help the professional educator and the political policymaker avoid the fate of the traveller who subsequently regrets having taken the wrong road.

Mark Hewlett, Richard Pring, Margaret Tulloch

1 A SOCIAL DEMOCRATIC EDUCATION SETTLEMENT

David Miliband, former Minister for Schools

The historian Peter Clarke divided 19th and early 20th century progressives into two camps: moral reformers and mechanical reformers. Moral reformers, taking their cue from Gladstone, aimed to change minds rather than remedy wrongs. Meanwhile mechanical reformers, perhaps best epitomised in the Fabian tradition, focussed on changing conditions, concerning themselves with practical reform not grandiose appeals to human idealism.

My belief is that successful, progressive educational reform requires moral purpose and mechanical efficiency, change of culture as well as change of structures and policies. My aim today is to persuade you that the Government elected in 1997 is pursuing this combination, and should be seen as the first serious attempt to build a social democratic education settlement in England's schools and colleges.

In this I will argue against the determinism that says education is doomed to perpetuate social and economic disadvantage, and against the voluntarism that says Government should withdraw and allow market forces alone to drive educational change. Not only does school matter, it matters most to those in greatest need; and not only can government intervention make a difference, it can make most difference to those who need it most.

What do I mean by a 'social democratic education settlement'? It is more than a set of policies. It is an attempt to embed new and enduring parameters for education policy, based on social democratic values. Specifically a social democratic education settlement must contain:

- a vision of educational purpose and practice based on the ambition of full and democratic citizenship for all, with curriculum, assessment and qualifications to match
- a commitment to teaching as a powerful, thinking and developing profession, with power devolved and accountability accepted
- a strategy to equalise life chances by tilting against inequality, spreading excellence and improving standards through innovation and collaboration
- sufficient funding, devolved to the school level and allocated according to need; I will not have time to address this today but the infusion of funds to schools between 1997 and 2005/6 – the most sustained rise in a generation, among the largest rises in European history – is a much needed corrective to neglect of educational investment by both parties
- and finally an understanding that culture matters as well as structure, and the dominant culture needs to support educational advance.

Equal worth. Active learning. Informed professionalism. Record resources. High expectations. These are the foundations of a new education settlement. The ultimate test is not that they hold firm for a few months, or even two Parliamentary terms, but that they endure. This is our ambition and this is what I want to set out today.

The First Social Democratic Education Settlement

I know I am surrounded by experts on our educational history. I therefore venture gingerly onto historical terrain. But for me, post-war educational history presents a paradox. On the one hand, substantial advance. On the other hand, missed opportunities.

Especially since the progressive introduction of comprehensive education, standards have risen across the board and notably for girls. And notwithstanding the diversity of circumstance, between the comprehensive in the market town and the comprehensive battling against the odds in the inner city, there has been no support from parents for a return to the status quo ante. Yet despite this progress, 50% of young people still leave secondary school without 5 good GCSEs. On other measures there is significant wasted potential.

I think four particular aspects of the reform story are noteworthy in explaining this evidence.

First, a recognition that education was the most ineffectual part of the war-time consensus and post-war settlement.

Ineffectual because although the 1944 Education Act raised the school leaving age, and made fee-charging illegal in state-funded schools, it was very much Butler's Act. His view, set out in 1943 in the debate on the Education White Paper, personified the complacency that bedevilled post-war education policy. He argued that fundamental change was unnecessary. He compared the inter-war education system to a "schoolboy's jacket", which had given wonderful service but was in danger of giving way to wear and tear. This patch and mend philosophy was no basis for a system in need of serious reform.

Complacent because the tripartite system was in fact loaded against children from working class backgrounds. There remained pervasive respect for genetic theories about the distribution of ability. The distribution of grammar school places across the country was arbitrary, and the schools funding system ensured that secondary moderns were consistently under-resourced. Yet the new Government after 1945 seemed to shrug its shoulders about all this, accepting that except for the few who made it through to grammar schools, 'poor would indeed mean worse'. Education hardly figured in Attlee's subsequent and often heroic social and economic reforms. It returned to the backwaters under Churchill, Macmillan and Home. Education thus became the great lost opportunity of the post-war settlement.

Butler's Act did not however extinguish the spark of reform. The dream of comprehensive schooling remained alive and progressively established itself as the social democratic prescription for schooling. As the 1950s unfolded, the comprehensive case gathered strength, driven as much by the vagaries and inequities of the selective system as through its own compelling vision of the future. In this second phase of reform, the growing comprehensive movement embodied important ideals: inclusion, aspiration, equality. But it was far clearer about what it was against – selective admissions and the 11 plus - than what it was for. Discussion of the curriculum was a second order question behind admissions; the idea of curriculum 'entitlement' in the form of the National Curriculum came thirty years too late. Meanwhile the organisation and experience of teaching and learning came a poor third.

This restricted notion of comprehensive education was then ill-served by the highly diffuse and variegated English education system of the time, a system which allowed mediocrity to flower alongside genius, and allowed rank failure to go unchallenged – all in the name of local autonomy. The result was what can only be described as 'disorganised idealism'. There was some fantastic innovation in the 1960s and 1970s – for example the Humanities Curriculum Project and Nuffield Science. I remember myself being put in a pioneering SCISP science class. But, while policy development was good, dissemination was poor. Training and retraining of teachers to spread good practice was weak, so some teachers were not ready for new demands, and where comprehensive pioneers built excellent practice, there were only the weakest means for these breakthroughs to become a general advance.

The strength of comprehensive pioneers in the 60s and 70s helped the new system establish itself. But even as it did so, backward-looking assumptions about the nature of the economy delayed its further advance. And the debate was conducted in a vacuum – the English business community, troubled enough with maintaining its own position in the face of fierce competitive pressures, neither made its voice heard in education debates nor made its contribution significant in education reform. We have neither the structured engagement between school and work of the German system, nor the diverse offers within a unified system of the French, American or Scandinavian systems. To this day, secondary education remains a series of hurdles to be overcome not a ladder to be climbed; vocational education remains undervalued; the academic track, notwithstanding the positive gains from AS Level, remains too narrow.

The fourth aspect of this chronicle is critical. The decade after Jim Callaghan's Ruskin speech was all but wasted. It is telling that after all the hoopla of the great Ruskin 'debate', the introduction to the party's 1979 manifesto, signed by Jim Callaghan and setting out the five priorities for the party, did not mention education.

There was no compelling Labour vision for the proper nature of secondary education and the ball again passed to the Conservatives. Although the Baker Reform Act included important innovations, it had a missing heart beat. The Tory flagships were about escape, not reform. The Assisted Places Scheme encouraged parents to opt-out of the state system. Grant Maintained Status sponsored innovation but isolation. The National Curriculum prescribed subject content and assessment arrangements in huge detail. But there was very little talk and still less action on the quality of teaching and learning, and there was shamefully no organised concern with truancy, suspensions and other manifestations of disaffection and social exclusion. The diversity sponsored by the Conservatives was between good schools and bad schools, inequitably resourced, with a scramble for scarce places that is still unwinding.

This inheritance is why I say the successive Labour governments since 1997 are no year zero but do represent the first serious attempt to build a social democratic settlement in education. Serious about funding, serious about pedagogy, about teachers, about quality and about culture.

Aims of Education

A social democratic education settlement must have at its heart a philosophy of teaching and learning. We stand for an expansive vision of the purposes of education:

- education must transmit and develop knowledge and culture from one generation to the next, promoting respect for and engagement with learning
- education must broaden horizons and develop high expectations, especially in a country scarred by a heritage of class division and socioeconomic disadvantage
- and education must empower children and young people with the skills that will enable them to learn further throughout life and take a full part in society

Ours is, therefore, a commitment to active learning – the engagement of the mind of the pupil in an enriched range of individual, group and IT-based learning tasks that develop their range of intelligence, and which are assessed in a way that helps pupils reflect on their learning, its goals and their potential. In this way, the pupil moves centre stage. He or she ceases to become the passive recipient of knowledge – an empty vessel to be filled – but is instead an independent learner, reflective and critical, ready to play an active role in a democratic community and dynamic economy.

This drives a view of how we teach. At each stage in the educational journey, children need to be encouraged and enabled to think for themselves and with others, as well as memorise and retrieve information, whether alone or in groups. This is the philosophy behind the Key Stage 2 literacy and numeracy strategies. It is also critical, in the commitment at Key Stage 3 to active learning as the basis of pupil engagement. Our aim is to move the early secondary years from too often being seen as fallow, transitional, and sometimes dull to being a real launchpad for education at 14-plus, marked by well-paced, challenging and exciting learning.

Active learning must also be embodied in the everyday life of the school as well as in the formal curriculum. In this context, the commitment to the development of citizenship in the curriculum and in the ethos of schools is significant. At a time when people are rightly worried about popular engagement with public affairs, as measured by election turnouts and community activity, study and activity about the rights and responsibilities of citizenship is important.

The commitment to active learning applies to all children – including those with special needs. There remain major issues about early identification of needs, about the right partnership between special and mainstream schools, about the support from outside the education system, but the drive since the 1998 Programme of Action has brought significant gains.

And it must extend beyond school - at the vital pre school stage, and during the school years in the crucial time out of hours when good work in school needs to be supported.

So the pedagogic foundation for a social democratic settlement is founded on a set of clear principles applied in a range of settings. It is now, I believe, increasingly matched by a delivery strategy built on the professionalism of teachers and head teachers, rejecting the false trails of paternalistic producerism on the one hand and unrealistic consumerism on the other.

Delivery through Informed Professionalism

Our emphasis on teaching and learning puts teachers and schools centre stage. Six years ago, the main tools for reform were ambitious targets, notably in primary schools, matched by specific allocations of money.

These were important innovations. But today there is a more mature educational project, and the model of delivery has developed too. The role of central and local government has changed; so have the responsibilities of teachers.

The model of delivery now being put in place represents a shift from the top-down 'informed prescription', mainly in primary schools, of the first Parliament. It can be described as 'informed professionalism', using national action to help develop and support professional learning communities within schools in both primary and secondary phases.

There are two principal drivers of change in the system.

First the decentralisation of authority to school level, with the legal flexibility to match local provision to local need, combined with incentives for collaboration and innovation at local level. This is our commitment to the professionalism of heads, governors and front-line staff.

Our new agreement on the school workforce encourages every school to think radically about the organisation of the school day and the deployment of staff, and gives guaranteed time for every teacher to collaborate with colleagues on preparation, planning and assessment of lessons.

Our new proposals on school organisation encourage existing popular schools to expand, new schools to be set up and new promoters to establish new types of schools to meet local parental demand. Our secondary transformation plans offer federation, Academy status, innovation and investment where systemic underperformance requires a new start.

Our new proposals for capital investment encourage local people to think about new ways of organising local education, with new and different provision as appropriate.

Our proposals for 14-19 encourage innovation to bring together schools, colleges and employers.

Our Leading Edge programme gives the teaching profession the opportunity, missed at the time of the Ruskin debate, to use outstanding practice and innovation to lead education reform.

Second, allied to this decentralisation is a more intelligent accountability framework that is the basis for targeted intervention.

We make no apology for ambitious targets. They have been lacking for too long – and their absence has hit poorest students hardest. But ambitious targets are necessary but not sufficient.

The accountability framework of tests and targets must promote assessment for learning as well as assessment of learning. Assessment for learning helps pupils and teachers develop appropriate teaching and learning strategies to fulfil individual potential.

For every school there should be a rich set of data about achievement by pupils to inform the respective decisions of parents, teachers, governors and government. The purpose is to help diagnose strengths and weaknesses, set the right incentives for raising performance, and establish an informed basis not only for decisions by parents about schools but by teachers about how they help fulfil the potential of individual children and by government about how it can help add value to the quality of learning.

The introduction of value added data in secondary education is an important step forward in this respect. So is the separate publication of KS3 data. So is the publication of average points score as well as the percentage of young people getting five high GCSEs.

Parental choices offer useful indications of perceptions about school performance. But they are not enough on their own to drive improvement. Data from the front line about what and how much children are learning, and how can they be helped to learn better, demands more.

Above all it demands more from teachers and support staff. They can ensure that for every pupil there is a clear analysis of learning styles and needs, the setting of agreed targets and a well-honed teaching strategy to match.

It demands more from heads. They must ensure that from each teacher and from every department there is a clear strategy for fulfilling the potential of each child.

The data also demands something different from central and local government.

The 1944 Act called for 'a national system...locally administered'. LEAs were in the pole position, often the arbiters of the curriculum as well as school organisation. Today the 'national system...locally administered' has a different vocabulary. 'Local' means the school. The role of the LEA is to add value to the work of schools, guaranteeing places for all children, tackling issues that cross school boundaries, and above all organising pressure and support for the raising of standards in underperforming schools.

As for local government so for national government – in addition to funding, providing the right curricula and qualifications framework for learning, identifying and targeting inequalities, sponsoring innovation with intervention where the system fails. That is now my focus.

Excellence and Equity

We know that if every primary school performed at the level of the current average for its own free school meal band, then the percentage of children reading and writing well when they leave primary school would be about 5 per cent higher. That is about 29,000 children per year. And we know that if every secondary school achieved at least the average performance of its free school meal band then the percentage of young people getting five good GCSEs would also be about 5 per cent higher. Another 28,000 children.

This is the school effect. But variation in performance within schools – the teacher effect – is also striking.

The OECD PISA study reported that in the UK within-school variation in performance is about four times between school variation. This partly reflects all-ability intakes. But it also reflects the variation in effectiveness between different teachers with the same pupils.

This variance shows that in all circumstances, inspiring teachers, departments and schools can provide excellent education. The central task of government is to help everyone be as good as the best practitioners facing similar challenges. We are focussed on four priorities to do so.

First, we know outstanding leadership is the foundation of a successful school. That requires a leadership team with the shared vision to inspire and support all their staff. The National College for School Leadership is designed precisely to help effect the shift from passive and isolated management to active and collaborative leadership, including in our most challenging schools through a new Leadership Incentive Grant worth £125,000 per year for 3 years.

Second, every successful institution in the public or private sector needs a clear sense of its own distinct mission, but also an outward-facing orientation, seeking collaborators in its work. We see specialist status as increasingly the norm, not because we want schools to have a fetish about particular subjects but because we believe a clear focus in every school helps drive improvement.

This institutional focus needs to be buttressed by local collaboration to spread excellence:

- this is why the Specialist Schools Programme requires the development of networks of collaboration that spread best practice and share outstanding facilities
- it is why the Government will encourage other collaborations between institutions, many of which already exist for post-16 provision.
- it is why school Federations will be encouraged to extend beyond the confines of one school its own success
- it is why the Excellence in Cities programme, now operating in 58 LEAs and covering 1000 secondary schools, is founded on the need to organise beyond as well as within the school special provision for pupils in disadvantaged areas.

In a specialist system every school has a centre of excellence, every pupil has opportunities in and out of school to develop their talents, every teacher is able to make a distinctive contribution to the school team. It is a recognition that isolation is the enemy of improvement, collaboration often the route to it, and that in gaining the benefits of collaboration diversity is a strength not a weakness.

Third, the full use of the whole school team, with heads and governors deploying a wide range of professional people to support teachers and support pupils, is absolutely critical to raising quality and tackling inequality. We are committed as a Government to an expanding teaching profession, with at least 10,000 more teachers this parliament (Labour's second term). Their pay, training and support are all improving.

But the demands of young people, and the demands on young people, are growing. That means more demands on teachers. The way to respond is an unyielding focus on supporting their professionalism – and supporting the individual learning needs of students. So we relieve teachers of chores that do not require professional teacher status. We promote continuous professional development. We set aside time for serious collaboration with colleagues to tackle problems – whether boys underachievement or girls lack of interest in physics. And the way to deliver personalised attention for pupils is to add the skills of sports and drama coaches, language specialists and learning mentors to the leadership of the qualified teacher in the classroom.

This is an agenda that is already transforming learning in schools up and down the country; we are ready to follow their lead.

Fourth, schools need to work in strong partnership with other institutions to expand the horizons of young people:

- partnership with parents is critical on issues of discipline and aspiration
- partnerships with universities are delivering new projects for gifted and talented pupils, especially in disadvantaged areas
- partnerships with business that are delivering 11,000 mentors for head teachers and around the country many more practical opportunities to give young people the benefit of business experience and expertise
- partnerships with other agencies to deliver the extra support demanded by children in care or with other disadvantages.

These four points are then the diamond of educational reform, dedicated to raising average performance across the system by learning from the experience of best practice, and tackling inequality within schools and between schools by spreading the benefits of excellence.

For each part of the strategy, greatest help goes to those who need it most. This is 'progressive universalism' – support for all to achieve their potential, but the greatest support to those who need it most. Not just money but support. The results are striking:

There were 515 schools in special measures on coming to office. 1415 schools have passed through special measures since 1997. The current number is 274.

In 1998 more than 600 schools were below the floor target of a quarter of pupils achieving 5 or more GCSE Grades A*-C. Today that figure is about 330.

There are 655 schools classified as facing Challenging Circumstances, beyond special measures but still facing serious challenges. They benefit from a tailored package of support, including up to £70,000 in funding, and access to advice and good practice. And I am delighted that in this year's results the rate of

improvement in schools facing challenging circumstances has been about 3 times
that of other maintained mainstream schools.

The improvement in primary school performance in areas of greatest
disadvantage has been faster than the average.

And figures for last year showed a historic reduction in social class inequality
in GCSE points.

So there is progress. Not just standards rising. But standards rising fastest in our
poorest communities.

Contested Terrain

My case is not that the Government has a monopoly of wisdom. In fact, the
dynamism and passion in the debate about further reform encourages me to
believe that the new settlement being built will endure. I want to highlight three
areas in this debate.

First, we need to ensure that the drive for strength in the basics complements
a broad and balanced curriculum.

The reason for ambitious targets is that so much of a young person's future
depends on their early achievement. The figures show that 69% of 11 year olds
who reach level 4 go on to get five good GCSEs, compared to 11% for those who
leave primary school below that level. So the stakes are high. At Key Stage 3 the
figures are equally striking: hit level 6 and you are 90% likely to get five good
GCSEs, fail to achieve level 5 and less than 10% do so.

Our belief is that the basics are best achieved in the context of a school-wide
commitment to a broad and creative school experience – whether in primary
school or the early years of secondary education. The figures suggest this is now
being achieved in about 40% of primary schools and 50% of secondary schools.
We need to spread it across the system.

Second, there is a major decision for the country when it comes to education
and training at 14-plus. There can be no social democratic education settlement
while the structure of curriculum, assessment and qualifications at 14-plus fails to
promote progression and attainment for up to half the cohort.

That is why the Government has unlocked the door to far-reaching reform.
There is a growing consensus in the education world, spanning SHA, HMC and
others, that an English Baccalaureate holds out the best hope of a high
aspiration, high achievement system of curriculum, assessment and qualifications
at 14-19. We have set up the Tomlinson Working Group to test this thesis. If we
are satisfied that such a system will meet the demands of higher education and
employers, as well as the needs of young people, then we will take forward
radical reform.

Third, there remains continuing debate about admissions. This is
understandable given the role of peer groups in schools. The Government's view
is founded on some simple premises;

- that the widespread end of selection at 11 has been beneficial
- that the Crosland approach of making local decisions the focus of school
  organisation is right

- that parents must be recognised; they have the right to express preferences about the education of their children, including for faith or single sex schools; the expression of that preference can be an important signal to governors and government as they seek to embed high aspirations and high standards;

These principles are important. But in a system where variation in performance between and within schools is stark, there remain real tensions:

- about responsibility for the most difficult pupils
- about the education of newcomers to the country
- about the dangers of social polarisation
- about the frustration when parental preferences are not met, a particular problem for parents in London
- and about the rights of children outside grammar schools in selective areas.

There are clear advantages from balanced intakes to schools. But we are equally clear that, first, we cannot impose our preference on local people, second that even if we did we cannot prevent housing decisions having a major impact on admissions, and third that we must not fall into the trap of believing that a debate about admissions can substitute for a debate about educational standards, whatever the intake.

The fundamental reason is not political but educational. There are too many clear rebuttals to the determinism that says poor pupils make poor schools to allow educational advance to wait for admissions reform.

Last year, 23 secondary schools with more than one in three pupils receiving free school meals were above the national median school result for GCSE performance.

These schools can remain fragile; they need extra support, because if admissions policy does not deliver balanced intakes then funding must compensate; they can benefit enormously from partnership with other schools; but they do not need to wait for reform of the admissions system to give a good start to pupils in need.

Conclusion: Culture Matters

I want to conclude by addressing the culture of education rather than the structure. It is, after all, the mistake of mechanical reform to underestimate the importance of cultural change.

Ernest Bevin famously said that the greatest poverty was 'poverty of aspiration'. Such poverty is founded on generations of social immobility, and the pervasive sense that things can't change. It is striking in this context that a child born into social class 1 is 32 times more likely to stay there in adult life, than a child from social class 7 is to make it there. It is even more striking that relative social mobility has hardly changed in the course of a century.

A social democratic education settlement must address issues of culture and language as well as structure.

We need to engage those who say vocational education is second class – especially when medicine and law are top rank professions.

We need to engage those who say money makes no difference to education however much you spend.

We need to engage both those who say that the pursuit of excellence creates inequality, and those who argue that unless excellence is associated with inequality it means a corrosive culture of equal prizes for all.

We need to engage those outside the education system who undermine respect for knowledge and learning when they use 'too clever by half' as an insult, but we also need to engage those inside who deny the importance of knowledge transfer and spread of best practice.

And we need to engage the core philosophical division in education policy – between those who see access and excellence as opposites, and those who see them as mutually reinforcing. Since Kingsley Amis famously said 'more will mean worse' in 1953, there has been a rearguard action in the name of standards against the expansion of educational opportunity. It has hugely benefited from the confusion, highlighted last Autumn by Mike Tomlinson, about the difference between the percentage of pupils achieving a particular standard, and the maintenance of that standard.

This is a battle that we have been too slow to engage, despite the shift to predominantly criterion-referenced examination in the 1980s. It is a fundamental nonsense to believe that because more people pass the driving test the standard of driving is falling. Similarly it is only the defence of unchanging elites that says more young people achieving well is a threat to standards.

More achievement in primary schools does not mean worse: in fact the proportion of 11 year olds not just reaching level 4 but attaining reading age of 12 or 13 – level 5 – has almost doubled in five years.

More achievement at GCSE does not mean worse – for the first time in this country more than half of young people are achieving five good GCSEs.

Similarly at A Level and beyond. Excellent provision promotes excellent performance. As standards of teaching rise, and students work smarter and harder, we should expect standards to rise.

This is my kind of comprehensive system, defined not only by who each school serves – the debate about admissions – but by how all the parts of the education system serve all pupils.

Different children have different talents and different intelligences. The challenge of a social democratic education settlement is to help develop all those talents.

Today I have set out how we seek to make it happen. A distinctive philosophy of teaching and learning, founded on respect for the craft and science of teaching, and the integrity and intelligence of the learner. A willingness to beat back the determinism of social class, by decentralising power and focussing resources within a context of national standards. The promotion of innovation and diversity backed by wide-ranging professional collaboration. In other words, a true partnership between school and society, backed up by national commitment of funding that is slowly making good the underinvestment of many years.

This is a project which combines moral purpose and practical efficacy. It is a great project, and I hope you will join me in seeing it through.

2 DOES NEW LABOUR BELIEVE IN COMPREHENSIVE?

Roy Hattersley: a précis of his seminar speech, Oxford 2003

These are difficult days for comprehensive education. And they ought to be quite the reverse. It is forty years since the end of secondary selection was accepted by all the major parties as essential to the future of the country. Remember it was Sir Edward Boyle, a Conservative minister, who won applause from his party conference by saying that he would believe that secondary modern and grammar schools had "parity of esteem" when he heard of a primary school pupil being given a bicycle for not passing the eleven plus examination.

There were, of course, comprehensive schools long before the sixties. But it is during the last forty years – when they have become the most usual form of secondary education – that we have been able to assess their success. The results are unequivocal. It is the comprehensive revolution which has produced such an explosion of good A level passes that the government can no longer afford to meet the costs of higher education and requires students to take out loans to cover "top-up" fees and living costs.

It is therefore extraordinary that any government should choose to undermine the comprehensive principle. That a Labour government should do so is almost beyond belief. But we are governed not by social democrats but by right of centre Christian democrats – or at least a Christian democrat Prime Minister. David Miliband's paper on a Social Democratic Settlement is very sound but the realisation of the aims and aspirations he carefully presents appears to me to fall foul of less enlightened and more superficial thinkers.

Part of the reason why the Prime Minister, and those who follow his lead, erode the comprehensive principle by creating a hierarchy of city academies and specialist schools, defend the existence of the remaining selective schools and allow the ten per cent selection in what are nominally comprehensives, is the desire to pander to the prejudices of middle class voters in marginal constituencies who regard a grammar school place as a "positional good" which defines their superior place in society.

But the hard truth is that Tony Blair does not believe in comprehensive education. Eight years ago, after I had continually criticised the Labour Opposition's education policy, I was convinced by colleagues that I could not avoid speaking on the subject at party conference. It turned out to be what will be remembered for David Blunkett's "read my lips" promise.

There was a party, given in honour of Tony Blair the night before the debate, to which I was invited. The same friends who told me I must speak also warned me against accepting. Tony Blair, they said, would take me aside and urge me not to rock the boat. And they assumed I would spinelessly agree.

I went. He did take me aside. But rocking the boat was not mentioned. Instead he tried to convince me of the merits of selection as a means of "providing escape routes for talented pupils". Despite the weight of evidence to the contrary, the fact is the Prime Minister believes in secondary selection.

The result is the death of my hopes that, after the election of a Labour Government, comprehensive education would cease to be a subject of controversy. Instead – as an alternative to thought which might lead thinking people to reject selection – we have constantly repeated meaningless mantras. "Standards not structures" and, worse still, "One Size Doesn't Fit All". Whoever suggested that it did? Comprehensive schools have, as part of their purpose, greater diversity.

The case for comprehensive schools needs to be made clearly and uncompromisingly. Politics deals in black and white simplicities. I perceive a possible undermining of the comprehensive education amongst those thought to be its champions: respected ideologists such as Clyde Chitty and Tim Brighouse arguing for comprehensive consortia – a combination of schools (often labelled successful and unsuccessful on grounds of misleading statistical data). This risks abandoning the comprehensive ideal and concedes the field to those who espouse selection: a combination of (de facto) grammar and (de facto) secondary moderns equals comprehensive.

Too much of that argument has been based on the (highly limited) experience of the metropolitan elite who believe that London is the world or that the rest of the world is like London. In fact the London comprehensive example is an aberration. A number of secondary modern schools have had their names changed on the notice board at the gate. They have been expected to compete for pupils with grammar schools. Add to that all the problems of the capital and you realise why judging the comprehensive principle on the basis of London alone is to produce the wrong answers.

Near where I live in central Derbyshire there is a comprehensive which is a genuine comprehensive accepted by the whole community covering every conceivable social group. This school has won the hearts and minds of its public who hold it in esteem. It is worth noting that this school, because of its ideological commitment to comprehensive education in the fullest sense, does not wish to apply for specialist status - thereby depriving itself of funding it could have made excellent use of. In a rural setting with no other school within ten miles specialism would be a nonsense though the prestige of specialism – spurious though it is - and the knock-on effects to recruitment and finance might well force the school to accede to government policies.

The Prime Minister now speaks of the "post-comprehensive era". In London – not to mention Kent, Ripon and half a dozen other boroughs – the comprehensive era has yet to arrive. Those of us who know that selection is a tragedy – for the whole nation as well as the thousands of pupils who it designates as "failures" – have an urgent duty to fight for what we know to be true.

We have to be more positive about comprehensive success. We have to explain the difference between genuine comprehensive education and what often masquerades as the non-selective system. We have to describe the real benefits of the comprehensive system – without being afraid to emphasise its role in building a socially united society.

Let us focus our attention on new Labour MPs, many of whom were actually educated at comprehensive schools, and remind them why Margaret Thatcher reorganised more secondary systems than any other Secretary of State for Education. She knew that the middle classes did not want seventy-five per cent of their children to be stigmatised as failures. And remind them of what the Prime Minister said in Bedford in 2000. "The worst start that any child can have in life is to be branded a failure."

3 A BRIEF HISTORY OF COMPREHENSIVE EDUCATION IN ENGLAND AND WALES

Ken Fogelman, Professor of Education, University of Leicester, UK

Acknowledgements: This chapter draws heavily upon the work of several past colleagues and collaborators and I particularly wish to acknowledge my debt to Alan Kerckhoff, David Crook, David Reeder, Jane Steedman and Jennifer Manlove.

Introduction

The story of comprehensive education in England and Wales is a long and complex one which begins before the Second World war and continues to evolve today. The variety of school structures now in place and labelled 'comprehensive' reflects the influence of political and educational debates, local circumstances and the contribution of many important individuals, nationally and locally. In this chapter I shall attempt to outline a chronology of the major events and developments and illustrate, with some examples, how these led to particular outcomes. As will be seen, many of the assumptions and explanations offered in modern debates on this topic, for example concerning the roles of particular political parties, are at best oversimplified.

Starting Points – The 1944 Act

Although the 1944 Education Act sets the scene for the development of secondary education in England and Wales in the post-war years, this in turn reflected debate and developments which had been taking place during the inter-war years. The main issue in this period was how to extend secondary education for children older than age 11 once the school-leaving age had been raised to 14. Earlier attempts had seen this mainly as an issue of extending elementary schooling for the majority of children, but throughout the 1920s there were demands for improving the education of children after the age of 11.

Even then there were advocates of a comprehensive or, as it was more commonly termed at that time, 'multilateral' system. Small but growing support from organisations such as the Independent Labour Party, teachers' trades unions and a few local authorities, can be seen as anticipating a demand for comprehensive education in the period after the Second World War.

However, the dominant view was that any reorganisation should protect the status of grammar schools and therefore should entail separate secondary schools. For example, the most influential of the inter-war reports on education (Hadow Report, Board of Education, 1926) concluded that children's secondary education should be determined on the grounds of ability, distinguishing between academic children, who would benefit from a traditional examination-orientated education in grammar schools, and the less able, who would benefit from courses of practical instruction in what came to be called secondary modern schools.

This was reinforced some years later by the Spens Report (Board of Education, 1938), which argued that a selective examination at the age of 11 was capable of selecting 'a) those pupils who quite certainly have so much intelligence, and intelligence of such character that without doubt they ought to receive a secondary education of a grammar school type; and b) those pupils who quite certainly would not benefit from such an education' (p.379).

The main concern of the Spens Committee was to respond to growing demands for diversification of the secondary curriculum, particularly with regard to technical education. They rejected representations which were made to them for incorporating technical education into a single secondary school, and instead proposed a tripartite solution of grammar schools, technical grammar schools and secondary modern schools. However, they did concede that multilateral schools might be the right solution in sparsely populated rural areas and new housing estates.

Thus it was the tripartite system which became enshrined in the 1944 Act. The essential framework for state-maintained education was set by the examination to be taken by all children at the end of their primary schooling at age 11, from the results of which children were assigned to a secondary school: the most academically able to a grammar school; those with technical aptitude to a technical grammar school; and the remainder to a secondary modern.

Local Education Authorities were required to submit detailed development plans. However, the 1944 Act did not close the door completely on multilateral / comprehensive education and the new ministry did not specify that non-selective secondary schools would be unacceptable.

To begin to understand how matters developed subsequently it is important to appreciate the traditions and ethos of educational administration as it was at that time (and essentially remained until the 1980s). A well-known phrase described British education as being a 'national system, locally administered'. In other words, the general framework was set by national policy, but much power resided with the LEAs, who were able to determine the detail of how they interpreted and administered this. Thus, the partial permissiveness of the Act and the balance of national and local power did leave the way open for some local innovation and variation.

The Immediate Post-War Years

Before and during the war the Labour Party had been a source of support for the development of comprehensive secondary schools. For example, a resolution at the Labour Party conference in 1942 called on the Board of Education 'to encourage, as a general policy, the development of a new type of multilateral school' (see Simon, 1991). However, this was not followed through once they were in power between 1945 and 1951. The exact views and roles of Labour Education Ministers in that period have been a matter of some debate (e.g. Rubinstein, 1979), but most statements and pamphlets from them assumed the tripartite system. Indeed one Minister warned, in 1950, that 'the (Labour) Party are kidding themselves if they think that the comprehensive idea has any popular appeal' (Parkinson, 1970). Rubinstein (op cit) has argued that the movement for comprehensive education was set back by up to 20 years by the lack of political will of the post-war Labour government.

Nevertheless, it remained open for local authorities to develop their own variations. Their ability to depart from the national framework is illustrated by the fact that the tripartite system never developed as had been envisaged. Technical schools were not widely introduced - and had virtually disappeared by the 1960s (see McCulloch, 1989). Thus the dominant system was bipartite, of grammar schools for those who passed the 11+ examination (the proportions varied between areas, but averaged about 30%) and secondary modern schools for the remainder.

Nevertheless, a small number of local authorities pressed ahead with plans to establish comprehensive schools. It is not possible to characterise these authorities in any straightforward way. For example, the first experimental comprehensive schools were in rural Anglesey. Also interesting is the Isle of Man, a deeply conservative, self-governing island, which implemented an entirely comprehensive system, but without labelling it as such (one of its schools continued to be called a 'grammar school') and apparently without any conscious ideological justification (Bird, H,1995).

On the other hand, other local authorities which produced plans for comprehensive schools included cities with Labour local governments such as London and Coventry.

It might have been expected that such cautious experimentation would have been curtailed with the election in 1951 of the Conservative government which remained in power for the next 13 years. However, this did not prove to be the case.

A Changing Climate

In the event, this period proved to be one of continuing, if still cautious, experimentation, influenced by a number of factors which together amounted to increasing encouragement for the ideas of comprehensive secondary education:

1. Educationists were increasingly aware of debate and changes taking place elsewhere, particularly in Europe. Sweden is perhaps the most notable example, where, after a short period of experimentation in the 1950s, legislation was introduced in 1962 to impose a uniform pattern of comprehensive schools from age 9 to 16. There were similar developments in other Nordic countries and in France.

2. The structures established by the 1944 Act depended crucially on the 11+ examination. During the 1950s, there developed increasing dissatisfaction with the role of the 11+. First, it was seen as having a very negative influence on the curriculum in primary schools which, particularly in their later years, devoted much time to the narrow content of the examination and to practising standardised tests. Secondly, there was concern about the apparently arbitrary variation among areas of the country in the proportions which went to grammar schools. Thirdly, there was an

accumulating body of research casting doubt on the technical efficacy of the examination (e.g. Yates and Pidgeon, 1958). Fourthly, there was concern about the all or nothing nature of the 11+, which came increasingly to be seen as inconsistent with the realities of child development. Although not published until a few years later, perhaps the seminal work here was Douglas' longitudinal study of children born in 1946, which produced strong conclusions about 'wastage of talent' (Douglas, 1968).

3. In the early part of this period, the dominant view of what a comprehensive school would be was of a single school, catering for all children aged 11-18 from a particular area. This created difficulties for many local authorities. A typical grammar school would have some 800 pupils in total. As most would continue with their education to the age of 18, such schools would have a viable sixth form. In a comprehensive school, the majority of pupils could be expected to leave at 15 or 16. Thus, in order to have a viable sixth form, 11-18 schools would have to be substantially larger than secondary schools had traditionally been. This raised a number of issues, not the least of which was cost. It was possible to consider establishing a large purpose-built comprehensive school in a New Town, on a large new housing estate or in some city areas which needed to replace schools damaged during the war, but most LEAs could not realistically consider schemes which were not based on their existing, smaller, school buildings.

   However, during the 1950s and early 60s, alternative structures came to be considered which gave local authorities more flexibility. Two examples are of particular note. First there was what came to be known as the 'Leicestershire Plan' (see Jones, 1988 and 1989), which is described in more detail below. Secondly, there was increasing interest in 'sixth-form colleges'. Under this system an area would have a number of comprehensive 11-16 schools, from which all those wishing to stay on beyond 16 would transfer to a separate sixth-form college. Again, in areas where this eventually happened, it was common for 11-16 schools to be created from secondary moderns and the former grammar school to become the sixth-form college.

4. The political climate was more encouraging than might have been expected. Particularly towards the end of this period, Conservative ministers were aware of the growing dissatisfaction with the 11+, and probably more sympathetic to change than the majority of their party members (Knight, 1990). It was towards the end of the Conservative administration in 1964, that legislation removed the compulsory requirement for school transfer at the age of 11. This allowed the possibility of a further alternative structure, for which some had been arguing for some time, incorporating 'middle schools' for children aged 9-13. This option came to be seen as attractive by many local authorities as it allowed reorganisation to take place with minimal extra building work, necessitated few, if any, school closures, and allowed former grammar schools to retain their academic courses and sixth forms.

All these factors combined to encourage those local authorities which wished to do so to develop and begin to implement proposals for introducing comprehensive secondary schools. A majority did so, but in virtually all cases in relation to only a small part of the area which they administered and affecting only a relatively small proportion of schools. Between 1960 and 1965 the total number of comprehensive schools in England and Wales increased from 130 to 262, but this still represented just 8.5 per cent of the total maintained secondary school population (Simon, 1991).

Circular 10/65 and After

We now arrive at the period of greatest interest and change, following the election of a Labour government in 1964. Although comprehensive secondary education was always a highly politicised issue, views about it certainly did not divide neatly along party political lines. As mentioned, among members of the Conservative Party, particularly senior ones, there were many who were sympathetic to alternatives to selection at 11; and at the local level there were many who had experienced at first hand the frustration and anger of parents whose children had failed the 11+. Conversely, in the Labour Party there were many who valued and wished to protect their local grammar schools, often because they saw them as having been the route for social mobility for themselves and their families.

Thus it was only in 1963, one year before the election, that the Labour Party had adopted a policy to establish universal comprehensive education and to end selection by the 11+. The resolution agreed by its annual conference did not indicate any time scale for this reorganisation. Nevertheless, virtually the first act of the new Secretary of State for Education, Michael Stewart, was to produce a proposal for his Cabinet colleagues for the issuing of a circular 'requiring local authorities to submit appropriate plans'. He also proposed that there should be new legislation 'to deal with uncooperative local authorities' (Stewart, 1980).

Although the proposal was generally well received, it became modified in some important respects. In particular, other Cabinet members did not wish to be seen to be disrupting the traditional relationship with local authorities and, in any case, several were ambivalent about the proposals. That there were contradictions in the views of government members is illustrated by an amendment which was passed in the parliamentary debate which 'welcomed the efforts of local authorities to reorganise secondary education on comprehensive lines which will preserve all that is valuable in grammar-school education for those children who receive it and make it available to more children' (quoted in Chitty, 1989). Prime Minister Harold Wilson frequently spoke of comprehensive schools as 'grammar schools for all'.

Thus when Circular 10/65 was issued in July, 1965, it 'requested' rather than 'required' local authorities to submit plans for reorganisation. Furthermore the plans for legislation were dropped. This was perhaps understandable given the extremely small parliamentary majority obtained by the Labour government in 1964, but this policy remained in place after the election in March 1966, when

Labour won a sufficient majority to be confident of remaining in power for the next five years.

Essentially, Circular 10/65 was a planning document, outlining several possible models for going comprehensive. The Department for Education and Science still saw the all-through school (i.e. the 11-18 comprehensive) as the favoured model, but LEAs were free to decide whether they favoured this solution or one of the two or three-tiered models.

Despite being only requested to submit plans, most local authorities did so, although 20 authorities indicated that they would not. Many of the submitted plans were not acceptable to the Department, particularly where, as was frequently the case, they proposed the retention of grammar schools alongside comprehensive schools. The situation was further complicated by local government elections in 1967, which saw a swing against Labour and the transfer of many large authorities into Conservative control. Several such authorities immediately withdrew the plans which they had previously submitted.

There was some progress. By 1968 there existed 748 comprehensive schools, attended by more than a fifth of the relevant population, but change was slow and the Labour government became impatient. Towards the end of 1969 it announced its intention to introduce legislation which would compel all authorities to submit plans for reorganisation. However, before this could happen there was another national election.

The new Conservative Secretary of State was Margaret Thatcher, who issued a new circular in 1970, withdrawing Labour's 1965 circular and freeing LEAs to determine secondary school patterns in their area. Whilst Thatcher was undoubtedly an opponent of comprehensive schooling and the 'progressive' educational ideas which she associated with it, her action did not have the desired effect. It did encourage those authorities which had refused to submit plans, but for most authorities their plans were too far developed to change or withdraw. LEA proposals continued to arrive at a steady rate. As Margaret Thatcher said some years later, '…this great roller coaster of an idea was moving, and I found it difficult if not impossible to stop' (Chitty, 1989).

The somewhat ironic consequence was that Mrs Thatcher presided over the creation of more comprehensive schools than any other Secretary of State before or since. By 1974, there were 2,677 comprehensive schools in England and Wales attended by 62 per cent of children. Nevertheless, her tenure did have some important influences on the developing nature of these schools She approved proposals, which would not have been approved under the Labour government, which retained grammar schools and others which established mixed systems in different parts of a local authority area. Furthermore she used her powers to veto proposals with regard to 94 individual grammar schools which had been nominated by LEAs for amalgamation or closure. Thus, whereas the majority of secondary age children now attended comprehensive schools, only 12 per cent were in LEAs with a fully comprehensive system. Therefore, many comprehensive schools had to compete with nearby grammar schools to attract the most able children (and with independent schools attended at that time by some 5% of secondary age children).

Examples of Local Developments

The above describes the context of national policy developments but, as already emphasised, what actually happened on the ground was also crucially influenced by local circumstances and personalities. This is illustrated by summaries of events in three local authorities, Leicestershire, Manchester and Stoke-on-Trent, taken from fuller accounts of ten case studies reported in Kerckhoff, Fogelman, Crook and Reeder (1996).

Leicestershire

Leicestershire provides an example of the importance of a particular individual in the implementation of educational change. Throughout the relevant period it had a Conservative local government, and most of its local politicians and education officials would have had no motivation to consider change or to promote the introduction of comprehensive schools. The crucial exception to this was Stewart Mason, its Director of Education from 1947-1971.

Mason was originally a supporter of selection, but became acutely aware, partly as the parent of a child who failed the 11+, of the distress which selection could cause. As he later wrote:

> a sense of success in a few was being paid for by a sense of failure in many; primary school friendships were severed, brothers and sisters artificially separated. A sense of social injustice was being engendered while reservoirs of talent were doomed to remain untapped. More and more people were coming to see that the 11+ reflected an outmoded 'we/they' society (Mason, 1965).

The options for change in Leicestershire were limited. There were the constraints of the 1944 Act, requiring transfer from primary to secondary education at the age of 11 and Mason did not wish to destroy Leicestershire grammar schools which had long traditions and excellent reputations. Nor did he favour large all-through comprehensive schools.

Mason claimed that the solution came to him in a 'blinding explosion' while he was shaving one morning, but there is strong evidence that he must have been influenced by the writing and lectures of Robin Pedley (Crook, 1992). The essential element in this solution was, as Mason explained in a newspaper interview, 'instead of having the schools parallel, as it were, they could be placed one on top of the other, i.e. with a system of 'High Schools' for children aged 11-14 and 'Upper Schools' for 15-18 year-olds. Mason moved quickly to set up consultation meetings with local head teachers. Accounts of these vary, but it does appear, not surprisingly, that most heads of secondary modern schools were positive about the proposals, whereas grammar school heads were less so. However, Mason was able to use his local contacts and knowledge to gain the support of the majority and of local politicians in influential positions.

With this support, Mason established such schools in two districts of the county. He was able to argue that his plans had several advantages. First, they responded to the increasing concerns about selection at 11, in that all children would transfer to a common high school at 11. The minimum school leaving age at this time was 15: those wishing to continue academic study beyond this age would transfer to an upper school, the remainder would stay at the high school for their final year. Secondly, reorganisation could take place in the two districts without any necessity for further building. Thirdly, as grammar schools would become upper schools they were not required to amalgamate, close or lose examination work. Indeed they could, if they wished, retain the title of 'grammar schools'. This feature was undoubtedly helpful in reducing controversy.

Although this was described as an experiment, there were no contingency plans for what should happen if it did not prove successful; Mason's biographer has suggested that, in his mind, it was not an experiment but a permanent feature (Jones, 1988).

Within two years, Mason produced proposals to extend the experiment to other parts of the county. Initially, these proposals passed through the relevant political committees with little opposition, but there then followed a further period of public consultation where the experience was somewhat different. In particular, there were protests from teachers and governors of several grammar schools, even to the extent of a deputation to the national ministry.

As a consequence progress was considerably slower than Mason would have wished. By 1962, five years after the initial experiment, only one further area within the county had been added to the plan. However, in the following year there was further movement in three new districts - again areas where no additional building was needed.

The 'Leicestershire Plan' was never presented as a move to comprehensive schooling as such. Because it retained selection by ability at age 14, it was not universally admired by supporters of comprehensive education. Those with doubts included members of the incoming Labour government and it became apparent that this structure would not be seen as an acceptable response to Circular 10/65. Therefore Mason developed a strategy for amending the plan. The major opportunity for this was given by the government's announcement in 1966 that it would raise the school-leaving age to 16 from 1971 (though in the event this did not happen until 1974). Thus, it was agreed that there should be a gradual move, phased in across different parts of the county, to a position where all pupils would transfer to upper schools at 14. This was achieved by 1972-73, by which time the structure had been adopted throughout the county. Interestingly, the controversy and objections which had been seen earlier in some parts of the county did not resurface at this time. This structure remains in place in Leicestershire to this day.

Manchester

By the particular nature of its plans and the skills of its Director of Education, Leicestershire succeeded in avoiding some of the political controversy surrounding the move to comprehensive education, despite its being a rural county, conservative in both its traditions and its local government. By contrast, Manchester provides an example of what is often presented, somewhat misleadingly, as the stereotype of comprehensive implementation - an urban movement, ideologically led by the Labour Party. Yet even this was far from straightforward.

As early as the 1940s there was some experimentation in Manchester, with one school designated as a 'secondary' rather than secondary modern and which offered examination courses to age 16. However, its status was always uncertain and it was the subject of a negative inspection report in 1952. This event was important in reinforcing the views of senior education officials who were unsympathetic to comprehensive education (Fiske, 1982).

Local elections saw Labour return to power in 1954, but this did not lead to any rapid changes. This was despite the efforts of Lady Shena Simon, a radical Labour councillor who was influential in local education policy for nearly three decades. She urged the local authority to establish comprehensive schools, co-ordinated fact-finding visits to such schools in other parts of the country and identified possible sites for an experimental comprehensive in Manchester. However, her aspirations were frustrated by three factors: she did not have the full support of all other local Labour politicians; she was opposed by successive Chief Education Officers; and the one attempt which was made to put forward a proposal to establish three comprehensive schools in the city was blocked by the Conservative Minister of Education on the grounds that it would involve the destruction of existing grammar schools.

Thus, by 1963 the only, relatively minor, development was that the secondary school referred to above had been officially designated as a comprehensive school. However that year did see a new pro-comprehensive chairman of the Education Committee, who circumvented the Chief Education Officer and persuaded the City Council to pass a resolution calling on the Education Committee to submit, within six months, detailed proposals for a wholly comprehensive secondary system. Interim plans were produced with the intention that more detailed plans would not be available until after consultation with teacher associations. However, this was thwarted by newspaper revelations which had the effect of rallying the opposition forces. These highlighted a number of issues about how individual schools would be treated and how catchment areas would be defined, which led to the withdrawal of the plans in the Spring of 1964.

New, though not substantially different, plans were soon produced, but still in an atmosphere of conflict and controversy. The new plans envisaged a mixture of all-through and two-tier comprehensives, with a sixth-form college in one district, whereas many local administrators and labour politicians favoured a uniform all-through scheme. Local teachers complained of a lack of consultation. A further revised plan was produced in June 1965, which proposed the ending of the 11+ in 1966 and the opening in September of that year of 29 comprehensive schools. 23 of these were to be 11-18 schools, with the remainder entailing transfer at 14. Despite considerable opposition, the revised plans were adopted as council policy and submitted to the Department of Education and Science a few days before the publication of Circular 10/65.

The Labour Secretary of State at this time was determined to support comprehensive plans from enthusiastic local authorities, and Manchester's were approved in June 1966. Implementation from this point was relatively rapid.

Manchester was one of several cities which elected a Conservative administration in 1967, and in some this had a delaying effect. In Manchester, however, Conservative leaders felt that there was now overwhelming public support for change, and also that administrative arrangements were too far advanced to withdraw. As Dame Kathleen Ollerenshaw, the new Chairman of Education, wrote at the time, 'To reverse plans... would have piled chaos upon chaos and would not have been in the best interests of the children' (quoted in Kerckhoff *et al*, 1996). A further important factor in Manchester was the existence of several highly prestigious direct-grant grammar schools. These were schools outside the maintained system, but which received substantial funding to enable them to offer a number of free places on a highly selective basis. The continued existence of these schools made it possible for Manchester to introduce a comprehensive system for the schools which it controlled, without being seen to fully deprive parents of the opportunity for a grammar school education for their children.

Stoke-on-Trent
In most areas the story of the introduction of comprehensive secondary schools is one of changes of direction, some ad hoc decisions and compromise, often resulting in mixed systems. Stoke-on-Trent is a rare exception to this, where the final outcome was largely the result of consistent and researched planning over a number of years, though it was certainly not without controversy. It also again illustrates the potential importance of influential personalities providing commitment and drive towards a clear objective.

Stoke-on-Trent has long been a traditional Labour stronghold and in the 1950s party members were expressing concern about the role of the 11+ examination. As early as 1955, Henry Dibden, the Chief Education Officer, produced a report in which he suggested that the city should introduce comprehensive schools. However, he reflected the dominant belief at that time that comprehensive schools had to be large institutions and there were major financial constraints that made it unrealistic to consider building new schools. Dibden was also influential, and unusual, in being opposed to suggestions that a small number of schools should be established as an experiment, as had happened in some areas. He recognised that as long as the 11+ and grammar schools continued to exist, any comprehensive school would be deprived of a significant proportion of able pupils (Dibden, 1965).

Progress was slow in the next few years, but the Education Committee sustained a commitment that future building programmes should be based on the comprehensive principle. In 1955 it was decided to establish two comprehensive schools, one purpose-built, the other based on extending an existing secondary modern. A special committee was set up to produce detailed plans. It has been argued that in their efforts to displease nobody they annoyed everybody (O'Rourke, 1978), producing plans which threatened existing schools but satisfied few people's notions of what comprehensive schools should be. For example, mechanisms were proposed whereby pupils could transfer from one of the schools to a grammar school at 13 or 16, and the other school was to have a special 'grammar stream which would be open to children from outside the school's catchment area. There was immediate criticism of the content of these proposals, but even stronger criticism concerning the lack of teacher consultation in the planning process. After a series of protests by teachers, parents and the local press, the plans were withdrawn.

There were other developments. In 1959, six secondary modern schools had accepted a special selective intake of 30 pupils who would, for the first time in such schools in Stoke, follow examination courses through to the age of 16. This was a limited and uncontroversial experiment, but it was envisaged that a high proportion of these children would in due course wish to transfer to schools offering A-level courses. It was therefore decided to re-designate an existing boys grammar school as a co-educational school which would have a sixth form of 360 pupils - as many as in the first five years of the school - with those from what were now known as 'junior high schools' joining those who had always been at the school after passing the 11+.

This was still seen as a limited experiment, and further plans for comprehensive schools remained inhibited by financial and building considerations. One option considered was the 'Leicestershire Plan' but there were doubts about the cost-effectiveness of a sixth form in every upper school. A further option which proved more attractive was of a single sixth-form college, serving 11-16 comprehensive schools throughout the city.

It is at this point that a second influential personality moved to the centre of the stage. Bob Cant, Chairman of the Education Committee and a Lecturer at nearby Keele University, prepared a memorandum for his committee in which he commended the development in the United States of 'junior colleges' for 16-18 year-olds. He proposed that he and Henry Dibden should undertake an eight week study tour of the USA. Reaction to this in the local press was hardly helpful, with much talk of wastage of local taxes, but their visit went ahead in the Spring of 1963.

The outcome was an influential booklet entitled *American Journey*, which confirmed the intention to establish a sixth form college. There continued to be vociferous opposition, mainly because the establishing of 11-16 schools would mean the demise of the local grammar schools, but the Education Committee pressed ahead and prepared detailed plans which were submitted to the ministry by the end of 1963. Originally it had been envisaged that the sixth form college would be based on the school with the enlarged sixth form, but this was abandoned in favour of proposing what would be the country's first purpose-built sixth form college.

The Ministry rapidly approved the sixth form college, although it was a further year before it also approved the funds to enable it to be built, but reserved judgement on the 11-16 schools. In 1965, after the election of the Labour government and shortly after the approval of the sixth form college funding, the Ministry announced that the 11-16 proposals were not acceptable.

This seemed like a major setback, but the way ahead became clearer when Circular 10/65 appeared. This included a possible model which had not been previously considered in Stoke-on-Trent, the three tier middle school system. It required relatively little modification to produce new plans which would entail school transfer at 8, 12 and 16. The major attraction was that this could be done at relatively little cost, requiring new annexes at just four secondary schools.

These plans were approved in August, 1967. The authority now decided to delay implementation until the building of the sixth form college was completed in 1970. This had the benefit of allowing time for negotiations with the city's denominational schools, which decided to opt for consistency by taking in their pupils at 12, although two Catholic schools also decided to retain their own sixth forms.

The opening of the sixth form college in 1970 attracted considerable national interest By the standards of that time its facilities were outstanding. Equal interest was paid to its curriculum, as its size in relation to the age group attending it enabled the college to offer an unusually wide range of Advanced level subjects.

After 1974

Although a Labour government was returned in 1974, the numbers of comprehensive schools continued to increase only slowly. By this time comprehensive education had become the focus of an intense political battle, subject to continuous negative comment from sections of the media and vociferous attack from right wing politicians A series of publications had appeared in which the authors made claims about the alleged failures of comprehensive schools and of what they saw as the progressive left wing authorities which supported them (e.g. Cox and Dyson, 1969; Cox and Boyson, 1975).

In the context of severe economic difficulties, many of these criticisms were echoed by the Labour government. A leaked paper from the DES contained what was described as a severe indictment of the failure of secondary schools to produce enough scientists and engineers. Such themes were repeated in a much-commented on speech by Prime Minister James Callaghan. However, in the dying days of the Labour government, the debate was not so much about school structures as about what was taught and how, and about the internal organisation of comprehensive schools.

This can be seen as paving the way for the many changes brought about by the Conservative government, elected in 1979 and in power until 1997. Of most general educational significance has been the introduction of a national curriculum and its associated assessment and inspection, but of more relevance here is the introduction of new forms of secondary schools. One such was the City Technology College, established with private and government money to specialise mainly in technological and scientific subject areas. In the event few such schools have been established, but there are undoubtedly some areas where comprehensive schools have been affected by the creaming off of able pupils by these schools. More significant numerically and in their impact were grant-maintained schools. Encouraged by substantial financial advantages, these schools were enabled to opt out of the control of local authorities and receive their funding directly from central government. Greater powers to parents to choose which secondary school their child attends, the encouragement of schools to see themselves as competing with each other for pupils, and legislation which permitted grant-maintained schools to select a proportion of their pupils by ability combined to have clear implications for the reality of comprehensive education.

The election of a Labour government in 1997 did not see a reversal of these trends. On the contrary, further variations have been introduced, such as Specialist schools and City Academies. There never was a standard model of a comprehensive school, but many would argue that, because such developments have frequently re-introduced at least partial selection and because of the continuing existence of grammar schools in many areas, the comprehensive 'ideal' was never quite achieved and that now it is being further diluted.

References

Bird, H. (1995) An Island that Led - The History of Manx Education (Isle of Man, Hinton Bird).

Board of Education (1926) *Report of the Consultative Committee on the Education of the Adolescent* (The Hadow Report) (London, HMSO)

Board of Education (1938) *Report of the Consultative Committee on Secondary Education* (The Spens Report) (London, HMSO).

Chitty, C. (1989) *Towards a New Education System: the Victory of the New Right?* (London, Falmer Press).

Cox, C.B. & Boyson, R. (eds) (1975) *Black Paper 1975: the Fight for Education* (London Dent).

Cox, C.B. & Dyson, A. (eds) (1969) *Fight for Education: a Black Paper* (London, Critical Quarterly Society).

Crook, D.R. (1992) 'The disputed origins of the Leicestershire two-tier comprehensive schools plan' *History of Education Society Bulletin*, 50, 55-59.

Dibden, H.C. (1965) 'Stoke-on-Trent' in Maclure, J.S. (ed) *Comprehensive Planning* (London, Councils and Education Press).

Douglas, J.W.B. (1968) *All Out Future: a Longitudinal Study of Secondary Education* (London, Peter Davies).

Fiske, D. (1982) *Reorganisation of Secondary Education in Manchester* Bedford Way Papers 9, London University Institute of Education.

Jones, D. (1988) *Stewart Mason: the Art of Education* (London, Lawrence and Wishart).

Jones, DK (1989) 'The Reorganisation of Secondary Education in Leicestershire, 1947-1984', in Lowe, R.A. (ed) *The Changing Secondary School* (Lewes, Falmer Press).

Kerckhoff, A., Fogelman, K., Crook, P. and Reeder, D. (1996) *Going Comprehensive in England and Wales: a Study of Uneven Change* (London, Woburn Press).

Knight, C. (1990) *The Making of Tory Education Policy in Post-War Britain, 1950-1986* (London: Falmer Press).

Mason, S.C. (1965) 'Leicestershire' in Maclure, J.S. (ed) *Comprehensive Planning* (London, Councils and Education Press).

McCulloch, G. (1989) *The Secondary Technical School: a Usable Past?* (London, Falmer Press).

O'Rourke, J.E. (1978) 'The National Union of Teachers and Education in Stoke-on-Trent, 1878-1978'. unpublished ms, Hanley Reference Library.

Parkinson, M. (1970) *The Labour Party and the Organisation of Secondary Education 1918-65* (London, Routledge and Kegan Paul).

Rubinstein, D. (1979) 'Ellen Wilkinson Reconsidered', *History Workshop*, 7, 161-169

Simon, B. (1991) *Education and the Social Order, 1940-1990* (London, Lawrence and Wishart)

Stewart, M. (1980) Life *and Labour: an Autobiography* (London, Sidgwick and Jackson).

Yates, A. and Pidgeon, D.A. (1958) *The Allocation of Primary school Leavers to courses of Secondary Education* (London, NFER)

4 THE ROAD NOT TAKEN: DECONSTRUCTING THE 1960s, THE FORMATIVE DECADE

Harry Judge, Brasenose College, Oxford

It may seem perverse, in a book made up of chapters exploring urgent questions about the future of "the comprehensive school", to include one contribution which is unashamedly about the past. But to ignore or misrepresent that past is to prejudice the future. Much of the current hostility to the principles and practice of comprehensive education, as the second half of the last century came to interpret them, is based upon a profound misunderstanding about what in fact then happened, and why. It has become fashionable, and not least within influential Government circles, to argue that the debilitating heritage of the 1960s must now be firmly and finally rejected. The comprehensive school movement of that romantic decade is now cynically misrepresented as a liberal and egalitarian aberration, as an attempt to impose upon a credulous society an ideology embracing at one and the same time the worst principles of philistine Old Labour and the romantic progressivism of a hippy culture. This chapter is therefore presented as a modest corrective to such misrepresentation, and as an alternative explanation of why comprehensive schools flourished, and why they were for a while quite widely accepted and even welcomed. The argument is illustrated by, but not confined to, a personal experience of involvement in that enterprise, at both local and (to a much more limited extent) national levels (Judge 1984). It is therefore appropriate that the first citation should be from the diaries of Richard Crossman, in a year when he was a cabinet minister and resident in North Oxfordshire, where I happened to be a recently installed grammar school headmaster:

Sunday November 7th 1965:
"A perfect day out on the hills behind Boddington watching the hunt career around us while we were exploring Hobbit country... Anthony Crosland and his wife Susan arrived at 5.30 and we gave a dinner party for them and Harry and Mary Judge from Banbury Grammar School... My evening was spoilt by what Harry Judge had to tell me about Banbury. We had been very much hoping that his plans for a middle school for the nine to thirteen age group, followed by a choice at thirteen, would form the basis for the reorganisation of secondary education in this part of the county. However, he tells me that this plan was incompatible with the Labour Party's definition of a comprehensive school and has been scrapped, so something much more unattractive will have to take its place... However, the headmaster and the Secretary of State got on very well, and I was impressed by Tony's proficiency in explaining his plans... Though he talked very well, Tony Crosland is only Minister of Education in order to be in the

"

Cabinet. He still feels that his real life as a politician will begin when he moves to an economic Department, preferably the Treasury" (Crossman 1975, pp 373-4).

Twelve years later Crosland died at the Radcliffe Infirmary in Oxford. Although he was Secretary of State for Education and Science for only two and a half of those years, he forced through far-reaching changes affecting both secondary and higher education, and in later becoming Foreign Secretary satisfied at least part of the ambition which Crossman detected in him. Eight years before in 1964 his party came to power, Tony Crosland had already redefined the new Labour policies of his day in the influential book, **The Future of Socialism** (Crosland 1956). The relatively few pages on education were correctly interpreted as an attack on the secondary modern school rather than a repudiation of the grammar school. The historic policy of the old Labour Party had been classically defined in the 1920s by R H Tawney. Genuine secondary education should be provided for all pupils from the age of eleven: this was to be very different from the part-time continuation schools which a coalition government had recently placed on the statute book, but had failed to build. But neither Tawney nor his successors for one moment supposed that secondary education for all implied that all pupils should receive the same kind of schooling: the academically more able should, without regard to parental income or social class, receive the traditionally valued education of the academic grammar schools. For the rest, other programmes and therefore other schools would be needed: "Equality of educational provision is not identity of educational provision, and it is important that there should be the greatest possible diversity of type among secondary schools" (Tawney 1922, pp.66-67).

Equality, identity and diversity soon however proved (as, fifty years later, they are yet again about to become) uncomfortable bedfellows. Diversity and the choice which it necessarily implies were popular enough as general principles in the years after the 1944 Act, but the practicalities of allocating pupils to one type of school or another proved, even for the most enlightened administrators, insuperable. For that reason in districts like the county of Oxfordshire (although, significantly, not yet in the City of Oxford) the distastefulness of the eleven-plus examination, and the injustices which it imposed, led to the peaceful introduction of more flexible forms of secondary school organisation. The traditions (and even, somewhat ingenuously, in some cases the name) of the grammar schools were carefully preserved. As Edward Boyle and other politically sensitive Conservatives recognised, the bureaucratic allocation of eleven years olds to a school that was inevitably perceived as second best (the secondary modern, that is to say) would never be popular with a growing number of disappointed and disgruntled parents. Any measure which could soften that harsh allocation to exclusive categories (such as the delaying of selection to a later age and a more flexible allocation of pupils to courses, which Crossman himself favoured) was assured of a wide measure of non-partisan support. Crosland, as he reflected on what a future Labour government might attempt, knew as well as anybody that "the problem" was not the grammar school, but the secondary modern school. But he gave tragically little detailed attention to the implications of such a distinction, and what he wrote in the 1950s – perhaps for that very reason – bore little or no relationship to what he did when in power.

This is one of the principal reasons why the future of the comprehensive school is now so contested and confused an issue.

The precise words of Crosland repay close attention: "Only a minority of education authorities at present favour a large-scale conversion to a comprehensive pattern; and no one proposes that the remainder should be coerced. It would, moreover, be absurd from a socialist point of view to close down the grammar school, while leaving the public schools still holding their present commanding position. It is curious that socialists... should fail to see that 'parity of esteem' within the State sector, combined with the continuation of independent schools outside, will actually increase the *disparity* of esteem in the system as a whole." (Crosland 1956, p. 205) Nevertheless, nine short years later – and before even setting up an impotent Public Schools Commission, of which he invited me to become a member – the same Crosland issued the celebrated circular 10/65, going as far as he then could to coerce those local authorities (Radice 2002, p.143). Although they were indeed to be "requested" and not "required" to submit appropriate plans, it soon became clear that they would get no money for capital programmes unless they behaved (Fenwick 1976, p.138; Jefferys 1999, p.104). So began the construction of a highly centralised educational system, a key element in that accelerating process which now makes Britain one of the most centrally governed in the world. The liberal establishment did not then protest, and it was left (paradoxically) for Keith Joseph very much later to agonise about the long-term yet inevitable consequences of this dramatic and accelerating shift of power to the centre. The Local Authorities found few real friends when they most needed them, and for that dismal dereliction a high cost has been paid. Alderman Broadsides may occasionally have been a problem, but it might just be better to be ruled by a selection of local lay people rather than by a few clever metropolitan ones less in touch with realities of education in the country at large. A high price had to be paid for the violation of consensus. Think only of Edward Boyle, who understood fully that the 11+ examination was as indefensible as it was electorally embarrassing, who had the courageous imagination to write the preface to the Newsom report, and who nevertheless protested, in his mild manner: "Public opinion may not like this, but we just don't know enough to be justified in describing any particular pattern of organisation as **the** [emph orig] right one." (Kogan 1978, p.127)

Crosland in power no longer harboured such debilitating doubts. After a predictably uncongenial dinner with indignant representatives of the Joint Four—teacher unions then representing the selective grammar schools – he went home to West London to explode: "If it's the last thing I do, I'm going to destroy every fucking grammar school in England. And Wales. And Northern Ireland." (Crosland 1982, p.148) This was not the language, nor were these the sentiments, of Harold Wilson, or Manny Shinwell or indeed of Crosland himself ten years before. Harold Wilson attracted a good deal of undeserved mockery for endorsing the ideal of "a grammar school education for everybody", while Shinwell, who left school at the age of eleven and died a Lord at the age of 101, protested: "We are afraid to tackle the public schools to which wealthy people send their sons, but at the same time are ready to throw over the grammar schools". (Judge 1984, p.68) This was of course the fatal flaw in Crosland's theory and practice. He had argued persuasively in the 1950s for the necessity of opening up the prestigious independent schools to meritocratic competition, of precisely the kind which had allowed the grammar schools to flourish. Yet, when in power he insisted that at one and the same time entry to state secondary schools should not be competitive *and* that the independent schools, which increasingly prided themselves on their academic reputation and success, should be integrated within a restructured public system. There was and is no way of squaring that circle. The bad tempered dissolution of the grammar school and the attempted (if half hearted) imposition of *the comprehensive school* (all three words glued together matter) led directly to hyperbolic claims for what such a school, or indeed any sublunar institution, could achieve, and therefore elevated to a dizzy height the criteria by which it would shortly be judged (Pedley 1978). Men and women who should have known better claimed that it would in short order reduce rates of juvenile delinquency, increase national productivity and competitiveness, erode the prejudices of a viciously class based society, restore the greatness of Britain, and cut out the roots of misunderstanding between posh employers and cloth capped trade unionists.

An intoxicated advance guard soon lost touch with the main body of opinion and sentiment, as adverbs crept insidiously into divisive sentences: hardworking schools just released from the iniquities and inequities of the 11+ process were now demeaned as being not wholly, genuinely, authentically, or fully comprehensive. Before the dust had even settled on a battlefield of mergers, redeployment, split sites and coeducation the prophets warned that "real" or "true" comprehensive schools had no business simply to replicate the threadbare curricula of grammar and modern schools, and had a compelling moral duty to abandon streaming or even setting. And this in spite of the fact that Crosland had himself carefully explained that the main reason why standards would not decline in comprehensive schools was that they had "not, as many feared (and some hoped), mixed children of different abilities in the same class, but have adopted a system of testing and differentiation designed to produce homogeneous classes of more or less similar standards of attainment... Division into streaming, according to ability, remains essential." (Crosland 1956, p.202) And still more was soon to be demanded of the schools (Midwinter, 1971). Fully comprehensive schools were required to be community schools serving the needs of the area in which they were set and grounded in local loyalties – and yet at the same time socially comprehensive, isomorphic with the larger society as a whole, embracing the happy children if not of dukes, then certainly of dentists and dustmen. Banding and bussing were proposed, as though schools could repair the failures of housing and other social policies.

Centrally determined prescription of the structures of schooling was accompanied by a ballooning obsession with a national curriculum, with the holy grail itself (Lawton 1980). British ministers of education seemed, quite unreasonably, ashamed when in international meetings they were unable to produce official texts defining what the national curriculum was. A general, if admittedly vague, sense that curriculum variety and teacher inventiveness were intrinsically good was supplanted by an uneasy suspicion that all pupils, whatever their abilities or aptitudes, should be prescribed the same basic educational diet. This search for the common curriculum was reinforced by a political and populist distrust of professionalism (teachers are the problem, rather than the solution) and surfaced with David Eccles' musings on "the secret garden of the curriculum". The open minded Edward Boyle dispersed much of the suspicion aroused by the attempt to define nationally and authoritatively what the curriculum should be by encouraging the creation of the Schools Council (Plaskow 1985, p.15). This was indeed a brave and virtuous effort to substitute corporatist consensus for ministerial direction. But it still encapsulated the plausible yet deeply dangerous doctrine that there is, or should be and could be, a single national curriculum. This led inevitably, as some of us argued ineffectually at the time, to a statutory definition of a national curriculum with all the attendant paraphernalia of key stages, tests and league tables.

By the end of the sixties we had therefore acquired a centrally defined view of what a secondary school should look like, a growing acceptance that there should be a national curriculum (with a frieze of nice theological distinctions as to whether the core or the whole should be defined and by whom and how), and a body of doctrine – by no means monolithic – wrapped around what *the-comprehensive-school* (those three treacherously adhering words again) should be. What we did not have was confidence in where we were and clarity about how we had got there. It was for that reason that I was presumptuous enough to argue in 1976 (twelve years before the critically important Education Reform Act of 1988) that "[the] comprehensivists have captured the city, and don't know what to do with it". This bald statement was expanded into an argument for a new approach to education at 16+ accompanied by a revaluation of the so-called vocational element in education, for a recognition that the age of fourteen does "usefully mark a stage in curricular planning", and for a federal or collegiate pattern within and between schools. On that basis it was possible, even as long ago as that, to assert that "'Secondary comprehensive school' is, in short, a term which has awkwardly outlived its usefulness." (Judge 1976, p.16) One of the few things which did dispirit me as the 60s edged into the 70s was the growing acceptance that large schools were always bad schools, and that our exhausted imaginations could neither move beyond the unitary notion of "the school" nor see beyond such pedestrian efforts to deal with size as house or year systems. With Prime Minister Callaghan's Ruskin speech, the renewed siege of the city began in earnest. The subsequent atomisation of the school universe, the still accelerating erosion of the importance of the LEAs, the pandemic of testing, the neurosis of league tables, the hypercompetitiveness among schools which in reality desperately need to support one another: all these call for fresh thinking about the patterns of schooling, about educational architecture, about how the parts relate to the whole.

Although history certainly can teach no straightforward lessons, its study does encourage the entering of certain caveats whenever new policies are proposed. These caveats deserve particular respect whenever such reformist policies are justified, to any significant degree, by appeals to a false reading of the history. The advance of comprehensive schools in the 1960s was not based on some currently fashionable ideology, now shown to be outdated and never accepted by more than a vocal minority. Comprehensive schools emerged because of a deep-rooted public disillusionment, not with the grammar schools serving a minority but with the secondary modern schools that offered to the majority only an inferior alternative. Conscientious attempts to improve the accuracy of selection at the age of eleven served only to underscore the inherent injustices, and to expose the anomalies of wide regional variations in grammar school provision (Yates and Pidgeon 1957). It was a mistake to suppose, and an even greater error to argue in a propagandist spirit, that the common secondary school could solve the wider and deeper problems of society, regenerate the local community or lead to the building of a new Jerusalem. Such claims, nevertheless repeated by a minority of the self-appointed advocates of such schools, inevitably led to the disappointment of unduly elevated hopes and to the discouragement of those dedicated professionals who were trying to make comprehensive schools work effectively.

It was an equally dangerous mistake to confuse a belief in the real advantages which comprehensive schools might bring with a principled disapproval of the grammar schools which they replaced. In this respect, Crosland himself obviously carried a heavy burden of responsibility. The grammar schools had extended to generations of young people from modest families the opportunities which had previously been enjoyed only by those who could afford to purchase an expensive and prestigious education. Grammar school values and curricula and traditions of learning and teaching should have been much more vigorously defended than in the event they were. Those who argued for such a defence were perhaps too easily demoralised by critics who unjustly accused them of lacking an adequately progressive and inclusive vision of what "the comprehensive school" should be.

Any attempt to impose a universal and uniform system (whether it be comprehensive schools for all in the sixties, or specialist secondary schools for all in Mr. Blair's current five year plan) should be resisted. If, as many believed a half century ago, comprehensive schools represented a reasonable and desirable development of a system which had been built up nationally since the passing of the 1944 Act, they should have been left to demonstrate their own virtues and develop at their own pace. The attempt by central government to set a uniform and accelerated pace generated hastily designed and inadequate schemes which resulted in the elimination of adequate (or better) schools before convincing alternatives could evolve. In some circumstances, however regrettably, an honest recognition of the difficulties inherent in so massive a systemic change would have allowed longer periods of time for transition and adjustment. It would doubtless have protected the continuing success of some inner city selective schools in conditions where no adequate plan of reorganisation could realistically be developed. Such a recognition of the desirability of gradualness would have eased the problems of those urban areas (and most significantly London), around which most of the recent discontent has congealed.

Instead, however, an insistence on the superior wisdom or virtue of central government fatally undermined the autonomy and responsibility of the Local Education Authorities, making it only too easy for their vitality to be remorselessly sapped during the next half century. Any sense of local accountability for the nurturing of a local system of secondary education adapted to serve the needs of the whole population was wantonly destroyed. Any system which deliberately elevates the status and achievements of some schools (be they grammar schools or city academies or specialist schools) without seriously weighing the implications for all schools is certain to fail. Nor, as Crosland himself acknowledged with brutal clarity, could maintained comprehensive schools enjoy a fair opportunity of success in a world where a party of the Left abolished grammar schools while leaving wholly undisturbed the historically entrenched independent schools – which owed their influence if not their existence to the long standing failure of the national government to provide a public secondary education that would have met the needs and aspirations of a rising middle class.

A harsh critic might therefore conclude that comprehensive schools fell into some disfavour not because of their inherent weaknesses and (still less) because they were the fruit of a superannuated ideology. At the root of their difficulties is the determination of central government in the sixties to proceed by edict rather than by building consensus. In doing so, that same Labour government failed to give appropriate weight to its own stated intentions – specifically, to avoid coercion and to address the social question raised by the dominance of the independent schools *before* tackling state secondary schools. There was then a choice: another road might have been taken, and then followed with greater determination and consistency. Although there is of course now no way back, it is at least clear that there are bad as well as good ways forward. The imperfections of public education will not be repaired unless and until central government ceases to insist that it knows best, until the integrity of accountable local government is restored, and until comprehensive and democratically controlled systems of schooling are seen to be more important than the market success of individual schools (Bridges and McLaughlin, 1994).

References

Barker, B. (1986) *Rescuing the Comprehensive Experience*. Milton Keynes: Open University.

Bridges, D. and McLaughlin, T. (eds.) (1994) *Education and the Market Place*. London: Falmer.

Crosland, S. (1982) *Tony Crosland*. London: Jonathan Cape.

Crosland, C.A.R. (1956 rev.edn. 1964) *The Future of Socialism*. London: Jonathan Cape.

Crossman, R. (1975) *The Diaries of a Cabinet Minister, Vol.I*. London: Hamish Hamilton and Jonathan Cape.

Fenwick, I.G.K. (1976) *The Comprehensive School 1944-1970*. London: Methuen.

Jefferys, K. (1999) *Anthony Crosland*. London: Richard Cohen Books.

Judge, H. (1976) *The Future of Secondary Education*. Swansea: University College of Swansea.

Judge, H. (1984) *A Generation of Schooling*. Oxford: Oxford University Press.

Kogan, M. (1978) *The Politics of Educational Change*. London: Fontana/Collins.

Lawton, D. (1980) *The Politics of the School Curriculum*. London: RKP.

Midwinter, E. (1971) *The School and the Community*. London: Macmillan.

Pedley, R. (1978 3rd edn.) *The Comprehensive School*. London: Penguin.

Plaskow, M. (ed.) (1985) *Life and Death of the Schools Council*. London: Falmer.

Radice, G. (2002) *Friends and Rivals*. London: Little, Brown.

Tawney, R.H. (1922) *Secondary Education for All : A Policy for Labour*. London: George Allen and Unwin.

Yates, A. and Pidgeon, D.A. (1957) *Admission to Grammar Schools*. London: National Foundation for Educational Research.

5 COMPREHENSIVE SCHOOLS: CONTINUING THE SUCCESS STORY

John Dunford, General Secretary of the Association of School and College Leaders

I hope that this paper helps to form the beginning of a re-energising process of comprehensive school education. I want to sound an optimistic note because I believe that comprehensive schools have been a success story and I believe, for various reasons, that this is an excellent time to set out the path of success for the future. But first, a little from the past.

I was educated at independent schools and spent the first two years of my career teaching in a grammar school in Nottingham. But then, with over ninety per cent of the secondary school population soon to be educated in comprehensive schools – a proportion that has remained steady over many years now – that was where my future lay and, I firmly believed, the future good of this country. And that was where I spent the next 26 years of my professional life.

From my present perspective as leader of an association with members across the UK, I have observed a greater commitment to comprehensive schools in Scotland and Wales than there has been for some time, or indeed ever, in England. In England we always seem to have first and second class options, especially in education. We had O level and CSE. We had – still have, in some places – grammar schools and secondary modern schools. We have academic courses and vocational courses. When we do attempt to bring these perceived first and second class options together, we soon begin to sub-divide them again, so the O level and CSE became the GCSE and almost from its inception, the GCSE has been divided and divided again into tiers and levels. It will be interesting to see if the government's (2005) attempts to achieve greater parity of esteem between academic and vocational courses go the same way. In the English culture, it won't be easy. In health and education, we seem always to be saddled with two levels of service and often your level of service depends upon your ability to pay.

Because other options have prevailed, there are many parts of the country in which the comprehensive system has never been given a chance. One sixth of children in England are educated in areas that retain selection.

But, according to the statistics of GCSE results, A level results and the percentage of 18-year-olds entering higher education, the comprehensive English secondary school system has been a success.

One of my problems in citing these statistics is the inadequacy of the measure. It is one of the ironies of our system that we judge it by such very inadequate measures. The proportion of the cohort of 16 year-olds gaining five or more passes at A* to C grades is a leftover from a time when five O levels was the acknowledged threshold for admission into the sixth form of a grammar school. The five A* to C measure has been particularly unfair towards schools working in disadvantaged areas. Equally, it has provided little – or even the wrong – incentive for schools working in more advantaged circumstances, for this measure gives no credit for helping a student to move from grade B to grade A or from grade E to grade D. The only credit to the school is when a grade D moves up to a grade C.

Inspection too has worked against schools in more disadvantaged circumstances. If you look back to the work of John Gray and Valerie Hannon in analysing the early published school inspection reports in 1983, you will find that the judgements were very much harsher on schools in difficult areas (Gray and Hannon, 1986). In spite of this research being in the public domain, lessons were not learned from it and I found when I replicated the research seven years later that the situation was exactly the same (Dunford, 1998). I believe that it still is.

Comprehensive schools have more complex aims than schools with pupils of more homogeneous ability and we need to find success criteria more appropriate to the breadth of these aims. Performance indicators should represent much more than exam results, attendance and truancy statistics. The often misleading nature of these statistics misinforms the public debate and misinforms the parents who rely on the statistics to guide their choice of secondary school. In fact, as we all know, the system of open enrolment has led to a situation in which schools choose children instead of children choosing schools. The convenient political rhetoric of parental choice is no more than a preference and, in many parts of the country, sophisticated tactics have to be adopted in order to ensure that a choice is not wasted.

It is, I know, different in urban and rural areas, and very different between London and elsewhere, but the fact remains that the quality of comprehensive schools is such that parents – even those who could afford to send their children to private schools – choose to send their children there. No selective system, once abolished, has ever been reintroduced in England for the simple reason that parents do not want it, a point often conveniently forgotten by proponents of more selection.

But is selection happening more covertly? Are faith schools and specialist schools creating a semi-selective system? The answer varies a great deal, depending on area. Specialist schools were originally intended to introduce a two-tier system – the old English disease, to which I refer above. In 2002 this was in the process of being refined – although that is too polite a word – into a multi-tiered system by Estelle Morris and Tony Blair, with their talk of ladders of schools and, even more bizarrely, escalators. With specialist schools of many different categories, beacon schools transforming into advanced schools, the vast majority lumped into a pejorative bog-standard category in the middle and, at the other end of the ladder, schools in special measures and schools with serious weaknesses, we were heading towards a depressing multi-tier system of secondary schools destined to make life very much more difficult for those at the bottom of the pile.

In spite of these early policy contradictions, specialist schools have succeeded, especially since 2003 when the emphasis changed from an exclusive, two-tier system to the more inclusive system of 2006, in which almost all secondary schools have a declared specialism.

With specialist schools now covering more categories – almost the whole curriculum – and with the removal of the early funding-driven caps on numbers, we are in a position where the specialist schools policy has at last become inclusive, where it can assist schools in developing their own ethos and, most important of all, where this can play a leading role in a collaborative framework.

In its earlier manifestations, the specialist school idea was based on some very shaky foundations – parental choice for a particular specialism (which parents almost never exercise in that way), pupil aptitude at 11 (which children rarely exhibit at age 11 in any permanent sense), selection by aptitude test (which cannot, in most subject areas, distinguish aptitude from general ability) and diversity of specialism (for which happenstance replaced planning of any coherent provision). Rarely can a government policy have had so little intellectual coherence. Above all, the policy was intended to create greater diversity *between* schools in a comprehensive system, the rationale of which is surely to provide diversity *within* each school to cater for all talents and abilities.

It has irritated me no end that in its rhetoric, the government has seemingly claimed to invent the idea of individual schools having their own mission and ethos. If, instead, ministers had said that it is already one of the great traditions of British, and especially English, schools that each develops its own mission and ethos and the government will provide funding to help them to do that, we would have had from the start a programme that promoted the areas of particular expertise in every school.

The comprehensive school system has suffered particularly badly from the culture of competition in which schools have been forced to work since the mid-1980s and it was good to observe the same ministerial team that removed some of the titles of categories of schools kicking away the hierarchical ladder and also emphasising greater collaboration between schools. Hierarchies will always be there, but that is no reason for governments to institutionalise them and, worse still, to emphasise them with differential funding. We still have some way to go before the funding drivers that promote competition cease to act against collaboration, but government thinking moved during 2005 (DfES, 2005b), producing obvious tensions between a drive towards greater autonomy for secondary schools and proposals for stronger collaboration.

The development of a 14 to 19 agenda holds both opportunities and threats to a comprehensive education system. First of all, it is good that at last the government is talking 14 to 19, although my own preference would be to articulate a 14+ agenda, linking more clearly the qualifications structure for the 14 to 19 age group with the promotion of lifelong learning. The carefully constructed Tomlinson report on 14 to 19 (2004), signalling a possible baccalaureate for the future, was welcome in taking on board so many of the messages from the summer 2002 consultation on the original 14 to 19 Green Paper, but the following 14 to 19 white paper (DfES, 2005a) was extremely disappointing in excluding A level reform, thus preventing the development of a comprehensive curriculum for this age group, which depends on reform of both curriculum and assessment. The qualifications structure is but one leg of a three-legged stool. Without strong curriculum and assessment structures, it will not stand up.

The development of comprehensive schools has been accompanied by no comparable development in the curriculum, except, perhaps, the HMI's nine areas of experience in the mid-1980s. There are many dangers lurking in the present discussions. One danger is the talk of a two-year key stage 3, ending at aged 13, in order to create space for a three-year AS and A level course. Almost inevitably, in the English context, this will create opportunities for early specialisation and we shall see youngsters specialising from 13 instead of 14, which is already quite bad enough. Government ministers often talk of the benefits of taking examinations a year early, as if examinations are the only form of education. Far better, surely, to bring greater depth and breadth to the education of the brightest students, instead of scurrying them through from one external examination hurdle to the next.

Another danger lies in the acceptance of a welcome degree of flexibility in the key stage 4 curriculum, but which has regrettably seen the overthrow of the gradual move towards a more broad and balanced curriculum for this age group – one of the original drivers behind the development of the national curriculum in the 1980s – as well as a league-table-driven surrender on modern foreign languages. It is difficult to both have your cake and eat it with curriculum flexibility *and* breadth, but it is possible if you have a *modular structure* to the curriculum and look at *breadth over time*. A 14 to 19 curriculum should be just that – a curriculum for learning during the whole of this period, not a strictly controlled subject diet for every week. If learning takes place in modules, it is not necessary to have a broad curriculum every week of every year during the 14 to 19 phase and breadth can be ensured over the whole time period.

Assessment too is a vitally important area. The structure of eight different grades at GCSE and the use of A level grades to divide not sheep from goats, but one type of sheep from another, has assumed a precision in the art of examining which does not exist. A comprehensive curriculum requires a different approach to assessment. We need to see more *assessment for learning* in place of the present reliance on the *assessment of learning*. And we need to move from a reliance on external examinations towards internal assessment, putting greater trust in the professionalism of teachers. The ASCL proposals for chartered examiners – experienced teachers accredited to uphold external examination standards in internal assessment – are a vital component in this. The Tomlinson report enthusiastically took up this proposal and it was the greatest disappointment of the 14 to 19 white paper that it rejected this idea out of hand, with the reactionary statement that there will be no change in the balance of external and internal assessment.

If we are to encourage comprehensive schools to grow and develop in the twenty first century, we must not constrain them with the suffocating accountability that is imposed upon them at present. Intelligent accountability demands better measurement of the performance of schools, better assessment of the work of children and the removal of some of the multiple lines of accountability which not only occupy so much time for heads and teachers, but which stem creativity and innovation as we all head for the safe options on which we will pass our inspections. The 'new relationship with schools', introduced in 2004, and the inspection framework started in 2005 have begun to make accountability more intelligent, but the lack of trust in teachers remains a major concern and will continue to prevent many sensible reforms to what remains a punitive system of accountability.

We need to develop the creativity of teachers and the innovativeness of schools, to build the professionalism of teachers, to create structures that promote collaboration not competition, and we need a curriculum for the comprehensive schools of the twenty first century. The answer here lies in the comprehensive values of the movement and in the communities that we serve. Values of equity, of equal opportunity for all, of increasing the life chances of our young people and of raising their educational achievement – irrespective of their background or circumstances – have underpinned the comprehensive school movement from its outset. Although these objectives have social consequences, they are fundamentally educational objectives and that is why it is right for us to concentrate, first and foremost, on developing the highest quality of teaching and learning in comprehensive schools.

Comprehensive schools of the future will have that high quality of teaching and learning and they will be firmly rooted in the communities they serve. Our schools of the future must be community learning centres, not working individually, but collaboratively as groups of schools, or groups of schools and a local college. Much of this is already taking place post-16 and in extending local 14 to 19 opportunities. There are already some 'hard' federations and many more collaboratives. Extended comprehensive schools, working in partnership with others, will move into the development of real community education, serving people from the youngest to the oldest. The range of services they provide will extend too so that the school, or network of schools, becomes the focal point of the local community. This goes further than Tim Brighouse's *collegiates*.

With shared policy on admissions, shared policies on behaviour and exclusions, sharing of expert teachers, shared provision of post-14 opportunities, and shared performance indicators, reported on jointly, we have a viable structure for the future of the comprehensive school movement. There is a place for diversity here too, with each unit of the collaborative having its own special area of expertise and diversity available within the group. That, I believe, provides an inclusive model that will ensure the continuation of the comprehensive school success story.

References

Department for Education and Skills, *14 to 19 Curriculum and Qualifications reform*, HMSO, 2004 [Tomlinson report]

Department for Education and Skills, *14 to 19 Education and Skills*, HMSO, 2005a

Department for Education and Skills, *Education Improvement Partnerships*, HMSO, 2005b

Dunford, J.E., *Her Majesty's Inspectorate of Schools since 1944: Standard Bearers or Turbulent Priests?*, Woburn Press, 1998, 103-106

Gray, J. and Hannon, V., 'HMI's interpretations of schools' examination results', *Journal of Education Policy*, I, no.1, 1986, 23-33

6 ACHIEVEMENT AND INCLUSION IN COMPREHENSIVE EDUCATION

Text of a talk given at the Department of Educational Studies,
University of Oxford, 29 January 2003

Geoff Whitty, Institute of Education, University of London

Let me start by quoting some findings from research I've carried out over the past twenty years with Tony Edwards, Sally Power and Valerie Wigfall, which will be published next month in a book on *Education and the Middle Class* (Open University Press). The original research on which it is based was carried out in the 1980s and widely cited at the time as showing that very few genuinely working class children were benefiting from the assisted places scheme. But it is not that aspect of our work that I want to dwell on today. Rather it is the subsequent work that we did from that study. The way we had designed the study, we had four groups of children identified as academically able at age 11, which was, of course, one of the eligibility criteria for the assisted places scheme. So we had a group of academically able children who participated in the scheme, another group who attended the same highly academic selective independent schools as full feepayers, a third group who attended state grammar schools in the same area and a fourth who attended comprehensive schools, again in the same area. We were therefore able to follow the progress of these four groups from age eleven onwards and the new book reports on their education and career trajectories up to their mid-twenties. You may think it odd that, in a talk on comprehensive education, which involves giving equal value to all learners and to all forms of learning, I choose to start by focusing on a study of academically able children most of whom were from middle class backgrounds. But I do so to make a point – *not* because I think that their education is more important than anyone else's.

In our study of these four groups of children identified as academically able at age 11, the mean score for those students who obtained A-levels in the elite independent sector was 23.1 points compared to 17.6 points in the state sector. However, overall point scores are potentially a misleading comparator, and mean scores per subject taken indicate a somewhat smaller difference. Thus, the mean subject grade for our independent schools was 7.7 (just below grade B), 7.2 for state grammar schools and 6.5 (just over grade C) for state comprehensives.

At first sight, these findings may not seem a great advertisement for comprehensive education. They suggest that comprehensive school pupils of high academic ability do rather less well at A-level than their peers in state grammar schools and both do less well than those in academically selective private schools. Our study also showed that those from the private schools were more likely to attend high status universities, read high status subjects and then enter the labour market in higher paid and more prestigious jobs. Most of today's brightest young people have relatively successful careers whether they have attended public or private, selective or non-selective schools, when measured by crude indices such as entry to higher education or entry to professional and managerial jobs. But it apparently remains the case that certain choices at 11 are still likely to bring a significantly greater chance of success than others, particularly when competing for the 'glittering prizes' associated with elite universities and elite occupations.

So it is perhaps hardly surprising that our findings were featured on the front page of *The Times* as showing that it was well worth ambitious parents spending £10,000 a year on their children's education. But, if you look at the figures another way, what is quite remarkable is how *small* the differences at A-level were – just over half a grade per subject – when you consider a whole range of factors that distinguish state comprehensive schools from the sorts of elite private schools in our study – whether we're talking about the nature of their mission, the nature of their intakes, their class sizes, the qualifications of their teachers, their facilities, etc. When you take these factors into account, it may well be that high status universities looking for the brightest and the best would have done better to sponsor more of those who had gained just slightly lower grades at comprehensive schools rather than those with straight As at private schools. And, even though it may be contentious to say this in some parts of Oxford, I think it entirely right that the government is now encouraging them to do so.

The other thing that is remarkable, given their differences in mission, is that within the sector differences in our study is hidden the fact some of the comprehensive schools actually performed better than some of our private school sample.

A similar set of thoughts strikes me when looking at the conflicting evidence about the relative performance of academically able children in comprehensive and maintained grammar schools that has been published in other places, including our own review of the research for Medway (Crook, Power and Whitty 1999). The fact that the difference is so marginal, and that successive studies by ourselves, David Jesson and NFER can contradict each other on which type of school is better for academically able kids, is a remarkable testament to the academic success of comprehensive schools. The point then is that, if the most able children in comprehensive schools can perform neck and neck with – and in at least some cases outperform – those in schools which have a mission that is geared directly to their needs and not much else, how come it is the comprehensive schools that are presented as failing? On this point, the failure to celebrate the success of comprehensive schools, I am unhappy with the government.

When you add to the equation the fact that comprehensive schools are part of the inclusion agenda as well the standards agenda, it is particularly puzzling that the present government should sometimes appear so reluctant to acknowledge the achievements of comprehensive schools. Instead, in the name of modernisation, we are now apparently going 'post-comprehensive' with a raft of specific policies that, taken together, are seen by some to constitute a retreat from comprehensive secondary education in all but name. People certainly have legitimate worries that the diversity agenda of specialist schools, faith schools and so on may recreate the tri-partite system, both academically and socially. And for a government ostensibly committed to evidence-informed policy to suggest, as it did in *Schools Achieving Success*, that there are no grounds for such fears is particularly worrying. The government may not intend specialist status to be divisive, but the research evidence it cites in support of its case that it won't be is not at all robust – as my colleague Harvey Goldstein and others have demonstrated.

But even if New Labour's policies prove – actually or potentially – damaging to the cause of comprehensive education, we've surely got to start from where we are. We are certainly not where, back in the 1960s – when many of us joined this struggle – we would have expected to be by now. I know I then expected that well before the turn of the last century we would have had a fully comprehensive system, little demand for private schools even if they still existed and, indeed, probably no single-sex or denominational schools. But we are not there and indeed society has probably changed sufficiently for some of those issues not to be quite as straightforward as I for one thought they were then.

And, in 1997, of course, Labour inherited not only a system that was being systematically dismantled and fragmented, but one in which the differences between the best and the worst schools were increasing and in which there was growing social polarisation between different types of schools. We should surely be pleased that, whatever else it did, New Labour narrowed the achievement gap between children from different social groups a little during its first term. And it was good that Estelle Morris saw closing that gap an even bigger priority in the second term and I believe Charles Clarke is equally committed to that goal. I am less clear that the government recognises what a huge task it will be to increase both the absolute and relative achievements of disadvantaged groups and make sure the benefits of improvement extend to all disadvantaged groups and not just some of them.

However, I want to make a rather different and perhaps more controversial point today. One which my colleagues who use private education find uncomfortable and one with which my hard left critics are unhappy for other reasons – although actually sometimes they're the very same people! Inclusion, as part of the comprehensive vision, is not in my view just a matter of engaging disadvantaged groups. As Tony Giddens has pointed out, 'social exclusion' is a dual process. It operates at the 'top' as well as the 'bottom' of society, with the wealthy often excluding themselves voluntarily from state-provided services. Certainly, the ruling and upper middle classes in England traditionally 'self-excluded' themselves from mainstream educational provision by their use of elite private education. The rapid growth of the middle classes since the second world war did not, however, lead to a similar growth in the size of that sector of education. So, although some of the newer fractions of the middle classes have made increasing use of private sector provision, others have successfully colonised specific parts of public education in ways that make it 'safe' for their own children. This is perhaps one of the reasons for the re-emergence of differentiated forms of public provision and for the 're-invented traditionalism' that we find in some comprehensive schools. But the effect – and sometimes even the intention – has too often been to exclude 'other people's children' from the best public provision. And that is why social inclusion in the comprehensive vision must, in my view, continue to entail both social and academic balance.

I believe that, for those of us committed to comprehensive education, it is thus important to ensure that the middle classes see mainstream public education as the right place for their children rather than opt out into their own schools, whether public or private. We need to have schools that meet the aspirations of all children and also provide that social and academic mix that has been shown to be essential for maximising the achievement of all. We know, as I said earlier, that there are comprehensive schools that perform with the best as far as academic achievement is concerned, while also doing many other things that private and grammar schools don't. The aim must surely be to learn from those schools and help other comprehensive schools to do the same, rather than finding ways for pupils to escape from them.

For, as my colleague Michael Young points out, exclusion 'at the top' and 'at the bottom' are interdependent in quite specific ways – families with high enough incomes to afford alternatives avoid the state secondary schools in many inner London boroughs precisely because many of the students in such schools are from families of the excluded 'at the bottom'. The falling quality of public services in the inner cities is partly an outcome of the withdrawal of support for them by growing numbers of relatively better off people. Even where better off families continue to use public secondary schools, they use other mechanisms of 'exclusion at the top', such as moving house into the catchment of what they perceive to be the best state schools.

In extreme cases, Young suggests, whole boroughs come to be regarded as unsafe for middle class children. In the 1990s, much of secondary education in Islington came into this category and much the same was true of Bristol when I took on the role of Chair of the Education Partnership Board there a couple of years ago. The falling quality of public services in large swathes of the inner cities is thus itself partly an outcome of the withdrawal of support for them by growing numbers of relatively advantaged people. School choice policies have often facilitated this strategic withdrawal of the middle classes, making it even more difficult for schools in those areas to succeed because, as Margaret Maden has indicated, it is important for such schools to have 'a "critical mass" of more engaged, broadly "pro-school" children to start with'.

Meanwhile, the sponsorship of a few 'meritorious' working class children into the suburban schools of the middle classes, whether public or private, helps to legitimate the system without threatening the so-called critical mass of middle class children in such schools. It might be concluded that the solution to working class failure in some inner city comprehensive schools could be an assisted places scheme targeted more effectively than the Tory one on working class students, and involving schools capable of retaining them beyond age 16 – or perhaps something like Peter Lampl's scheme. However, the broader problem of working class failure is barely addressed by the existence of a privileged route out for the few – and, indeed, their very existence can serve to reduce the pressure for a more fundamental reform of provision.

Now, despite what I said earlier about specialist schools, there are those who see them as a way of making schools more socially inclusive in just the way I am suggesting is necessary if we are to realise the comprehensive vision. Gill Penlington, when at the Social Market Foundation, argued that 'it is unusual (for a government) to base an entire policy on spin' – and without any apparent sense of irony! But in the case of specialist schools, she went on, 'spin may be the most effective way to achieve two antagonistic goals: encouraging the middle classes to use the state sector while simultaneously raising levels of provision in Britain's worst-off communities'. If she were proved right, then the government's specialist schools strategy might ultimately contribute to, rather than detract from, the achievement of the comprehensive vision. Unfortunately, some of the figures on free school meal take-up must raise serious questions about the extent of the social inclusivity at least of the initial tranches of specialist schools.

Nevertheless, I have little doubt that diversity will remain the name of the game for the foreseeable future. And, of course, advocates of comprehensive education have never actually denied the importance of a degree of diversity – indeed, they were not responsible for the phrase 'bog standard'. Each comprehensive school has its own ethos and we celebrate that. And many schools now are adept at responding to diversity within. But we must always beware of legitimate differences turning into unjustifiable inequalities – and of particular social groups monopolising particular sorts of schools or curricula.

Whatever the mix of different types of schools, it remains vitally important to rebuild a comprehensive *system* of secondary education. To avoid diversity producing a hierarchy, all schools in an area need to work together in the interests of optimum provision for all pupils. My own view, as I've said before, is that genuine collegiality among schools would be much easier if they were all put on a similar legal and budgetary footing, whatever private and voluntary sector partners are involved in their governance. But even without that I am rather hoping that we might be able to do it another way if we can pursue Tim Brighouse's notion of collegiates, which you will be discussing in a later session.

But whether we are talking about individual schools or collegiates, the key issue is admissions policies and we must continue to push really hard on that. And I am pleased to see that you will be addressing that too in more detail in a later session, because it is clear that the degree of social polarisation between schools correlates with the proportion of schools controlling their own admission policies. While the government still appears unwilling to address that issue head on, local admissions forums and harmonisation of admissions timetables should certainly make some difference. But I fear it will need far more than that to encourage some of the so-called comprehensive schools I know to become genuinely comprehensive. For all its faults, ILEA's banding arrangement prevented extreme polarisation, while before the Greenwich judgement some degree of planning could take place at LEA level. But even with the present system, with multiple admissions authorities, one would have thought that a government so wedded to the audit culture would, at the very least, institute a far more rigorous and regular audit of actual admissions practices than is currently envisaged. Perhaps we need an access regulator like that proposed last week for universities!

Of course, even if we achieve fair admissions policies, a comprehensive system will need to go much further than an aggregate of comprehensive schools and involve the creation of a comprehensive and inclusive approach to education in those schools. But my main point here today is that we need to recover a sense that comprehensive education needs to be both academically and socially comprehensive and that it will not be if *any* social group is effectively excluded from it – either by choice or by default.

7 THE IMPACT OF SCHOOL DIVERSITY

Stephen Gorard, University of York

This chapter presents a summary of the findings from a series of investigations conducted by the author into the relationship between school organisation and school outcomes in England and Wales. It shows that increased diversification of secondary schooling in the UK is generally associated, by commentators and advocates, with two inter-related claims. First: increased diversification does not lead to increased segregation of students between schools. Second: the new school types driving diversification are more effective in producing higher levels of student attainment with equivalent student intakes than their predecessors. Neither claim can be shown to be true. Then the chapter considers a relatively new type of school – the Academy – that adds an apparent complication. It shows that Academies do, in fact, fit the same overall pattern of 'sleight-of-hand' school improvement as grammar, faith-based, specialist and Welsh-medium schools (among others). If all types of schools produce pretty much the same level of student attainment once their intakes are taken into account, why then does the segregated nature of schooling matters. If the drive to increase standards through diversification has merely produced more segregated schools, apparently nothing has been gained but nothing lost. The chapter ends by arguing that segregation matters, not for school outcomes as narrowly envisaged, but for schools as mini-societies in which students develop a sense of what is just and what is not.

School diversity and segregation

In a major study of the composition of secondary schools in England and Wales from 1989 to 2001, I have demonstrated that increased diversity of school types is strongly associated with increased segregation of student intakes (Gorard et al. 2003). 'Segregation' here refers to the unevenness of student allocation to schools in terms of their background characteristics – most notably in terms of official designation as 'living in poverty'. It is a measure of the extent to which poor children are clustered in specific schools (Gorard and Taylor 2002). At the start of the period of study (1989) the school system in England and Wales was largely comprehensive in structure (with a minority of selective and faith-based schools), so that most state-funded schools were open to students of any ability or socio-economic background, and students tended to use their local designated school. This meant that the student body in most schools reflected the nature of local housing and its residents more than anything else. The historical long-term trend of both residential and school segregation was down.

By 1995 this long-term trend towards comprehensive school intakes had stalled, and from 1997 onwards began to reverse. The growth in segregated school intakes coincided with considerably increased diversity of school types both temporally and spatially. As the proportion of 1989-type local comprehensives declined so segregation increased, and was highest in those areas with a low proportion of comprehensives (Gorard and Taylor 2001). Once the nature of local housing patterns had been taken into account, the least segregated areas were those with no selection by schools, little or no diversification of school types, where choice prevailed over the rigid allocation of school place via catchment areas, and finally where schools were constrained to admit a proportion of students across all of the ability bands represented in the area ('banding').

Readers are recommended to pursue the references given throughout this paper in order to gain a more sophisticated picture of the problem. However, in summary it would be fair to say that, *ceteris paribus*, diversity of school types is clearly linked to increased segregation of school intakes. This applies whether the diversity is in terms of fee-paying:state-funded, faith-based:secular, local:central control, selection:all-ability, specialist:traditional, or Welsh:English medium (Gorard 2000a). Some conservative commentators, especially in the UK research community, objected to the findings of this analysis, presumably on ideological grounds given that their substantive objections were flimsy and sometimes even dishonest (Gorard and Fitz 2006). For advocates of increased diversification of schools it is important to maintain the fiction that introducing new types of schools does not drive up segregation, because their advocacy is generally based on the claim that new type of schools produce superior academic outcomes without changing their intakes. How true is this?

School diversity and improvement

In order to show that a school is differentially effective we have to establish that exactly equivalent students would achieve lower test scores after education at another school. In order to show that a school has improved we have to establish that there has been an improvement in test scores that cannot be explained by a change in the nature of the school intake. Otherwise, SESI (School Effectiveness and School Improvement) is 'sleight-of-hand'.

It is not possible to compare directly the progress of the same student in two schools. Trying, instead, to match the characteristics of students, curricula, qualifications and schools, leads to multiple difficulties of comparability (Gorard 2001).

This leads to an asymmetry in the burden of proof. A commentator claiming to have evidence that one type of school is differentially effective has, therefore, to explain how they have overcome the problems of comparability and of matching equivalent students. A commentator denying evidence of differential effectiveness, on the other hand, needs only point to any lack of *prime facie* evidence or to a contextual difference between types of schools that has been omitted from the analysis.

In any study of school effects, typically between 0 and 25% of the variation between school outcomes remains to be explained, and this residual includes a very important error component. This major finding of work in the school effectiveness genre has been quite consistent over time (Gorard and Smith 2004a). The larger the study, the more variables available for each student, the more reliable the measures are, and the better conducted the study, the stronger is this link between school intake and outcomes. Where sufficient background or prior attainment data is available, it is possible to explain apparent raw-score differences between types of schools simply in terms of differences in student intake (Gorard 2000b). Once their intake is taken into account, specialist, grammar, faith-based and Welsh-medium schools appear no more effective than 'bog standard' comprehensives. In fact, it becomes quite difficult to establish any school effect at all (Gorard and Smith 2004a). But school effectiveness and school improvement (SESI) forms an entire field of research and policy endeavour based on the dual premise that some schools are differentially effective with equivalent students, and that is possible to transfer good practice from the more successful schools to the less successful ones.

SESI advocates try to guard against being misled by not using raw-scores outcomes, and using value-added models instead. Such models are intended to take the prior attainment of each student into account, and so to produce scores that are 'a measure of the progress students make between different stages of education' (DfES 2005). Unfortunately, these models fail for a very simple but important reason – the value-added (VA) scores they produce are so little different from the raw-score figures they are derived from (Gorard 2006a).

The DfES value-added school 'performance' figures have a correlation of +0.84 with the raw-score outcomes they are intended to replace, which themselves have a +0.87 correlation with the prior KS2 scores (Figure 1). This means that 71% of the variation in school value-added scores is explicable in terms of their raw-scores alone. There is a clear pattern of low attaining schools having low VA, and high attaining schools having low VA. Value-added scores are no *more* independent of raw-score levels of attainment than outcomes are independent of intakes. This means that all policies concerning schools, and judgements about the relative effectiveness of different schools and types of schools, will have been misled where they have been based on such a 'value-added' analysis. School improvers and school improvement researchers, relying on value-added analyses, will have been misled in their explanations and in making recommendations for practice. Once accepted, this re-consideration suggests that school improvement policies, at least in this narrow sense, are always likely to be ineffective. Therefore, all claims to differential effectiveness of one kind of school over another are suspect, and the risk of increased segregation through diversification is being taken for no reason at all.

Figure 1 - The link between GCSE A*-C benchmark and KS2 to GCSE value-added, all secondary schools in England, 2004

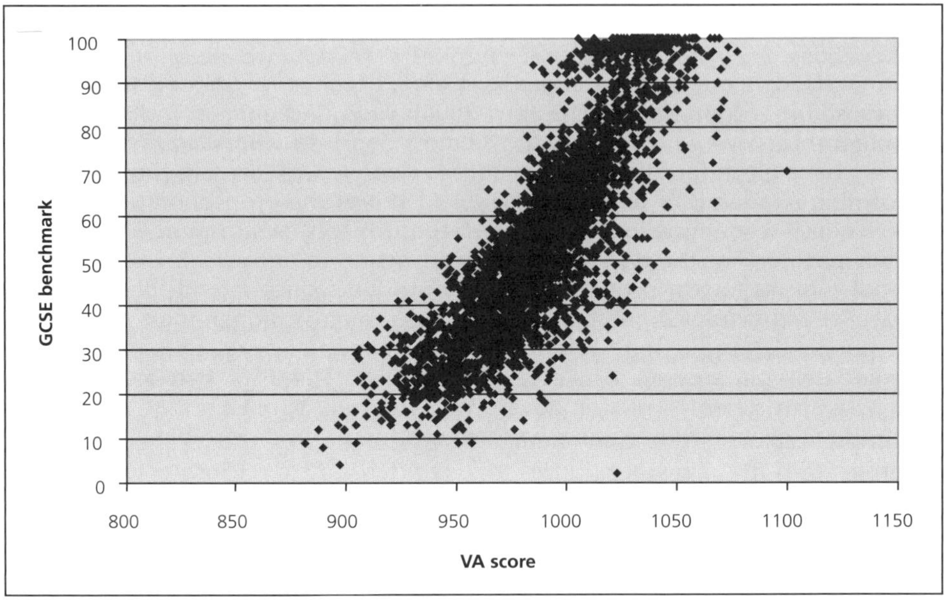

Note: figures provided by DfES. The figures exclude special schools, school with no GCSE entries, no GCSE 'passes' or no Key Stage 2 results, independent schools opting out of the value-added scheme, those whose results were suppressed by the DfES on grounds that individuals might be identifiable, and those with fewer than 30 cases in the cohort.
Note: the value-added scores are those published by the DfES, with a mean of around 988.
Note: the perceived 'width' of the scatter depends upon the scales used. The correlation coefficients quoted are a better guide.

The Academies programme

One recent model of school diversification in England appears, at first sight, to break this link between increased segregation as a price to pay for less than convincing academic improvement. This is because these new schools were intended to be selected as those with the highest levels of disadvantage, so that a change in their intake towards less deprived families would inevitably lead to *less* local segregation, rather than more. In 2004, the BBC reported the considerable success of the Academies (originally City Academies) programme, wherein troubled schools in deprived areas were rebadged, given extra funding, new management, and curricular freedom. The report stated: 'The government has released GCSE figures from three of its new flagship Academies in England. All the schools, which were set up in deprived areas, showed remarkable improvements in results' BBC (2004). The first three Academies were set up in 2002, so that by 2004 it was only these three about which one could tentatively draw before-and-after comparisons. One of these was the Business Academy, Bexley, where the Prime Minister stated that he had 'seen the future of education'. 'In its first year, the Business Academy, Bexley achieved an increase in pupils attaining 5 or more A*-C grades at GCSE from 7% in 2002 to 21% in 2003' (DfES 2004).

In fact, of course, Academies did not break the link between school composition and attainment (Gorard 2005). Many Academies, including one of the first three, were nowhere near the most deprived schools in their areas. The others have all reduced the proportion of deprived children in the school since becoming Academies. For example, Table 1 shows the proportion of students in the Bexley Academy eligible for free school meals, which is an indication of family poverty. For the two years after conversion to an Academy (2002-03), this school took its lowest proportion of FSM students since records began in 1989. The proportion of FSM students was, and remains, higher than the national average so this reduction could have been claimed as a success of the policy of turning schools around. However, this reduction in FSM had to be ignored because the school and the government wished to claim that a purported increase in examination success was achieved with no discernible change to the school intake.

Table 1 – Pattern of disadvantage over time in Bexley							
Business Academy	1997	1998	1999	2000	2001	2002	2003
Percentage eligible for FSM	53	49	52	50	49	46	42

But just how 'remarkable' were the improvements in GCSE scores acclaimed by the Prime Minister? Table 2 shows that, in recent years, the best year for GCSE results in the school that became an Academy in Bexley was 1998, long before the change to Academy status. When the DfES claimed success for the early Academies, because the GCSE benchmark for the Business Academy rose to 21% in 2003, they neglected to mention that the predecessor school had a benchmark of 24% in 1998 at a time when national benchmarks were lower on average anyway. The historical sequence of events here is quite wrong for a successful claim to a policy intervention.

Table 2 – GCSE results over time for the Business Academy							
Bexley	1997	1998	1999	2000	2001	2002	2003
GCSE points per candidate	-	23	20	20	22	-	23
Percentage obtaining 5+ A*-C GCSE	13	24	14	10	17	-	21
Percentage obtaining no qualification	10	6	7	9	11	-	5
Note: the DfES Standards Site does not provide results for 2002, the year of changeover							

In addition, the more recent GCSE 'success' remarked on by the government occurred when the school had a lower level of disadvantage. This makes the 1998 success more remarkable. Of course, the intervention is still at a very early stage, and perhaps we should not expect to see differences until an entire cohort has gone from entry at age 11 to GCSE. The point is that by 2004 success *was* already being claimed by some (see above), and that claim does not stand up to even superficial scrutiny. Because the strong link between school compositions and school outcomes remains, the apparent improvement of Academies is, just like other attempts at improvement through diversification, sleight-of-hand.

The true impact of school composition?

Diversification of schools tends to lead to increased student segregation, which is a concern for some commentators. But if, as appears superficially to be the case, the precise mix of students in any school makes no substantive difference to their levels of attainment (Gorard 2006b), then increased diversification of schools appears somewhat pointless but also relatively harmless. Why does it matter who is educated with who? I have two tentative responses to that important policy question.

First, if there is no need to re-mix school intakes in order to improve attainment (because that has been shown to be ineffective) then we can feel free to use other criteria for deciding on the pattern of intakes to schools. These criteria might include efficiency or convenience, but we could also try equity as a guiding principle. This was the approach that led to comprehensive schools in the first place, and to area-level ability banding in particular.

Second, it is important to bear in mind that the outcome measure in all of the foregoing is based on examination outcomes. Schools are, however, about much more than these. The school mix appears to matter most because it provides the context for creating students' awareness of equity (Halstead and Taylor 2000, Meuret 2001). Close to the heart of developing a model of citizenship among students is the need to encourage children to develop their own concepts of fairness (DfES 2002). Probably the fundamental influence on pupils in developing their perceptions of what constitutes a fair and equitable society is their experience of school (Howard and Gill 2000, Davies and Evans 2002). Inclusive schools are generally more tolerant (Slee 2001), and exhibit that tolerance in racial, social and religious terms, and this is also associated with greater civic awareness (Schagen 2002). In fact, the simple act of segregating students, whether by race, class or ability, might be considered an affront (Massey and Denton 1993).

This matters because the level of ethnic, and other, segregation in schools can affect racial attitudes, subsequent social and economic outcomes, and patterns of residential segregation (Clotfelter 2001). The experience of Northern Ireland shows that, if true, this can be a force for even greater *societal* segregation, where the segregation in schools feeds back into society (Smith 2003), and where teachers in schools are, therefore, unwilling even to discuss issues of sectarianism with their (segregated) students (Mansell 2005). In divided societies, citizenship education can actually generate *negative* results, including the ghettoisation of minority communities, perhaps culminating in greater social unrest as it has in some central European countries (Print and Coleman 2003).

My own research shows that school students have a clear notion about what constitutes a fair and equitable national education system (Gorard and Smith 2004b). The system should be an egalitarian one which benefits all students equally. In general, most students in EU countries were of the opinion that a fair and equitable national education system would be one in which all students were treated in the same way, although there was also considerable support for the notion that the less able students should receive a disproportionate amount of the teacher's attention. However, the extent to which the students report that this was what they actually experienced in school varied across the EU. There are preliminary indications that the nature of their national school system is related to students' formation of views of justice (Smith and Gorard 2006). Perhaps, therefore, we should be more concerned with the experience of schooling as something in its own right, and not always *for* something at a later date (qualification, participation, employment and so on). Perhaps the school mix *is* the school effect, affecting pupils' views of school, and therefore of later educational opportunities, but also affecting their notions of social justice in the present. And perhaps it is this that is most at risk from some of the proposed changes to school organisation presented in the Schools White Paper for England before the UK parliament at time of writing.

References

BBC (2004) Academies getting results at GCSE, http://news.bbc.co.uk/go/pr/fr/-/1/hi/education/3602818.stm, (accessed 17/11/04)

Clotfelter, C. (2001) Are whites still fleeing? Racial patterns and enrolment sifts in urban public schools, *Journal of Policy Analysis and Management*, 20, 2, 199-221

Davies, I. and Evans, M. (2002) Encouraging active citizenship, *Educational Review*, 54, 1, 69-78

DfES (2002) *Citizenship: the National Curriculum for England*, http://www.dfes.gov.uk/citizenship [Accessed August 2003].

DfES (2004c) Academies that are open, http://www.standards.dfes.gov.uk/academies/projects/openacademies/?version=1, (accessed 2/11/04)

DfES (2005) Value-added Technical Information, http://www.dfes.gov.uk/performancetables/schools_04/sec3b.shtml, (accessed 25/2/05)

Gorard, S. (2000a) *Education and Social Justice*, Cardiff: University of Wales Press

Gorard, S. (2000b) 'Underachievement' is still an ugly word: reconsidering the relative effectiveness of schools in England and Wales, *Journal of Education Policy*, 15, 5, 559-573

Gorard, S. (2001) International comparisons of school effectiveness: a second component of the 'crisis account'?, *Comparative Education* , 37, 3, 279-296

Gorard, S. (2005) Academies as the 'future of schooling': is this an evidence-based policy?, *Journal of Education Policy*, 20, 3, 369-377

Gorard, S. (2006a) Value-added is of little value, *Journal of Educational Policy*, (forthcoming)

Gorard, S. (2006b) Is there a school mix effect?, *Educational Review*, 58, 1, 87-94

Gorard, S. and Fitz, J. (2006) What counts as evidence in the school choice debate?, *British Educational Research Journal* (forthcoming)

Gorard, S. and Smith, E. (2004a) What is 'underachievement' at school?, *School Leadership and Management*, 24, 2, 205-225

Gorard, S. and Smith, E. (2004b) An international comparison of equity in education systems?, *Comparative Education*, 40, 1, 16-28

Gorard, S. and Taylor, C. (2001) Specialist schools in England: track record and future prospect, *School Leadership and Management*, 21, 4, 365-381

Gorard, S. and Taylor, C. (2002) What is segregation? A comparison of measures in terms of strong and weak compositional invariance, *Sociology*, 36, 4, 875-895

Gorard, S., Taylor, C. and Fitz, J. (2003) *Schools, Markets and Choice Policies,* London: Routledge Falmer

Halstead, J. and Taylor, M. (2000) Learning and Teaching about Values: a review of recent research, *Cambridge Journal of Education*, 30, 2, 169-202

Howard, S. and Gill, J. (2000) The pebble in the pond: children's constructions of power, politics and democratic citizenship, *Cambridge Journal of Education*, 30, 3, 357-378

Mansell, W. (2005) Don't mention the troubles, *Times Educational Supplement*, 18/2/05, p.16

Massey, D. and Denton, N. (1998) *American Apartheid: Segregation and the making of the underclass*, Harvard: Harvard University Press

Meuret, D. (2001) School Equity as a Matter of Justice, in *In Pursuit of Equity in Education,* Hutmacher, W., Cochrane D., Bottani N. (eds.), Kluwer Academic Publishers, Dordrecht.

Print, M. and Coleman, D. (2003) Towards understanding of social capital and citizenship education, *Cambridge Journal of Education,* 33, 1, 123-149

Schagen, I. (2002) Attitudes to citizenship in England: multilevel statistical analysis of the IEA civics data, *Research Papers in Education*, 17, 3, 229-259

Slee, R. (2001) Driven to the margins: disabled students, inclusive schooling and the politics of possibility, *Cambridge Journal of Education*, 31, 3, 385-397

Smith, A. (2003) Citizenship education in Northern Ireland: beyond national identity, *Cambridge Journal of Education*, 33, 1, 15-31

Smith, E. and Gorard, S. (2006) Pupils' views of equity in education, *Compare*, 36, 1, 41-56

8 SCHOOL ADMISSIONS AND 'SELECTION' IN COMPREHENSIVE SCHOOLS: POLICY AND PRACTICE

Anne West, Audrey Hind & Hazel Pennell, London School of Economics and Political Science*

Originally published in the Oxford Review of Education, Volume 30 Number 3, 2004. Reproduced by kind permission of Carfax Publishing, Taylor and Francis Group.

This article examines secondary school admissions criteria in England. The analysis revealed that in a significant minority of schools, notably those responsible for their own admissions – voluntary-aided and foundation schools – a variety of criteria were used which appear to be designed to select certain groups of pupils and so exclude others. Specialist schools were more likely than non-specialist schools to report selecting a proportion of pupils on the basis of aptitude/ability in a particular subject area but voluntary-aided/foundation schools were far more likely to select on this basis than community/voluntary-controlled schools. Criteria giving priority to children with medical/social needs were given for nearly three-quarters of schools; however, community/voluntary-controlled schools were more likely to include this as a criterion than were voluntary-aided/foundation schools. Nearly two-fifths of schools mentioned as an oversubscription criterion, pupils with special educational needs; these were predominantly community/voluntary-controlled schools as opposed to voluntary-aided/foundation schools. The evidence reported here reveals that despite attempts by the Labour Government to reform school admissions, considerable 'selection' takes place. Implications for policy are addressed.

Introduction

A 'quasi-market' in school-based education resulted from the education reforms introduced by Conservative Governments in the 1980s. One of the consequences of these reforms is that twice as many state secondary schools than in 1988, the year of the Education Reform Act, now determine their own admissions: in January 1988, 15% of schools were their own admission authority whereas now this figure is 30% (West & Pennell, 2003). Schools that are their own admission authority are in a position to 'cream skim'; that is, they can, if they choose to do so, select pupils who are likely to maximise their examination 'league table' results or, conversely, not select those who are likely to have a negative impact on school examination results. However, only oversubscribed schools that are their own admission authorities are in this position, namely foundation and voluntary-aided (in the main religious) schools.[1]

This paper focuses on reforms to secondary school admissions made by the Labour Government since 1997 and, more specifically, the impact they have had on policy and practice. The following section examines the policy context and in particular the changes that have been made in an attempt to make the process

---

* Corresponding author. Centre for Educational Research, Department of Social Policy, London School of Economics and Political Science, Houghton Street, London, WC2A 2AE, UK.
Email: a.west@lse.ac.uk

of admissions fairer and more transparent. It also reports on objections made to, and decisions by, the schools adjudicator – a new system of quasi-regulation. The research methods are also outlined. The next section examines admissions criteria in place in English state secondary schools (excluding academically selective grammar schools), and presents examples of ways in which individual admissions authorities 'select in' or 'select out' particular types of pupils via these criteria and other admissions policies. The final section concludes with a summary of the main findings and their implications for policy and practice.

Policy context

Under the previous Conservative Government a variety of commentators expressed concerns about the administration of school admissions in various parts of the country. These included the lack of policy co-ordination and equity issues surrounding admissions policies and practices, particularly those used by the former grant-maintained schools (now mostly foundation) and voluntary-aided (mostly church) schools[2] (see Gewirtz *et al.*, 1995; West & Pennell, 1997; Audit Commission, 1996; West *et al.*, 1997, 1998).

The Labour Party in its 1997 election manifesto committed itself to a fair system of admissions to schools: 'We support guidelines for open and fair admissions...' (p. 9). The 1998 School Standards and Framework Act and accompanying regulations set a new legal framework for admissions. Associated with the legislation is a Code of Practice on School Admissions. This legislative framework can be seen as an attempt to alleviate problems created by the development of a largely unregulated market as regards school admissions. It also provides a new mechanism – the adjudicator – for resolving local disputes in relation to, amongst other issues, school admissions.

The first Code of Practice came into force on 1 April 1999 (DfEE, 1999) and applied to arrangements leading to admissions from September 2000. A new Code of Practice came into force on 31 January 2003 (DfES, 2003). Key aspects of the Code of Practice relate to the provision of information for parents and guidance concerning the admissions process. Information on oversubscription criteria that admission authorities (LEAs, voluntary-aided and foundation schools) should use is also provided: where more parents have expressed a preference for a particular school in a given year than it has places available, the admission authority must apply the oversubscription criteria in its published admission policy in deciding which parents' preferences it should meet.

Specific reference is made to partial selection that is permitted in some circumstances but not others. The first Code of Practice addressed the issue of interviews stating that schools or admission authorities should not interview *parents* at any part of the application or admission process, although church schools may do so, but only in order to establish a person's religion, including religious denomination or practice. There was no mention of interviewing children. It is significant that the revised Code of Practice (DfES, 2003) states that for the admission round leading to September 2005 intakes and subsequently, '*no parents or children* should be interviewed as any part of the application or admission process, in any school except a boarding school' (s3.15) [our emphasis]. The Code also notes that 'auditions which are part of objective testing for aptitude conducted by a school with a specialism in a prescribed subject' may be carried out in accordance with the school's published admission arrangements.

Turning specifically to oversubscription criteria, the Code of Practice (DfES, 2003) states:

The admission authority has a fairly wide discretion in deciding what these oversubscription criteria should be, provided that:

- The criteria are not unlawful
- The admission authority has considered the factors which it believes to be most important in ensuring that children receive an efficient and suitable education and has had regard to guidance in the Code
- The criteria are clear, fair and objective and are published (sA.51)

One of the mechanisms introduced by the Labour Government was the 'schools adjudicator', designed to resolve local disputes in relation to, amongst other issues, school admissions. Objections can be made to adjudicators by admission authorities; by community and voluntary-controlled schools (since 2003); and in the case of certain existing partially selective arrangements, by parents.

West & Ingram (2001) investigated objections to school admission decisions made to the Office of the Schools Adjudicator during the first 13 months of its operation (July 1999 to the end of July 2000). Over this period, the adjudicators ruled on 57 objections relating to admissions. Objections related to admissions policies in different parts of the country, but the vast majority were in London and the South East of England. In almost all cases these were in local education authorities (LEAs) where there is a 'highly developed' market in operation (West *et al.*, 1998), with a variety of school types co-existing – foundation schools, voluntary-aided schools, fully selective schools, partially-selective schools and so on.

Objections to the Office of the Schools Adjudicator concerned different aspects of the admissions process but in the main related to partial selection by ability/aptitude, interviews, whether employees/children of former pupils should have priority for places, concern about the testing procedures, and feeder schools to secondary schools (see West & Ingram, 2001). The majority of objections relating to partial selection were not upheld by the schools adjudicator. In some cases the objection was upheld in part (e.g. by partial selection being reduced) but in only two cases was the objection fully upheld. In both these cases the partial selection by ability was deemed unlawful on the grounds that it had been introduced after the cut off date, namely the 1997/98 school year.

Interestingly, across all the examined adjudications, none of the objections to priority being given to children of former pupils of the school provided evidence showing specific examples of adverse effects, but each time the adjudicator decided that such admissions criteria were unfair and objections were thus upheld. In several cases an admissions criterion referred to priority being given to children with a parent employed at the school; this, it was reasoned could discriminate against traveller and refugee children who had moved to the area and was thus contrary to the Race Relations Act 1976. Objections to the practice of interviewing pupils prior to admission were made in relation to one voluntary-aided school for non-religious places. The school claimed that it was not breaking the law as the (first) Code of Practice did not explicitly state that interviews with pupils were not allowed. However, the adjudicator upheld the objection. Other objections to interview-like processes (e.g., sports trial, musical audition) were similarly upheld (West and Ingram, 2001).

As noted above, the use of interviews is not permitted in the *revised* Code of Practice. Moreover, the Code (DfES, 2003) also specifically addresses some of these issues raised in rulings made by the adjudicator:

> Bearing in mind the provisions of the Sex Discrimination Act 1975, the Race Relations Act 1976 (as amended by the Race Relations (Amendment) Act 2000), and the Disability Discrimination Act 1995 (as amended by the Special Educational Needs and Disability Act 2001), admission authorities should carefully consider the possible impact, direct or indirect, on equal opportunities of their proposed oversubscription criteria. For example, criteria which give preference to children whose parents or older siblings had previously attended the school or whose parents followed particular occupations, such as teachers, could disproportionately (even if unintentionally) disadvantage ethnic minority, Traveller or refugee families who have more recently moved into the area. In such cases, the criterion could be unlawful unless objectively justified. Such criteria have been determined by the Schools Adjudicator not to be in the interests of all local children and have been ruled out when the subject of an objection. It would not be good practice for admission authorities to set or seek to apply oversubscription criteria that had the effect of disadvantaging certain social groups in the local community, including disabled pupils. Examples would be explicit or implicit discrimination on the basis of parental occupation, employment, income range, standard of living or home facilities (s3.12).

We now turn to our own investigation of admissions criteria, which augments and complements earlier research carried out by White *et al.* (2001), who analysed secondary school admissions arrangements relating to 40 LEAs in England and Wales. Their analysis was at the LEA level, and so focused on *community schools* and in some cases voluntary-controlled schools, not on voluntary-aided and foundation schools. One of their key findings was the considerable variation between LEAs in terms of the criteria they used for allocating places.

Our study, by way of contrast, focused on admissions criteria used for state secondary schools – community, voluntary-controlled, voluntary-aided and foundation. The research involved setting up a database of criteria to individual state-maintained secondary schools for pupils entering in year 7 (age 11) in September 2001. In a minority of cases criteria for September 2002 were used. The schools in the sample were secondary schools (or high schools in the case of those LEAs with middle/high schools). Data were collated for the vast majority (95%) of secondary/high schools in England (N=3013) (excluding the 15 city technology colleges that are officially classified as 'independent'). Data were obtained from LEA brochures and from individual admission authority schools (voluntary-aided and foundation schools) where information was not provided in LEA brochures. The missing schools were foundation/voluntary-aided schools that were not included in LEA brochures and did not provide us with admissions information when we contacted them to request details. The sample consisted of 69% community schools, 14% voluntary-aided schools, 14% foundation schools and 3% voluntary-controlled schools. As certain voluntary-aided and foundation schools did not provide information our sample under-represents these school types. Full details of the research findings are provided by West and Hind (2003) and West *et al.* (2003). This paper, which draws on these, focuses specifically on admissions criteria for non-selective secondary schools in England (N=2862) (and not the 164 grammar schools in England that select all pupils on the basis of ability).

Key findings

Admissions – overall picture

Some admissions criteria were used by a high proportion of secondary schools. Table 1 gives those reported most frequently.

Table 1: Most frequently used admissions criteria

Criteria	Percentage of schools (N=2862)
Siblings	96
Distance	86
Medical/social need	73
Catchment area	61
'First preference'	41
Pupils with special educational needs	39
Feeder schools	28

A high proportion of schools reported giving priority to siblings and to distance; medical and social needs were frequently referred to; and catchment areas were also widely used.

Comparisons were made between schools of different types. Some statistically significant differences were found between community/voluntary-controlled and voluntary-aided/foundation schools; these included more community/voluntary-controlled schools reporting the following admissions criteria: siblings (98% versus 90%); distance (91% versus 71%); medical/social need (80% versus 52%); catchment area (67% versus 43%); first preference (48% versus 22%); and pupils with special educational needs (48% versus 15%); however, more voluntary-aided/foundation than community/voluntary-controlled schools reported admissions criteria mentioning feeder schools (32% versus 26%).

A wide variety of other criteria were used by admission authorities in order to prioritise who should be offered places (see Annex A). These included: religious criteria (13% of schools); children of employees (9%); a difficult journey to another school (6%); children of former pupils (5%); travel time (4%); 'banding' by ability (3%); partial selection by ability/aptitude in a subject area (3%); compassionate factors (3%); children from other religions (3%); children in public care (2%); children with a family connection (2%); and partial selection by general ability (1%).[4]

We now move on to examine a range of criteria that provide opportunities for particular categories of pupils to be 'selected in' and 'selected out' during the admissions process. The criteria considered include: partial selection by ability or aptitude, which has been the subject of intense debate in recent years; giving priority to children of employees or former pupils; the use of religious criteria; the use of 'banding' to obtain a 'balanced' intake; and criteria giving priority to children who have special educational needs or who have particular medical/social needs.

Admissions criteria and opportunities to select
In this section we investigate criteria that may be considered to be 'unfair' because, for example, they give preference to pupils with certain abilities or aptitudes or because they could contravene current legislation. Some of these criteria could be considered to be forms of covert, if not overt, selection.

Criteria relating to ability/aptitude. The 1998 School Standards and Framework Act defines 'ability' as 'either general ability or ability in any particular subject or subjects'. It does not define aptitude, but the Code of Practice notes that a pupil with aptitude is one who 'is identified as being able to benefit from teaching in a specific subject, or who demonstrates a particular capacity to succeed in that subject'. It is not clear how demonstrating a 'capacity to succeed' differs from 'ability'. However, given the complexity we have included partial selection by either ability or aptitude, although we have excluded 'general ability'. Thus our focus was on partial selection by ability or aptitude in *particular subject areas* (e.g. technology, music, dance, art, languages). The distinction between aptitude, ability and achievement is not at all clear. For example, one school made reference to selecting up to 10% of pupils on the basis of 'proven aptitude in music'; the accompanying notes state that children applying under this criterion 'must have achieved at least Grade III of the Associated Board…in an instrument or voice'. This can be construed as a measure of ability or aptitude or achievement – or all three.

It is noteworthy that the relevant subjects, set out in regulations, are: physical education or sport or one or more sports; the performing arts or one or more of those arts; the visual arts or one or more of those arts; modern foreign languages or any such language; design and technology and information technology (DfES, 2003). Amongst the schools in our sample, we found examples of schools selecting pupils on the basis of these subjects, but also on the basis of science and mathematics.

Some schools had more than one criterion relating to pupils' aptitude. One foundation school, for example, had three such criteria: 10% of places for pupils by aptitude for music by audition; 5% of places for pupils by aptitude for dance by audition; and 10% of places for pupils with technological aptitude (see also Annex B).

The legislation governing partial selection by aptitude is not straightforward, as certain pre-existing partial selection (i.e. partial selection that took place prior to the election of the Labour government in 1997) is allowed to continue. New partial selection (introduced after 1997/98) is permitted for schools with a specialism (including specialist schools) and in these cases schools may select up to 10% of pupils on the basis of aptitude in the subject(s) in question.

Given the debate about specialist schools selecting pupils on the basis of ability/aptitude (see West *et al.*, 2000; Flatley *et al.*, 2001; Gorard and Taylor, 2001; Fitz *et al.*, 2002;) we examined whether designated specialist schools were more likely than non-specialist schools to be selecting pupils by ability/aptitude in a subject area. As our database related to admissions in October 2001, we compared specialist schools in operation in September 2001 with non-specialist schools (our sample included 90% of specialist schools in operation at that time[5]).

Overall, in our sample, 3% of secondary schools were found to select a proportion of pupils on the basis of ability/aptitude in one or more specific subjects; just 2% of these schools were non-specialist schools, whilst 6% were specialist. This difference was statistically significant (chi-squared = 27.8, p<0.001). One might therefore assume that the reason that more specialist schools are selecting is as a result of their 'specialist' status (which allows such schools to select up to 10% of pupils on this basis).

However, it can also be argued that as the early specialist schools were either grant-maintained or voluntary-aided (see West *et al.*, 2000, Gorard, 2003), partial selection by ability/aptitude might be more a function of school type than specialist status – with schools in control of their own admissions being more likely to select on this basis than other schools. This is confirmed by our data. If we look at the percentage of schools of different types selecting a proportion of pupils on the basis of ability/aptitude in a subject area, we find that the highest percentage of schools selecting in this way are foundation schools, followed by voluntary-aided schools, then community and voluntary-controlled schools (see Table 2).

Table 2: Percentage of secondary schools selecting a proportion of pupils by aptitude/ability

Type of school	Percentage of schools selecting by ability/aptitude	N
Foundation	11.2	357
Voluntary-aided	6.5	401
Community	0.3	2023
Voluntary-controlled	0.0	81
All schools	**2.5**	**2862**

It is clear from this table that the schools in our sample that were selecting a proportion of pupils by aptitude/ability were predominantly those that were their own admission authority. Looked at another way, 8.7% of voluntary-aided/foundation schools and just 0.3% of community/voluntary-controlled schools selected pupils on this basis.[6] Moreover, within specialist schools, we found that 0.7% of community/voluntary-controlled schools were selecting pupils in this way compared with 16.1% of foundation/voluntary-aided schools. This difference was statistically significant (chi-squared = 56.8, p<0.001).

To see if there were *independent* effects of specialist school status and school type (community/voluntary-controlled versus voluntary-aided/foundation) on whether schools partially selected pupils by ability or aptitude we carried out a logistic regression. The results are shown in Table 3.

Table 3: Logistic regression analysis of partial selection

Model	Odds ratio	Probability
School type	27.64	<0.001
Specialist school status	3.2	<0.001

Note
School type: voluntary-aided/foundation versus community/voluntary-controlled
Specialist school status: specialist school versus non-specialist school

Table 3 shows that there was a statistically significant association between school type and partial selection (with voluntary-aided/foundation schools selecting more than community/voluntary-controlled schools). The odds ratio revealed that voluntary-aided/foundation schools were over 27 times more likely to be partially selecting pupils by ability/aptitude than community/voluntary-controlled schools. Specialist schools were about three times more likely than non-specialist schools to be partially selecting on this basis. Thus, both factors had a statistically significant association with partial selection by ability/aptitude but the odds ratio was greater for the 'school type' variable (voluntary-aided/foundation versus community/voluntary-controlled) than for specialist school status.

Finally, whilst only 1% of schools selected a proportion of pupils on the basis of *general ability*, we again found that such selection was not observed in voluntary-controlled schools and was exceedingly rare (0.2%) in community schools. More voluntary-aided and foundation schools (2% and 4% respectively) selected a proportion of pupils on this basis. In some cases, selection by aptitude was combined with selection on the basis of general ability; in one voluntary-aided school 10 places were allocated for 'pupils demonstrating musical aptitude' and 65 places for pupils with high levels of general ability (measured by verbal reasoning test scores and additionally tests of English and mathematics).

Banding. The School Standards and Framework Act 1998 permits secondary schools to select pupils in order to gain a balanced intake of pupils based on their ability; this is commonly referred to as 'banding'. Overall, 3% of secondary schools in our sample reported the use of some form of banding (2% of community/voluntary-controlled schools compared with 5% of voluntary-aided/foundation schools).

Under the legislation (s101), banding is allowed so long as no level of ability is 'substantially over-represented or substantially under-represented'. The meaning of 'substantially' is open to debate, but our research revealed examples of schools banding in a way that gives rise to an intake 'skewed' towards higher ability pupils. Below we give two examples:

Places are offered in the following ratios: Band 1 [the highest]: 40%, Band 2: 40%, Band 3: 20% (foundation school).

The girls chosen for admission will be drawn from across the ability range, i.e. above average, average and below average...The Governors' expectation is that the ...entrants to the school will be approximately made up of [27% of] girls of above average ability, [56%] of average and [18%] of below average. These proportions are in no way rigid...(voluntary-aided school).

A different approach was adopted where community schools used banding (predominantly in London, see West *et al.*, 2003); this involved the LEA allocating places rather than individual secondary schools:

A quarter of the total places available at each of these schools are allocated to each of the four reading bandings [25% in each].[7]

The main purpose of the [mathematics and reading] tests[8] is to make sure that each secondary school has, as far as is possible, an even balance of pupils of different abilities and is therefore a truly comprehensive school. [There are five bands of ability with 20% in each.] Children with the greatest difficulty in the tests will be in band 3 and those with a high score will be in band 1a. The rest will be in bands 1b, 2a or 2b..

There are two main reasons why 'banding' systems used by LEAs can be construed as being fairer than those used by individual schools. First, the LEA-wide system involves all pupils attending primary schools within the LEA (and those applying from outside the LEA), whilst a school-based system involves only those primary pupils who *apply* directly for places at the secondary school in question. This is important, as there may be particular reasons why some parents may be deterred from applying to a particular school – for example, there may be a perception that there is little chance of success (see Noden *et al.*, 1998). Second, if the admission authority is the LEA the system is more likely to be clear and transparent as the LEA has no vested interest in the process. Evidence indicates that where banding takes place on an LEA-wide basis, its introduction was an attempt to obtain a fully comprehensive intake to schools in the area, whereas in the case of *some* school-based systems, as we have noted above, the banding system could be skewed in favour of those of higher ability. It is also noteworthy that banding at the LEA level appears to be associated with decreases in school segregation over time (Fitz *et al.*, 2002), suggesting that it also serves a 'social justice' function.

Criteria giving priority to children of employees/former pupils etc. The Code of Practice on School Admissions makes specific reference to admission authorities giving priority to certain categories of pupils such as the children of former pupils or employees, stating that these should not be used as they may contravene the Race Relations Act 1976. Nevertheless, we found that 9% of secondary schools in our sample were giving priority to the children of employees/governors: 5% community/voluntary-controlled schools versus 20% voluntary-aided/foundation schools. An example is given below:

Children of present school staff who are normally employed for a minimum of 10 hours per week. Headteachers will have the discretion to include children of other staff employed at the school (community schools in one LEA).

Overall, 5% of secondary schools in our sample gave preference to the children of former pupils (2% of community/voluntary-controlled schools versus 11% voluntary-aided/foundation schools). A small percentage of schools (2%) gave preference to pupils with a 'strong family connection' or equivalent (1% community/voluntary-controlled schools versus 4% voluntary-aided/foundation schools). Altogether we found that 11% of schools were giving priority to one or more of these categories of pupils (priority to employees, the children of former pupils or some other family connection).

Religious schools, criteria used and 'other' faiths. Just over one in ten secondary schools (13%) in our sample made reference to religious criteria. As might be expected, over nine out of ten (92%) voluntary-aided schools had such criteria and 16% of voluntary-controlled schools.

Just under a quarter (23%) of voluntary-aided schools made explicit reference in their admissions criteria to pupils from other faiths or another 'World Faith'. Below is one example:

> If after considering applications made which meet any of the above criteria or a combination of one or more of the same, there remains a shortfall in the planned admissions, then the governors will consider all applications made by parents of children of other Christian denominations. It would be necessary for such parents to have expressed a genuine desire for them to be educated in a Catholic School and to be fully supportive of its Catholic ethos. Such admissions will be limited to 5% of the relevant age group (such an application would need to be supported, in writing, by the appropriate Minister of Religion. Also parents of such applicants may be required for interview).

It is noteworthy that some voluntary-aided schools did not even mention pupils from other Christian denominations. However, we found an example of a school that not only had a criterion relating to those who were not Christians, but also provided details of the proportion of 'non-Christians' admitted the previous year. An unusual example, was a voluntary-aided school that used the same admissions criterion as the LEA (which was very rare) but also noted: 'However, in addition, as we are a Church and a multi-faith school, we request that students are sensitive to, and respectful of, religious worship and prayer' (voluntary-aided school).

Admissions criteria and 'social justice'

In this section, we examine a number of criteria, the presence of which might be construed as indicating that the admission authority has considered issues related to what we have called broadly 'social justice'. This does not mean that these categories are, in practice, used in an equitable manner, however.

Table 4: Percentage of schools with admissions criteria referring to medical/social needs

Type of school	Percentage of schools with medical/social need criterion	N
Community	80	2023
Voluntary-controlled	80	81
Foundation	69	357
Voluntary-aided	35	401
Total	**73**	**2862**

Criteria relating to medical/social need. Nearly three-quarters (73%) of schools in our sample had an admissions criterion relating to medical or social needs of the child. However, as can be seen from Table 4, community/voluntary- controlled schools were more likely to specifically include such a criterion than were voluntary-aided/foundation schools (80% versus 52%, chi-squared = 229.6, p <0.001).

Interestingly, medical/social need did not necessarily need to be supported by a professional, so leaving the possibility of administrative discretion being used by an admission authority to admit certain categories of pupils and exclude others – who may, in terms of social justice considerations, have more 'need' for a place.

Below we show the admissions criterion for one foundation and one community school in one LEA. As can be seen, the former allows discretion as to what constitutes 'personal or medical need' whilst the latter is less likely to be amenable to administrative discretion:

Where there are special medical/social grounds for admitting the girl (foundation school).

In exceptional circumstances, the Director of Education has discretion to give a higher priority where a parent provides professionally supported evidence, at the time of application, that their child has an acute personal or medical need for a place at the college (community school).

Special educational needs. Nearly four out of ten schools in our sample (39%) had an admissions criterion making reference to pupils with special educational needs (or 'special needs', 'physical or psychological conditions' etc.). As shown in Table 5, more were community/voluntary-controlled schools than voluntary-aided/foundation schools (48% versus 15%, chi-squared = 245.3, p<0.001).

Table 5: Percentage of schools with special educational needs admissions criterion

Type of school	Percentage of schools with SEN criterion	N
Community	48	2023
Voluntary-controlled	44	81
Foundation	20	357
Voluntary-aided	11	401
Total	**39**	**2862**

It thus appears that children with special educational needs may be less likely to be admitted to secondary schools that are their own admission authority than to schools where the LEA is the admission authority. However, in some LEA brochures and individual schools' admissions information, the admission of children with special educational needs and more particularly for those with statements of special educational need[3] is not explicitly mentioned as an admissions criterion. This information therefore needs to be treated with caution. It is also important to note that where a school is named in a statement of special educational need, the pupil concerned is required to be admitted to that school.

However, when we examined admissions brochures from LEAs where special educational needs was included as an admissions criterion for community schools it was generally not included as an admissions criterion for voluntary-aided or foundation schools. In one LEA, for example, the first admissions criterion for community schools was: '[Children] for whom a statement of special educational needs has been made under the Education Act 1996 and for whom the school has been named in that statement'. By way of contrast, none of the foundation or voluntary-aided schools in this particular LEA had such a criterion and only 16% of the schools in this category mentioned 'special needs' as either an admissions criterion or in the admissions information provided to parents.

Support for the hypothesis that 'faith' schools are not accepting their 'fair share' of pupils with special educational needs comes from recent government data (House of Commons, 2001) revealing that in January 2000, pupils with statements of special educational need accounted for 2.2% of the population of Church of England secondary schools, 1.9% of Roman Catholic secondary schools, 1.5% of Jewish secondary schools and 2.6% of all other secondary schools.

Children in public care. Just under 2% of schools in our sample (1.7%) had children in public care as an admissions criterion. More of these schools were community/voluntary-controlled than voluntary-aided/foundation (2.3% versus 0.1%).

Idiosyncratic practices to 'select in' and 'select out' pupils
We found a wide range of idiosyncratic criteria and practices that are potentially unfair. These include interviews, imprecise, unclear criteria, and reference to the pupil's academic record or the record of siblings.

Interviews. The first Code of Practice (DfES, 1999) stated that 'Church schools may carry out interviews, but only in order to assess religious or denomination commitment' (s5.25). In 2% of secondary schools in our sample, parents were reported to be interviewed. All of these schools were voluntary-aided; overall, 10% of voluntary-aided schools reported interviewing parents (27 were Roman Catholic schools, 11 Church of England and 4 other religions or denominations).

We also found that 2% of schools in our sample reported interviewing pupils. The vast majority of these schools were voluntary-aided; overall 16% of voluntary-aided schools reported interviewing pupils (of these 45 were Roman Catholic, 13 Church of England and 11 other religions or denominations). In addition, one voluntary-controlled school and three foundation schools reported interviewing pupils.

In some cases, the interviews were to assess religious commitment, for example: 'An interview to confirm Catholicity' or to determine religious commitment. In other schools, however, this was not their sole aim:

> Applicants and their families making a Foundation application will be invited to come for interview. The function of the interview is to assess whether the aims, attitudes, values and expectations of the applicant and her family are in harmony with those of this Anglican school as detailed in the school prospectus …and to explore further the family's commitment to their faith [our emphasis].

> Catholicity of home and pastoral benefit to be derived by child [our emphasis].

Moreover, in some schools, no reference was given to 'religion':

> Admission criterion 1: The outcome of an interview with the pupil to ascertain their *potential to contribute to or benefit from a small school with a caring family atmosphere* [our emphasis].

In the case of this criterion, it is hard to see how any child would not benefit from a 'small school with a caring family atmosphere'.

Criteria that are not clear, objective or fair. Some criteria were not clear or fair in that they were vague and allowed administrative discretion. One, used by a voluntary-aided school was 'compassionate factors'; another, also used by a voluntary-aided school was 'any pastoral, social or educational benefit to be gained from the pupil's education'.

Other criteria related to the behaviour of siblings, which again would seem to be unfair, enabling schools to 'select out' some pupils on account of the behaviour of others, for example:

> Whether the candidate has a brother or sister with a satisfactory record at the school and whose parents have supported the school (for this purpose, a pupil's record will be regarded as satisfactory if she or he has: (i) consistently achieved A or B grades for effort in all subjects, general attitude to work and school, and conduct (as shown in interim and annual reports); (ii) good records of punctuality and attendance; and (iii) taken part in extra-curricular activities or made a contribution to the school in another way) (voluntary-aided school).

Although not an 'admissions criterion' some schools as part of their admissions procedure reported taking up references from pupils' primary schools:

> The school will also require each application to be supported by a reference from the applicant's primary headteacher…The purpose of taking [this] up is to give the primary heads the opportunity to show that the applicant and her family's attitudes, values and expectations are in sympathy with this…school (voluntary-aided school).

Finally, in one case the criteria, relating to religious commitment appeared to be unachievable:

> Baptised fully practising children of families where at least one Catholic parent/guardian is a Baptised fully practising member of the Catholic Church, *whose first priority is a Catholic education for the child where both child and parent/guardian have attended Saturday evening/Sunday Mass every week since the child started Primary School.* This must be supported by:
> - An interview at the school to confirm Catholicity
> - A signed statement by the parent/guardian stating that they have not applied nor taken steps to apply (including the sitting of a selective test) to a non-Catholic school (voluntary-aided school).

The requirement to have attended Mass every week is likely to be unachievable, with childhood illnesses and holidays. Moreover, the requirement for parents to confirm that a non-Catholic school has not been applied to would appear to be unreasonable as there is no guarantee that an application to *any* Catholic school would be successful; such a requirement could leave parents without a school place for their child.

Conclusions

Our analysis has revealed that the admission criteria used by the majority of schools in England appear to be fair in that they do not seem to have been designed to select any specific categories of pupils at the expense of others. This is particularly the case with those for community schools. However, a significant minority of schools, notably those that are their own admission authorities, use a variety of criteria that appear to be designed to select certain groups of pupils but exclude others – there are thus clear opportunities for schools to 'select in' and 'select out' pupils. It is important to stress that the results reported here almost certainly underestimate the amount of 'selection' that takes place as our sample did not include *all* voluntary-aided and foundation schools in England. The missing schools were foundation/voluntary-aided schools that neither appeared in local education authority admissions brochures, nor responded to our request for information about their admissions criteria. Our sample therefore under-represents those schools that are more likely than others to have 'selective' admissions criteria.

The fact that certain types of schools have lower levels of poverty than others lends support to the notion that some schools are more likely than others to 'select out' certain groups of pupils. For example, in England in January 2001, the percentage of pupils known to be eligible for free school meals was 11.4% for Church of England schools, 15.6% for Roman Catholic schools, 6.2% for Jewish schools and 6.5% for Sikh schools, compared with 16.1% for all other maintained secondary schools in England (House of Commons, 2001).

Given the links between social background, prior attainment and later examination performance, various selective practices enable some such schools to obtain higher positions in examination 'league tables' than others. Indeed, an analysis of the overall increase in terms of the percentage of pupils gaining five

or more General Certificate of Secondary Examination (GCSE) passes at grades A*
to C between 1997 and 2000 found an increase of 3.6 percentage points across
all types of maintained secondary schools in our database.[10] However, this figure
was only 2.8 for voluntary-controlled schools and 3.4 for community schools,
whilst for voluntary-aided schools it was 4.3 and for foundation schools 4.4
percentage points (both of which are in control of their admissions).

Schools that are their own admissions authorities are clearly placed in a
favourable position compared with other schools, particularly in urban areas
where the 'quasi-market' is most highly developed. Such schools are in a position
to 'cream skim' as we have demonstrated. There is also the question of the
complexity of the admissions system (e.g. multiple preferences) which is likely to
affect parents who are less well versed in the educational system, for example,
those from minority ethnic groups (see West *et al.*, 1997).

Although the Labour Government has made attempts to reform school
admissions, there is still considerable room for improvement. Some admissions
criteria that are not objective, clear or fair continue to be used and some may
contravene legislation, for example the Race Relations Act, 1976. The new Code
of Practice reiterates the concerns raised in the previous version about
oversubscription criteria that are potentially discriminating, but were
nonetheless in operation at the time of our study (e.g. criteria giving preference
to children whose parents or older siblings had previously attended the school or
whose parents followed particular occupations, such as teachers). Guidance is
not being adhered to by certain admission authorities and the body that has
been set up to regulate school admissions – the Office of the Schools Adjudicator
– needs more power if it is to have the impact that is needed for unfair
admissions policies and practices to be removed.

One issue raised in the Code of Practice, but addressed by very few admission
authorities, relates to children in public care, who are a particularly
disadvantaged group. The Code recommends that 'all admission authorities give
these children top priority in their oversubscription criteria'. It remains to be
seen which admission authorities will take up this recommendation.

Another issue that is mentioned in the Code of Practice relates to children with
statements of special educational needs; where a school is named in the
statement, pupils are required to be admitted to that school: 'It is good practice
for LEAs to mention this in their composite prospectuses' (s7.20, DfES, 2003). This
is another area where current practice could be improved. The admissions
criteria and brochures we analysed were not consistent in terms of what was
reported. It would be in the interests of the parents of children with special
educational needs to have information about this issue. In our view, the
secondary transfer process needs to be further reformed so that some groups of
parents and pupils – and schools – do not continue to benefit at the expense of
others. By encouraging academically and socially-mixed schools that do not give
unfair advantages to some categories of pupils, policy makers have an
opportunity to improve educational outcomes for the majority at the same time
as promoting social justice (see West & Pennell, 2003).

Additional problems will arise with the advent of academies (formerly known
as city academies); although subject to the Code of Practice they are nonetheless

responsible for their own admissions (and will also be able to select a proportion of their pupils on the basis of aptitude in subjects in which they specialise). Thus they may be more likely than, say community or voluntary-controlled schools, to seek to select higher performing or more motivated pupils. The advent of such schools will also add to the complexity of the admission process for parents in the urban areas where they are to be located and where the admission process is already at its most complex (see Flatley *et al*, 2001).

Various changes could be made to school admissions to overcome some of the problems we have identified; for example, the adjudicator could adopt a more pro-active role, which would regulate school admissions more effectively (see also West & Ingram, 2001). This would require legislation. However, we feel it may be necessary to go much further. The House of Commons Education and Skills Committee in a recent report that examined secondary admissions as part of an investigation into the diversity of types of schools noted:

> Legislation now requires coordinated admissions arrangements both within and between LEAs. This change calls into question the whole issue of schools retaining the role as their own admissions authorities. (House of Commons, 2003, p. 35)

We would concur and urge that a thorough investigation be conducted to consider whether the admissions problems that have been examined in this paper and elsewhere would be better addressed by removing the rights of schools to act as their own admission authority rather than by the current method of quasi-regulation via Codes of Practice and the schools adjudicator. To date, these reforms do not appear to be working and more radical steps may well be needed in order to deliver an admissions system to parents that is fair and equitable.

Acknowledgements

The research reported here was undertaken in conjunction with the Research and Information on State Education (RISE) Trust. Thanks are due to all those who provided information for this research, in particular the local education authorities and schools concerned. We would like to thank all those who provided research and administrative support, in particular, Matthew West, Laura Bracking, John Wilkes and Dabney Ingram. Thanks are also due to the two anonymous reviewers of an earlier draft of this paper.

Notes

1. Admission authorities are legally required to admit children, on demand, up to the physical capacity of the school except in the case of selective or religious schools; religious schools will be required to admit children up to this limit from 2004/05 (DfES, 2003).
2. Following the School Standards and Framework Act 1998, grant-maintained schools either reverted to voluntary status or were, in the main, designated foundation schools.
3. There are currently 150 LEAs in England.
4. This list is not exhaustive. For examples of other criteria see Annex B.
5. 613 out of the 676 specialist schools that were not special schools – the remainder did not provide information. Of the specialist schools, 69% were community/voluntary-controlled and 32% voluntary-aided/foundation.
6. In the main, for purposes of simplicity, percentages have been rounded; in some cases, for clarity, they are reported to one decimal place.
7. A reading comprehension test, taken in Year 6 (age 10 to 11 years) of primary school, is used to allocate pupils to bands.

8. The English Qualification and Curriculum Authority's optional mathematics and reading tests for children in Year 5 (age 9 to 10 years) are used.

9. A statement of special educational needs is associated with additional funding.

10. This is of significance as school performance tables published by the Department for Education and Skills have as a key indicator the percentage of pupils achieving five or more GCSEs at grades A* to C.

Note on Contributors

ANNE WEST is Professor of Education Policy in the Department of Social Policy at the London School of Economics and Political Science. She is also Director of the Centre for Educational Research. Her research interests include market reforms in education and their impact on equity, in particular regulation and school admissions. Her other interests include financing education and international education policy.

AUDREY HIND is a Computer Analyst at the London School of Economics and Political Science. She works at the Centre for Educational Research on both data analysis and associated research.

HAZEL PENNELL is a Research Fellow based in the Centre for Educational Research at the London School of Economics and Political Science. She has extensive research interests; these include market reforms; higher education; and equity. She has a particular interest in issues associated with access to higher education.

References

Audit Commission (1996) *Trading Places: The supply and allocation of school places* (London, The Audit Commission).

Department for Education and Employment (1999) *Code of Practice on School Admissions* (London, DfEE).

Department for Education and Skills (2001) *Statistics of Education: schools in England 2001* (London, The Stationery Office).

Department for Education and Skills (2003) *Code of Practice on School Admissions* (London, DfES). Available online at: http://www.dfes.gov.uk/sacode (accessed 18 February 2004).

Fitz, J., Gorard, S. & Taylor, C. (2002) School admissions after the School Standards and Framework Act: bringing the LEAs back in? *Oxford Review of Education*, 28(2&3), 373-393.

Flatley, J. Connolly, H., Higgins, V., Williams, J., Coldron, J., Stephenson, K., Logie, A. & Smith, N. (2001) *Parents' experiences of the process of choosing a secondary school* (London, DfES). Available online at: http://www.dfes.gov.uk/research/data/uploadfiles/RR278.PDF (accessed 26 July 2004).

Gewirtz, S., Ball, S. J. & Bowe, R. (1995) *Markets, Choice and Equity in Education* (Buckingham: Open University Press).

Gorard, S. (2003) Verbal evidence to the House of Commons Education and Skills Committee, 34-35. House of Commons, Secondary Education Diversity of Provision. Fourth Report of Session 2002-3 (London, House of Commons).

Gorard, S. & Taylor, C. (2001) The composition of specialist schools in England: track record and future prospect, *School leadership and management*, 21(4), 365-381.

House of Commons (2001) *Hansard written answers for 22 October 2001*.

House of Commons (2003) Secondary Education: Diversity of Provision. Fourth Report of Session 2002-3, House of Commons Education and Skills Committee (London, House of Commons).

Noden, P., West, A., David, M. & Edge, A (1998) Choices and destinations at transfer to secondary schools in London, *Journal of Education Policy*, 13(2), 221-236.

West, A. & Hind, A. (2003) *Secondary school admissions in England: Exploring the extent of overt and covert selection*, (London, Research and Information on State Education Trust). Available online at: http://www.risetrust.org.uk/admissions.html (accessed 18 February 2004).

West, A. & Ingram, D. (2001) Making school admissions fairer? Quasi-regulation under New Labour, *Educational Management and Administration*, 29(4), 459-473.

West, A. & Pennell, H. (1997) Educational reform and school choice in England and Wales, *Education Economics*, 5, 285-306.

West, A. & Pennell, H. (2003) *Underachievement in Schools* (London, The Falmer).

West, A., Hind, A. & Pennell, H. (2003) *Secondary school admissions criteria in London secondary schools: Examining the extent of cream skimming* (London, Research and Information on State Education Trust). Available online at: http://www.risetrust.org.uk/london.html (accessed 18 February 2004).

West, A. Noden, P. Kleinman, M. and Whitehead, C. (2000) *Examining the impact of the specialist schools programme* (London: DfEE).

West, A., Pennell, H. & Noden, P. (1997) *Secondary School Admissions: Towards a national policy?* (London, Research and Information on State Education Trust).

West, A., Pennell, H. & Noden, P. (1998) School admissions: increasing equity, accountability and transparency, *British Journal of Educational Studies*, 46(2), 188-200.

White, P., Gorard, S. Fitz, J. & Taylor, C. (2001) Regional and local differences in admission arrangements for schools, *Oxford Review of Education*, 27(3), 317-337.

Annex A – Secondary school admissions criteria

Data in the following tables relate in the vast majority of cases to admission in September 2001. Information was obtained from LEA composite prospectuses and from individual schools for those voluntary-aided and foundation schools not included in prospectuses (in some cases information relating to admission in September 2002 was provided); not all such schools provided data. Data were available for 3013 state-maintained secondary schools out of 3165 secondary schools in England (excluding middle schools and city technology colleges) (DfES, 2001). Of these, 151 were designated grammar schools (out of 164 in England) and 2862 were not. The latter are the focus of this paper.

Table A1 England: secondary schools admissions criteria (excluding grammar schools)

Criterion	Percentage of secondary schools N=2862
Siblings	96%
Distance	86%
Medical/social need	73%
Catchment area	61%
First preference	41%
Special educational needs	39%
Feeder school	28%
Religion	13%
Children of employees	9%
Difficult journey	6%
Children of former pupils	5%
Banding	3%
'Other faiths'	3%
Ability/aptitude in subject area	3%
Pupil interviews	2%
Strong family connection	2%
Parent interviews	2%

Note: This table does not provide an exhaustive listing of admissions criteria/practices used

Annex B – Examples of admissions criteria

Community school

1. Applicants who have a brother or sister already at the school.
2. Applicants who live nearest to the school. Nearness to the school will be measured on a large-scale map of the area. For this purpose measurement will be over the shortest reasonable walking route and accessibility by private or public transport will be disregarded.
3. In exceptional circumstances the … Director of Education … will admit children on grounds of particular medical or social need for [named school].

Community school

Priority for places will be allocated strictly against the following criteria in the order listed.

1. A proven medical need relating to your child: (the requirements are strict and need certification by an appropriate doctor or psychologist).
2. The attendance of a brother or sister at the time of admission.
3. Children living in the area served by the following [five named] primary schools
4. The desirability of maintaining relationships while transferring from primary to secondary school.
5. The distance from home to school and the ease of access.

Voluntary-aided school

Where there are more applications for places than the total of 120 places available, places will be offered according to the following order of priority:

1. Roman Catholic children baptised into and practising their faith, whose parents can produce a letter of priestly support.
2. Other Roman Catholic children baptised into the faith.
3. Christian children whose parents wish their daughter to attend [named school].
4. Non-Christian children whose parents wish their daughter to attend [named school].

Voluntary-aided school

The Governors consider that it is reasonable to ensure that prospective pupils can demonstrate their clear wish to be educated within an environment that has clear and strong emphasis on nautical activities and seafaring traditions. The criteria to be applied in rank order are:

1. Demonstration of a clear commitment to [the school's] nautical ethos, and a wish to pursue a nautical career. (The Governors would assess this through an interview in which prospective pupils are given the opportunity to demonstrate their interests and ambitions with regard to the school, and express how they would take full advantage of the specialist education offered. The assessment criteria used for the interviews will be available from the school.)
2. Sibling links
3. Geographical distance

Voluntary-aided school
a) Pupils will be admitted at age 11 without reference to ability or aptitude. Clear priority will be given to pupils drawn from the former [named Urban District Council area] as at 1972. The children of staff have a right to attend the school.
b) Where applications for admissions exceed the number of places available, the following criteria will be applied, in the order set out below, to decide the children to admit:-
   1) Where the child has a sister or brother currently attending the school;
   2) Where there are medical grounds (supported by a doctor's certificate) for admitting the child;
   3) Proximity of the child's home to the school, with those living nearer being accorded the higher priority.

Voluntary-aided school
Group A
1. Children of worshipping members of the Church of England including those worshipping at the Cathedral (up to 58 places).
2. Cathedral day choristers (up to 8 places).
3. Children of staff currently at the school at the time of application.
4. Brothers and sisters of children attending the school at the time of application.
5. Children of other worshipping members of other Christian denominations and faiths.
6. Children of any other applicants to the limit of the places available, according to proximity to the school.

Group B
Pupils selected by ability as measured by the school's assessment procedures in merit order for a maximum of 15 places.
1. 12 of these places will be selected on overall academic ability.
2. 3 of these places will be selected on musical ability.

Voluntary-aided school
Category A1
i. Children of families … actively involved in local RC communities (max 118 places).
ii. Children of families … actively involved in Anglican Church Communities (min 40 places)

Should the numbers in any one sub-category exceed the number of places the following criteria will be applied
(a) evidence of significant involvement … in the church …
(b) evidence of some involvement …
(c) number of years the family has been involved …

Category A2
 Children of families who are members, but not active members of the local
 RC and Anglican Church communities ... with reasons ... which deserve
 priority.

Should the numbers in this category exceed the number of places the following
criteria will be applied
(a) evidence of some involvement ...
(b) number of years family involved ...
(c) weight of reasons ...

Category A3
 Notwithstanding all of the above...special consideration ... child with special
 educational needs, medical problems, or exceptional domestic or social
 problems ... with appropriate evidence.

Category A4
 ... applications from parents of other Christian denominations ... supported
 in writing ..

Tie break
 i. brother or sister attending
 ii. greater number of years the siblings would be part of the same school
iii. weight of reasons ...

Foundation school
1. Residents within [three named] parishes.
2. Children with a brother or sister attending the school.
3. Children who have benefited from a period of residence outside the UK
   leading to experience of a language/culture other than English.
4. Children influenced by the culture/language of another country as a result of
   residence there of one or more parents.
5. Children influenced by the culture/language of another country as a result of
   work/interests of one or more parents.
6. Children with a proven interest in language/culture outside the UK.
7. Children whose parents work/interests are connected with other countries.
8. Proximity of home to school, those living closest being accorded higher
   priority.

Foundation school
- Allocation of places will follow the criteria in order as published:
- Siblings of pupils at present on roll at the School
- 10% places for pupils by aptitude for Music by audition
- 5% places for pupils by aptitude for Dance by audition
- 10% places for pupils with Technological Aptitude
- Pupils whose parent works at the School
- Remaining places allocated by geographical proximity to the School

Foundation school
1. Children with a brother or sister currently attending the school.
2. A number of children, up to a maximum of 21, who have high levels of ability and aptitude in music and/or drama – proportions in each subject to be determined by the Applications and, if there are sufficient, in the ratio of 2:1 respectively, i.e. 14 children of high ability in music and 7 in drama. Preference will be given to those who have high abilities and aptitude in both subjects.
3. Medical grounds (supported by a doctor's certificate) for admitting the child.
4. Proximity of the child's home to the school, with those living nearer being accorded the higher priority.

9 USING NATIONAL VALUE-ADDED DATASETS TO EXPLORE THE EFFECTS OF SCHOOL DIVERSITY

Ian Schagen and Sandie Schagen
presented at BERA, Exeter, 12 September 2002

Abstract

The advent of large-scale matched datasets, linking pupils' attainment across key stages, gives new opportunities to explore the effects of school organisational factors on pupil performance. Combined with currently-available sophisticated and efficient software for multilevel analysis, it offers educational researchers the chance to develop objective evidence about issues both old and new. Previously-reported research, based on separate datasets from KS2 1997 to KS3 2000 and KS3 1998 to GCSE 2000, focused on the impact of selective, specialist and faith schools. We now have access to a national dataset with 380,000 pupils' KS2 levels in 1996 matched to their GCSE performance in 2001, and this has enabled us to rework these analyses based on value-added results across all five years of secondary education. Results of the analysis will be compared with the previous work, and the paper will emphasise the important contribution that the marriage of these datasets and multilevel modelling will continue to make to educational research.

Introduction

In order to assess the effectiveness of individual schools, or school types, it is necessary to carry out a value-added analysis of their pupils' performance. The 'raw' results published in league tables tell us little, since a high level of attainment could simply indicate a more able, privileged intake.

The introduction of national testing at the end of every key stage has made it possible to measure and compare pupil performance across key stages. National value-added datasets (NVADs) provide the matched pupil-level information to facilitate effective value-added analysis. However, test results were collected in this form from 1996 onwards, so the first NVAD linking key stage 2 and GCSE results (1996-2001) was not available until early in 2002. Using this NVAD, it is now possible to measure the value added by schools across the whole of compulsory secondary education.

Using earlier NVADs, it was necessary to carry our separate analyses for key stages 3 and 4. In this way, the authors explored the impact of selection on pupil performance (Schagen and Schagen, 2001) and the impact of specialist and faith schools on performance (Schagen *et al.*, 2002).

The selection project aimed to assess whether comprehensive or selective education produced the best overall results. We found that, at GCSE level, there was little difference between comprehensive and selective LEAs, in terms of value-added performance. However, at key stage 3, selective LEAs had a clear advantage. The analysis indicated that this was because 'borderline' grammar school pupils (those with level 4-5 at key stage 2) performed very much better than pupils of the same ability in comprehensive schools. Exploring possible reasons for this, we examined entry to higher tiers in mathematics and science at key stage 3; we found that grammar school pupils were 9-20 times as likely to be entered for higher tiers than pupils of equal ability in comprehensive schools.

Like the selection project, research into the impact of specialist and faith schools explored a range of outcomes at both key stages (key stage 3 and GCSE). Broadly, the key findings were that:

- technology colleges and language colleges performed slightly above the norm on all of the outcomes investigated
- Jewish schools performed exceptionally well on all but one of the outcomes
- church schools performed consistently well in English.

It was our intention to repeat the analyses when the new NVAD became available, to see whether our findings could be replicated with a different cohort of pupils, when looking across the whole five years of compulsory secondary schooling, rather than individual key stages. This paper describes the findings from that analysis. The approach used, based on multilevel modelling, was basically the same as that employed in the original projects; however, we investigated a wider range of outcomes, and the models were refined in the light of analysis recently undertaken for a related project, which explored the impact of school size and single-sex education (Spielhofer *et al.*, 2002). The technical details are given in the following section.

Models fitted and background variables

The GCSE outcomes investigated were:

- total GCSE score[1]
- average GCSE score
- mathematics score
- English score
- total science score[2]
- average science score
- number of GCSE entries.

The following background variables were used in the model to predict each of these GCSE outcomes:

pupil-level
- sex (girl or boy)
- levels achieved at key stage 2 in mathematics, English and science
- an indicator to show if the average key stage 2 level achieved was less than 3.0 (previous research has shown that there is a significant positive progress effect for pupils with low values of prior attainment)

---

1 Points were derived from subject grades in the standard manner, i.e. A*=8, A=7, B=6 … G=1.
2 Points were derived from science grades in the manner described above, e.g. grade CC for double balanced science = 10 points.

school-level
  • school percentage of pupils eligible for free school meals (FSM)
  • square of the above percentage, divided by 1000 (analysis has shown the relationship between performance and FSM is non-linear)
  • grammar school indicator
  • percentage of pupils in the LEA attending grammar schools
  • specialist school indicator (default type = technology college)
  • percentage of pupils in the LEA attending specialist schools
  • indicators for arts, language and sports colleges
  • faith school indicator (default affiliation = Church of England)
  • percentage of pupils in the LEA attending faith schools
  • indicators for Catholic, Jewish and other Christian schools.

Extra variables were created to allow for the fact that the relationship between prior attainment and GCSE outcome may be affected by certain key background factors (sex, low prior attainment, percentage eligible for free school meals, grammar school, specialist school and religious school).

The multilevel model was fitted at three levels: LEA, school and pupil. Over and above the 'fixed' part of the model, which consists of the regression against the background factors outlined above, there is a random part of the model which relates to variations in outcome which are specific to particular pupils, schools or LEAs. There is a random variance at each level: i.e. we assume that pupils differ in their GCSE outcomes, over and above what might be predicted; schools differ between themselves in average outcomes, as do LEAs. In addition, the relationship between key stage 2 prior attainment and GCSE outcome was assumed to vary from school to school.

The model was fitted to data from 377,583 pupils in 3044 schools in 149 LEAs.

Outcomes

Figures 1 to 7, one for each of the outcomes, show graphically the effects of different school types. The lines illustrate 'expected' GCSE performance for pupils with different key stage 2 average levels in different school circumstances, taking average values for the other background factors.

As would be expected, all outcomes were strongly related to prior attainment (levels gained at key stage 2), although the performance of those with the lowest key stage 2 levels (average < 3) was better than would have been predicted from a simple linear model. Gender was also significant for all outcomes, with boys outperforming girls in mathematics and science, and girls doing better than boys in all other outcomes.

One school-level factor had a strong negative impact on outcomes: the percentage of pupils in the school eligible for free school meals (FSM). In other words, GCSE performance relative to key stage 2 attainment tends to be reduced in schools with high numbers of FSM pupils. However, this effect was reduced as the FSM percentage increased, i.e. after %FSM reaches a certain level (about 50-60%), further increases will have less of an impact on pupil performance.

After controlling for all of these variables, school type had an impact, as described below.

Grammar Schools

Grammar schools had by far the biggest impact of any school type. They would obviously be expected to have the best raw results, so it is important to remember that here we are examining performance in value-added terms.

As Fig. 1 shows, the line representing grammar schools is much flatter than the lines representing other school types. In other words, in grammar schools the difference in the range of performance at key stage 2 is significantly reduced at GCSE. Pupils at the highest ability level (average 5 or higher at key stage 2) appear to achieve better results in comprehensive[3] schools; by contrast, borderline grammar school pupils with level 4-5 at key stage 2 perform much better than pupils of equivalent ability in other types of school.

Grammar schools obtained similar results (illustrated by flatter lines) on most other outcomes (see Figs. 2-4 and 6-7). The exception was total science score, for which pupils across the whole grammar school ability range obtained better results that students of the same ability in other schools. This probably reflects the fact that grammar schools are more likely to offer three separate science subjects than comprehensive schools.

Fig. 7, illustrating expected number of GCSE entries, is interesting as the grammar school line is particularly flat, and intersects with the lines representing other school types at an earlier point. It appears that grammar schools tend to enter their pupils for the same number of GCSEs, since the range shown is so limited (from about 9.6 entries for the least able grammar school pupils, to 10.2 for the most able). In other school types, there is much greater differentiation, and a large number of pupils would be likely to take more GCSEs in a non-selective school.

Specialist schools

Specialist schools also achieved better value-added results than non-specialist schools, although their impact was very much less than that of grammar schools. In Figs. 1-6, the line representing specialist schools is usually just above, and roughly parallel to, the line representing 'ordinary' comprehensive schools. This is the case in Fig. 2, illustrating average GCSE point score; however, in Fig. 1 the lines start very close (at the low end of the ability range) and gradually diverge. This suggests that the more able pupils in specialist schools tend to take an extra GCSE, an inference which is confirmed by Fig. 7, which illustrates number of GCSE entries.

Here the difference between specialist and non-specialist schools is much greater than for any other outcome; the relevant coefficient was 0.229, showing that an 'average' pupil would take an extra quarter of a GCSE in a specialist school. The specialist school line is slightly steeper than the other lines, indicating again that in specialist schools the more able pupils are likely to take an extra GCSE. Examination of Figs. 5 and 6 suggests that the extra subject may be

---

3 In the context of the analysis, the term 'comprehensive' is used to denote all schools other than grammar schools, although we recognise that this includes schools in selective areas which are not comprehensive in the sense of catering for the full ability range.

science, since total science score increases with ability (compared with the norm represented by non-specialist schools) while average science score does not.

The graphs illustrate the performance of all specialist schools taken together, but the models included indicators which distinguished language, sports and arts colleges from the default technology colleges. In most cases, the differences were not significant; however, arts colleges performed below the general level of specialist schools in total science score, and sports colleges in total GCSE point score.

Faith schools

Faith schools in general had a positive impact on two GCSE outcomes: total score and number of entries. On most other outcomes (Figs 2-6) the line representing faith schools is barely distinguishable from that representing ordinary comprehensives. However, in terms of total point score (Fig. 1) the faith school line is consistently above the comprehensive line, although the difference is small. Since there is no corresponding advantage in terms of average score, this suggests that pupils in faith schools may take an extra GCSE (perhaps, in this case, because religious education is compulsory).

As with specialist schools, this is confirmed by Fig. 7, illustrating the number of entries. Indeed, the lines representing faith and specialist schools are close, although they diverge towards the top end of the ability range, suggesting that faith schools differentiate less than specialist schools in terms of GCSE entries for pupils of different abilities.

The models distinguished Roman Catholic, Jewish and 'other Christian' schools from the default Church of England schools, but in most cases the differences were not significant. However, in value-added terms, RC schools performed above the norm in English, and Jewish schools in terms of average GCSE point score.

Impact on LEAs

One aim of our research was to discover what impact, if any, the existence of different school types had at LEA level. In selective LEAs, the existence of grammar schools, which can be expected to perform better than comprehensive schools, presupposes the existence of secondary modern[4] schools, which cannot be expected to perform as well. How do the overall results of selective LEAs (grammar and secondary modern schools combined) compare with those of fully comprehensive LEAs?

Similarly, it has been suggested that, because specialist and faith schools are popular with parents, an informal system of selection will operate, leading to increasing 'polarisation' between these schools and the 'ordinary' comprehensives in neighbouring areas (see Gorard and Taylor, 2001). A 'virtuous circle' can be created, as the 'better' schools tend to attract the children of informed, supportive parents, and therefore obtain better results, which

---

4 The term is used here to denote schools in selective areas which are not grammar schools, although we acknowledge that many now prefer different designations.

improves their reputation and makes them more likely to attract the children of informed, supportive parents... The corollary is that ordinary comprehensives will take fewer children from 'better' families, their results will drop and they may tend towards becoming 'sink' schools. We wished to discover whether there was evidence to support this theory.

We therefore carried out an analysis of the performance of an 'average' school within different types of LEA. In the first instance, selective LEAs were classified as 'low' or 'high' selection, and the performance of schools within both types were compared with that of schools in 'no selection' or fully comprehensive LEAs. On all but one of the seven GCSE outcomes, schools in selective LEAs obtained better value-added results than those in comprehensive LEAs – but none of the differences were statistically significant.

LEAs were likewise classified according to the percentage of their pupils in religious or specialist schools. Schools in 'high' or 'low' religious LEAs obtained better results than those in non-religious LEAs,[5] but again, the differences were not statistically significant. Similar results were obtained by 'high' and 'low' specialist LEAs, in comparison with LEAs with no specialist schools, but in this case one of the GCSE outcomes emerged as significant – the number of GCSE entries. In low specialist LEAs, the number of entries was just over a third (0.348) of a GCSE higher than in non-specialist LEAs, while in high-specialist LEAs the difference was slightly greater (0.373).

Comparison with previous findings

The research described above replicated research undertaken earlier, but was based on a different dataset (2001 GCSE outcomes linked with 1996 key stage 2 levels) and used a wider range of outcomes and an improved methodology. The findings were broadly the same, but there were a few (relatively minor) differences, which will be highlighted below.

Selection

In terms of selection, the 'grammar school effect' identified in the original research (Schagen and Schagen, 2001) was demonstrated clearly in the new analysis. For almost every outcome, the line illustrating grammar school performance is much flatter than any other school type, showing that the difference in the range of performance at key stage 2 is significantly reduced at GCSE. In particular, both old and new analyses demonstrate clearly that grammar schools enhance the performance of their least able pupils, raising it to a level well above that which would be achieved by pupils of the same ability in comprehensive schools.

However, in contrast with our earlier findings, the new analysis indicates that selection has no significant impact on the overall performance of LEAs. The original research showed little difference at GCSE level (indeed, high selection

---

5 I.e. LEAs with no religious schools. It should be noted that there are very few LEAs in this category, and they may not be a representative group.

LEAs had slightly lower total point scores than comprehensive LEAs) but at key stage 3 both high and low selection LEAs were significantly ahead.

One possible explanation can be deduced from a closer examination of the graphs (Figs. 1-7) in comparison with similar graphs illustrating earlier findings (see Schagen and Schagen, 2001). On the new graphs, the crossover point (where the grammar school line crosses the comprehensive school line) occurs at around level 5 (key stage 2) rather than level 5.5. This suggests that, in contrast with earlier findings, pupils with average key stage level greater than 5 fare better in comprehensive schools than in grammar schools; although there are fewer pupils in this category, this would help to counterbalance the advantage of borderline pupils in grammar schools, and explain why there was no significant difference between selective and comprehensive LEAs.

Specialist schools

Our earlier research (Schagen *et al.*, 2002) considered four types of specialist schools separately. It showed that while language and technology colleges performed slightly above the norm (represented by non-specialist schools) on all GCSE and key stage 3 outcomes, the performance of arts and sports colleges was more variable.

The revised analysis looked at the performance of specialist schools as a whole, taking technology colleges as the default but using indicators to enable any significant differences to be identified. The analysis confirmed that specialist schools were significantly ahead of non-specialist schools on all outcomes (though the differences were relatively small, and did not compare with the grammar school effect). However, arts and sports colleges appeared to perform better, falling below the level of specialist schools as a whole on only one outcome (total science score for arts colleges, total GCSE score for sports colleges).

In the report based on our earlier research, we noted that the advantage of technology colleges in terms of total GCSE point score was relatively higher than their advantage in terms of average point score. The inference was that pupils in technology colleges were taking more subjects than their peers in non-specialist schools. The new research clearly confirms that hypothesis. Once again, specialist schools are further ahead in terms of total score than in average score. In addition, we included number of entries as an additional outcome, and here there was a statistically significant difference between specialist and non-specialist schools.

Faith schools

In the earlier research, different categories of faith schools (like different categories of specialist schools) were considered separately; this time, they were considered together, with Church of England schools as the default type. The original findings showed a mixed picture; Roman Catholic schools performed mainly above expectations at GCSE, but below at key stage 3, while C of E schools performed in line with expectations on some outcomes, and ahead on others, at both key stages. Only in English were church schools consistently ahead at both key stages (in line with findings from other research). Jewish schools, however, performed exceptionally well on all outcomes except key stage 3 science. Faith schools of all types obtained good results in terms of GCSE total point score, but (as with specialist schools) their advantage was much less clear in terms of average score, which again suggested that pupils were encouraged to take an additional GCSE (in this case, perhaps, compulsory RE).

The findings from the latest research presented a broadly consistent picture, but with some variations. Taking key stages 3 and 4 together this time, faith schools as a whole were significantly ahead on only two outcomes: total point score and number of GCSE entries. This clearly confirms the hypothesis that pupils in faith schools are encouraged to take an additional GCSE. In this analysis, Roman Catholic schools performed above expectations in English, but other faith schools did not (and even RC schools were only slightly ahead on this outcome). In addition to total point score and number of entries, Jewish schools were ahead in terms of average point score, but not in English, mathematics or science.

Conclusions

National value-added datasets make it possible to carry out a fair and effective comparison between different types of school. This year, for the first time, an NVAD matching key stage 2 and GCSE results for individual pupils is available. We were therefore able to repeat some research undertaken earlier, in order to see whether the findings could be replicated with a different cohort of pupils, looking at key stages 3 and 4 together, and using a refined multilevel modelling approach. A wider range of outcomes was investigated.

Despite these differences, the findings from the latest analysis were broadly consistent with those from the earlier research. There were some relatively minor variations which have been discussed in the previous section, but the overall picture remained the same, and the analysis therefore provides confirmation of the following key points:

- There is a large 'grammar school effect', which shows that borderline pupils – those who narrowly obtain a grammar school place – obtain much better GCSE results five years later than pupils of equal prior attainment in comprehensive schools. The new research, however, indicates that pupils of higher prior attainment (key stage 2 average level greater than 5) may fare better in comprehensive schools. In general, the difference in the range of pupil performance at key stage 2 (restricted, of course, in grammar schools) is further reduced in terms of GCSE outcomes.
- Compared with grammar schools, the impact of specialist schools is relatively minor, but it is positive and consistent, with pupils in specialist schools obtaining better results in every GCSE outcome investigated than those in non-specialist schools. This applies to all types of specialist school – in the latest analysis, arts and sports colleges failed to reach the level of technology and language colleges in just one of the outcomes investigated.
- On the whole, faith schools seem to make very little impact, although there are exceptions to this general rule: Roman Catholic schools perform above expectations in English, and Jewish schools in terms of average point score.

The earlier research suggested that pupils in faith schools of all types were encouraged to take an additional GCSE; this was confirmed in the recent research, which showed that faith schools are ahead of ordinary comprehensives in terms of total point score (but not average point score) and number of GCSE entries.

This paper has demonstrated again that statistical analysis of national value-added datasets can be a powerful tool to help us investigate the effectiveness of different school types. However, it is important to note the limitations of the data included in the NVADs. Thus, although the analysis took into account prior attainment and other key background variables, there are relevant factors for which data is not available, such as ethnicity, and level of parental support. It could be, for example, that Roman Catholic schools get better English results because they have fewer pupils with English as an additional language, or that specialist schools' above-average performance is linked with the additional funding which they receive. In order to explore these issues further, a more in-depth exploration would be required, looking at factors which cannot be included in statistical analyses.

The research project on which this paper is based was funded by the NFER's Research Development Fund. The authors wish to thank Christine Boateng-Asumadu and her colleagues at QCA and DfES for supplying the matched value-added datasets used in the research.

References

GORARD, S. and TAYLOR, C. (2001). The composition of specialist schools in England: track record and future prospect, *School Leadership & Management,* 21(4), pp. 365-381.

SCHAGEN, I. and SCHAGEN, S. (2001). 'The impact of selection on pupil performance.' Paper presented at the NFER's Annual Conference, Institute for Civil Engineers, London, 19 October.

SCHAGEN, S., DAVIES, D., RUDD, P. and SCHAGEN, I. (2002*). The Impact of Specialist and Faith Schools on Performance* (LGA Research Report 28). Slough: NFER.

SPIELHOFER, T., O'DONNELL, L., BENTON, T., SCHAGEN, S. and SCHAGEN, I. (2002). *The Impact of School Size and Single-sex Education on Performance* (LGA Research Report 33). Slough: NFER.

Figure 1: Expected Total GCSE Score v. Average KS2 level for Different school Types
100
90
80
70
60
50
40
30
20
10
0
Total GCSE Score
3
4
5
6
Average KS2 level
Comprehensive
Grammar
Specialist
Faith

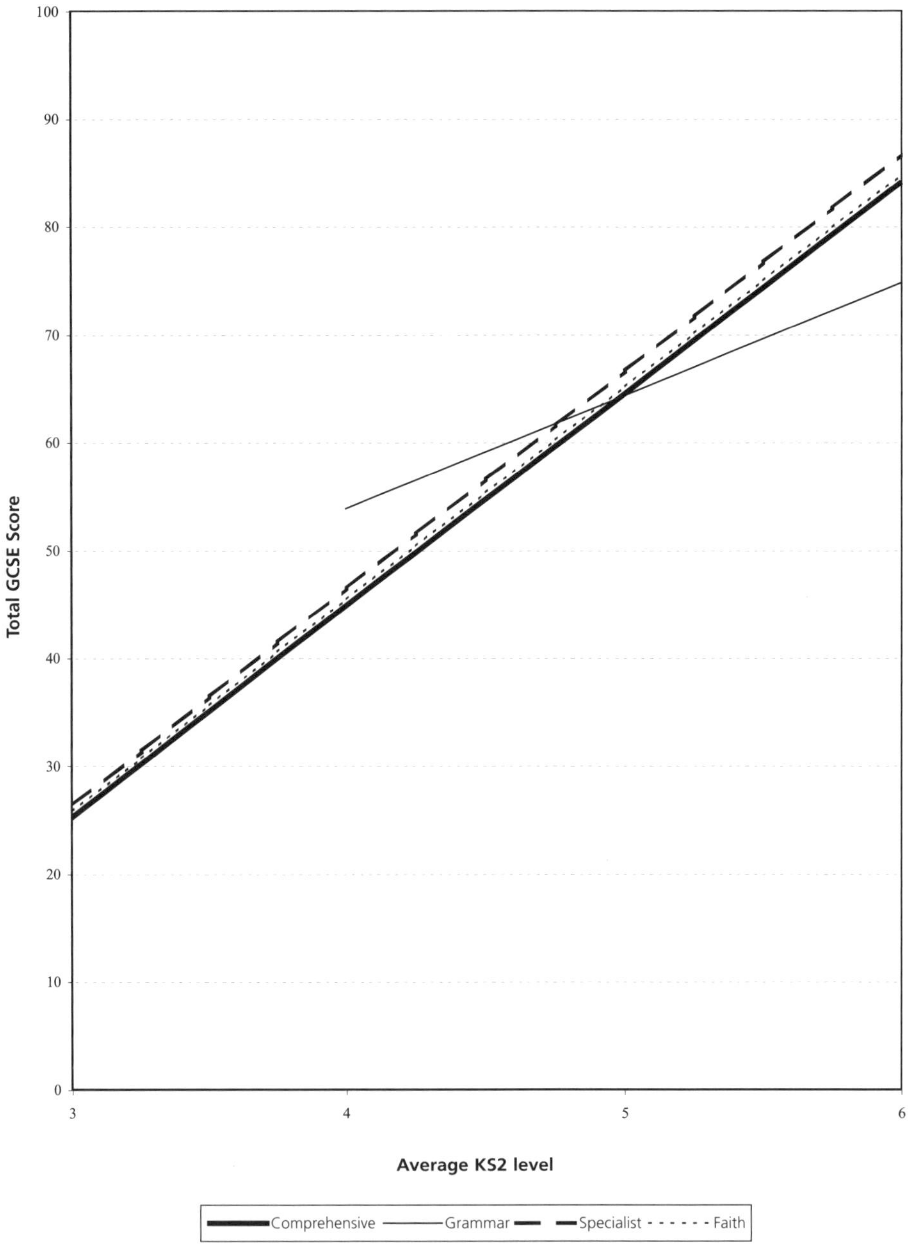

Figure 2: Expected Average GCSE Score v. Average KS2 level for Different school Types

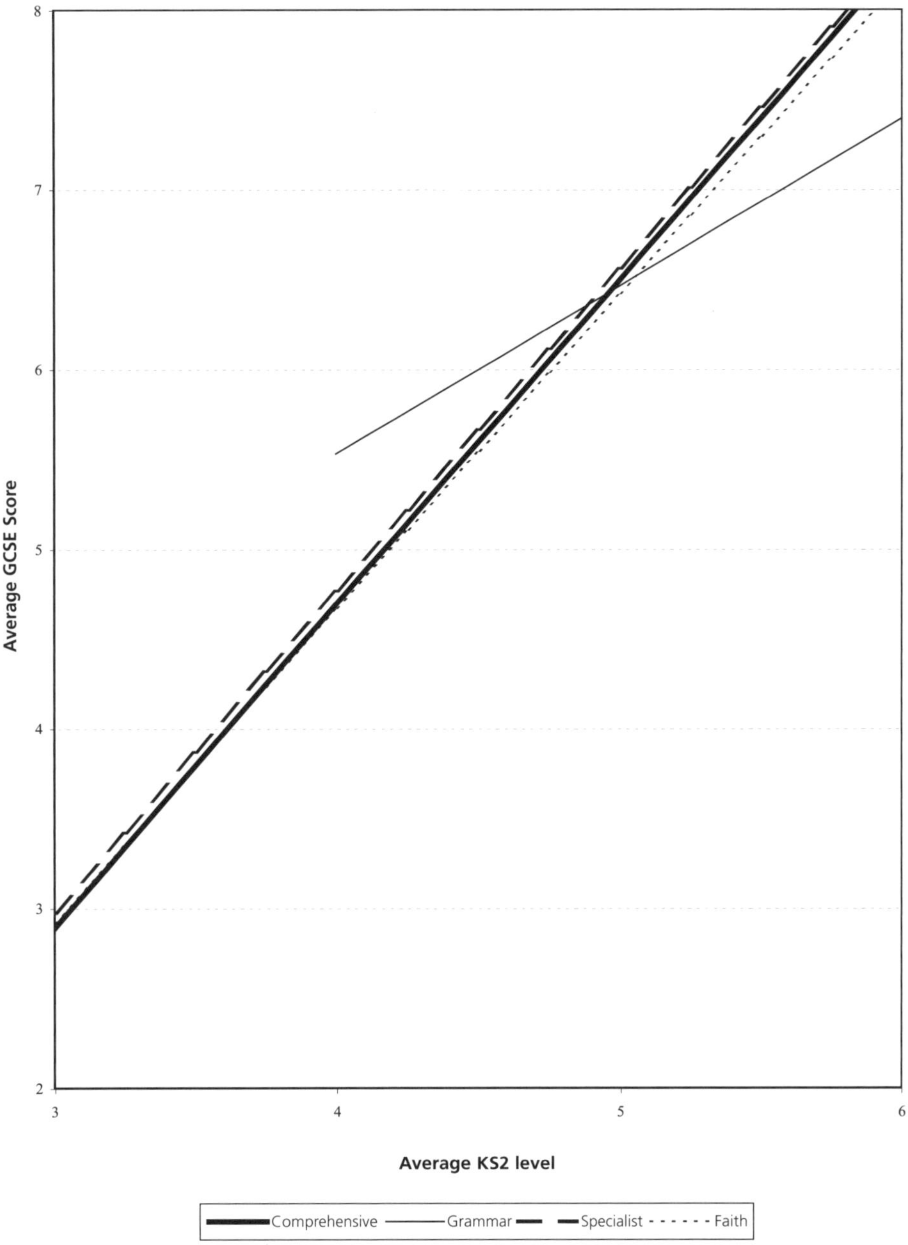

Figure 3: Expected Maths GCSE Score v. Average KS2 level for Different school Types
8
7
6
5
4
3
2
Maths GCSE Score
3
4
5
6
Average KS2 level
Comprehensive
Grammar
Specialist
Faith

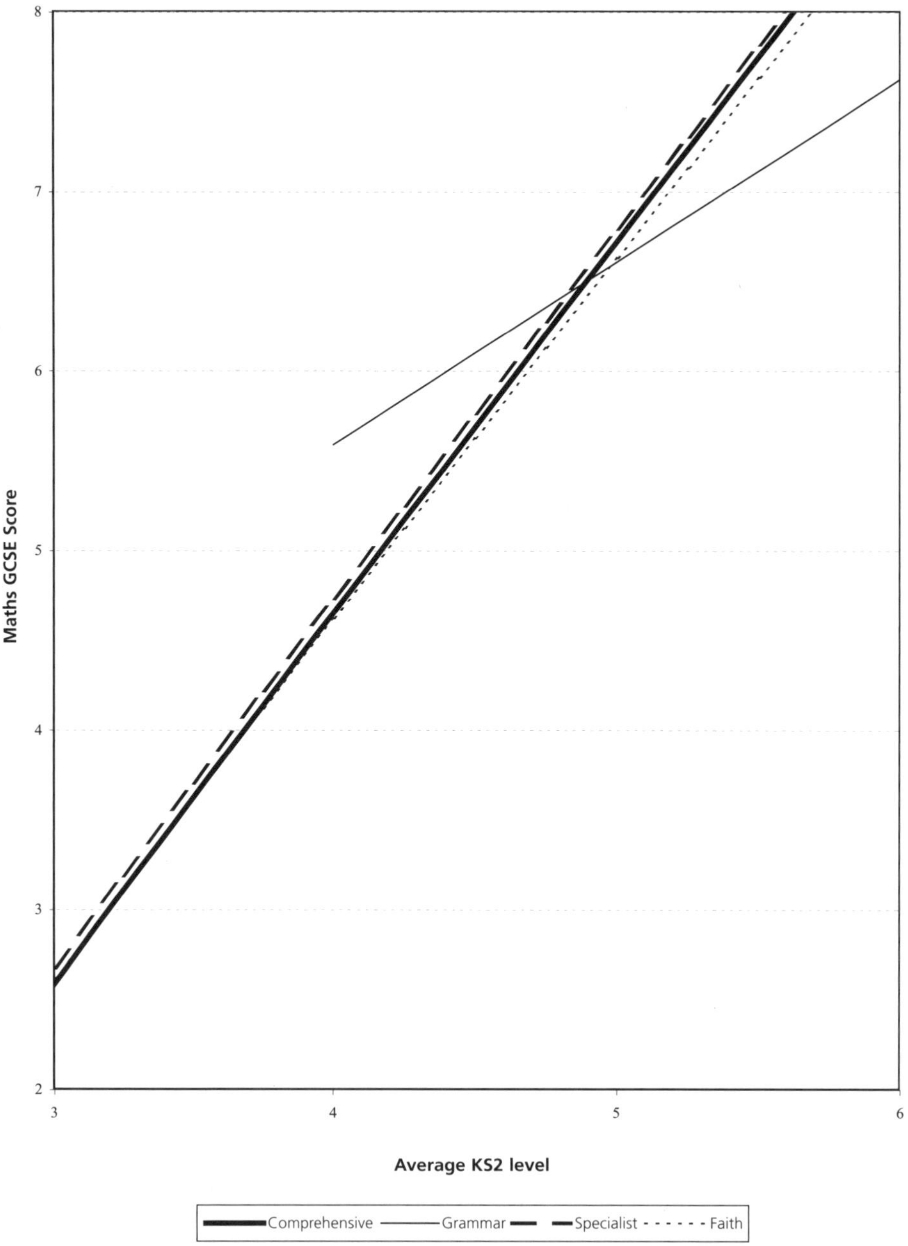

Figure 4: Expected English GCSE Score v. Average KS2 level for Different school Types

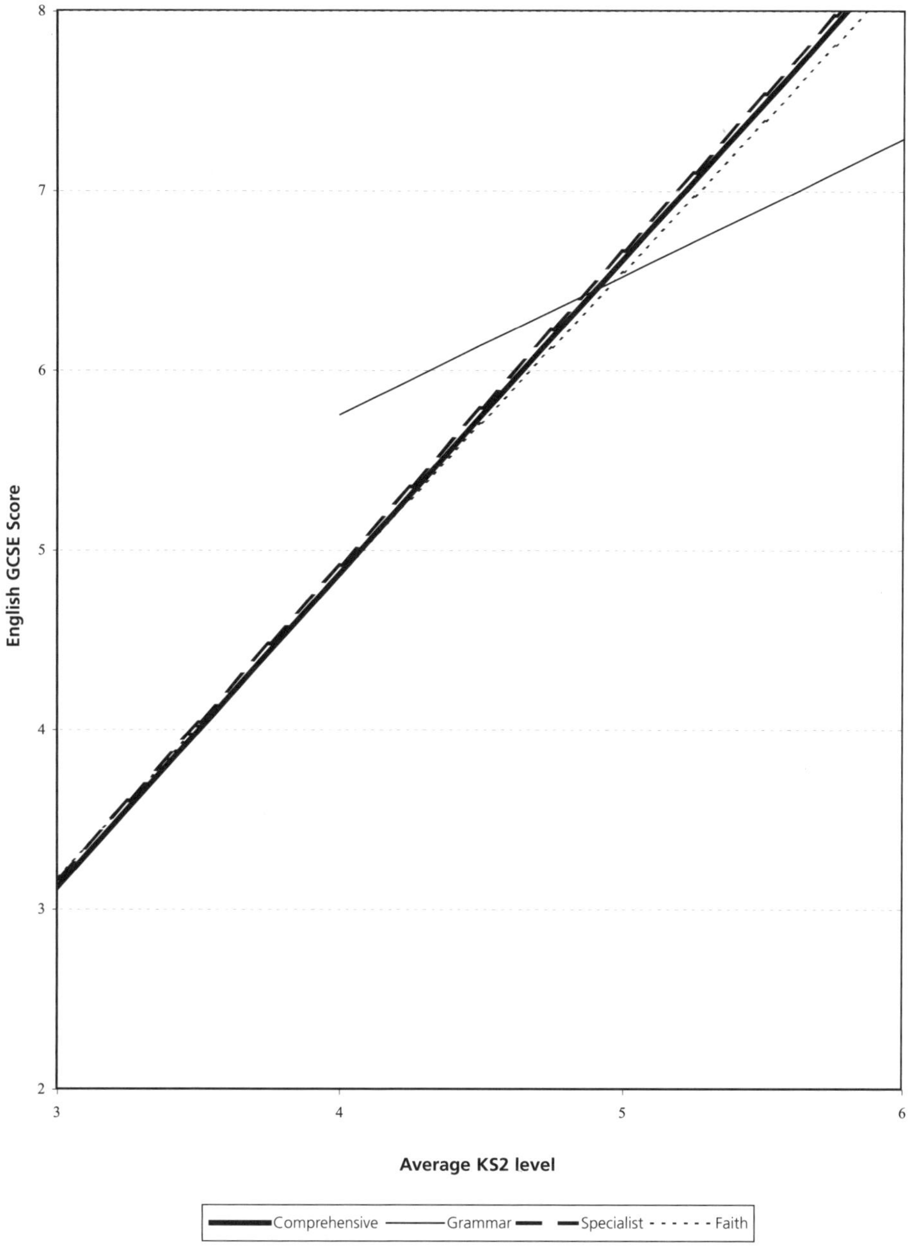

Figure 5: Expected Total Science GCSE Score v. Average KS2 level for Different school Types

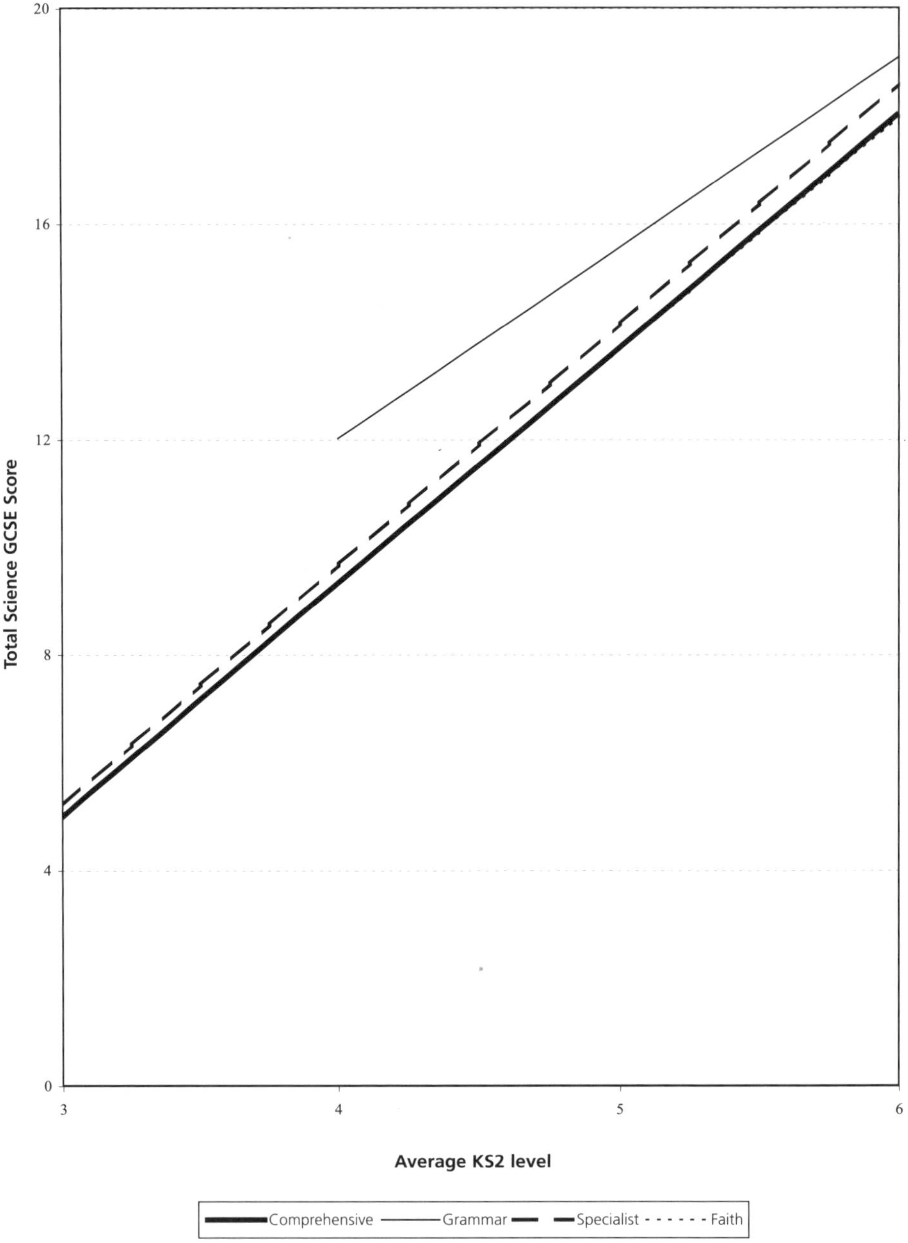

Figure 6: Expected Average Science GCSE Score v. Average KS2 level for Different school Types

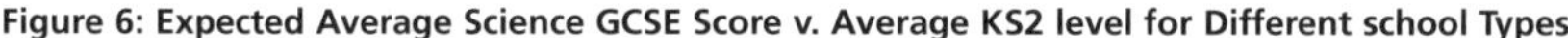

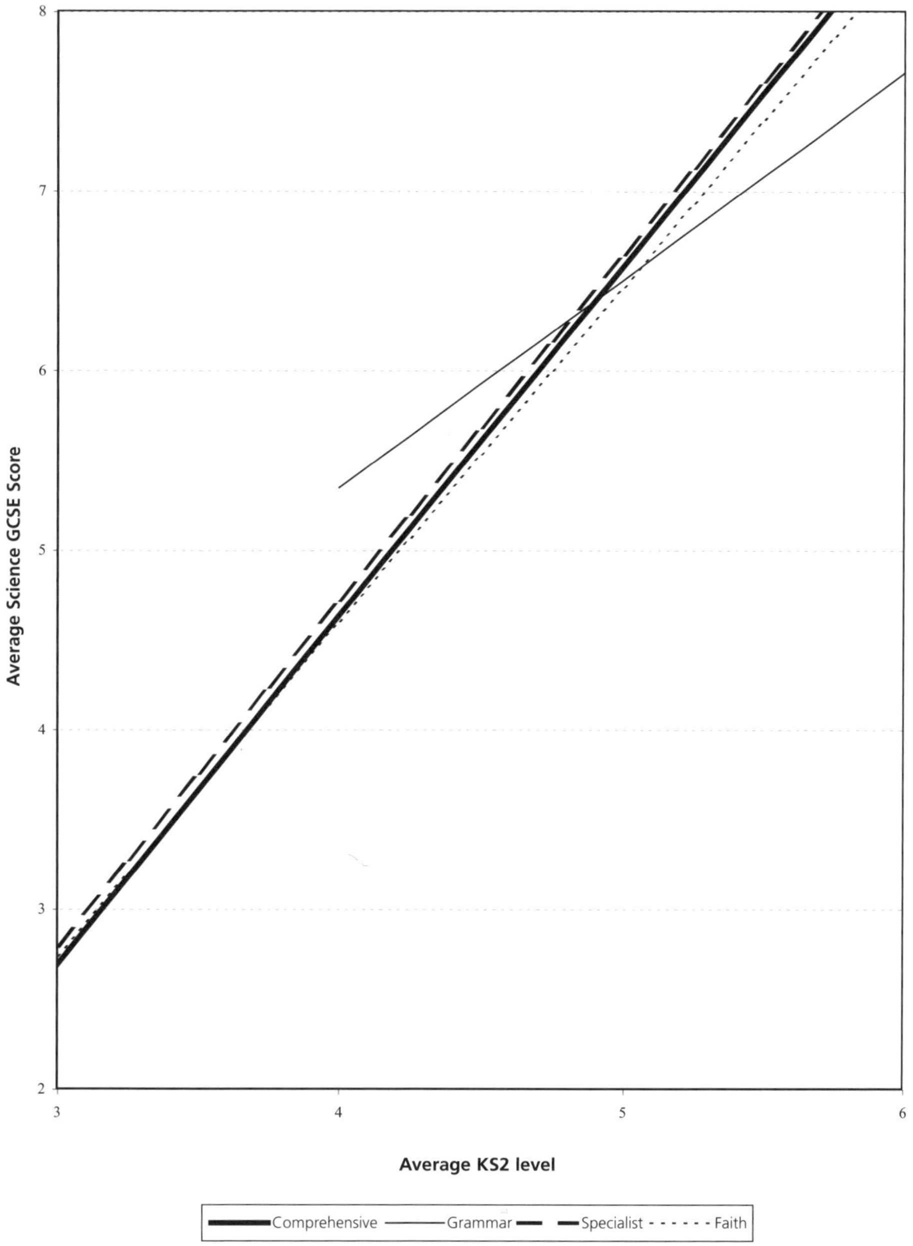
Average Science GCSE Score
8
7
6
5
4
3
2
3
4
5
6
Average KS2 level
Comprehensive
Grammar
Specialist
Faith

Figure 7: Expected GCSE Entries v. Average KS2 level for Different school Types

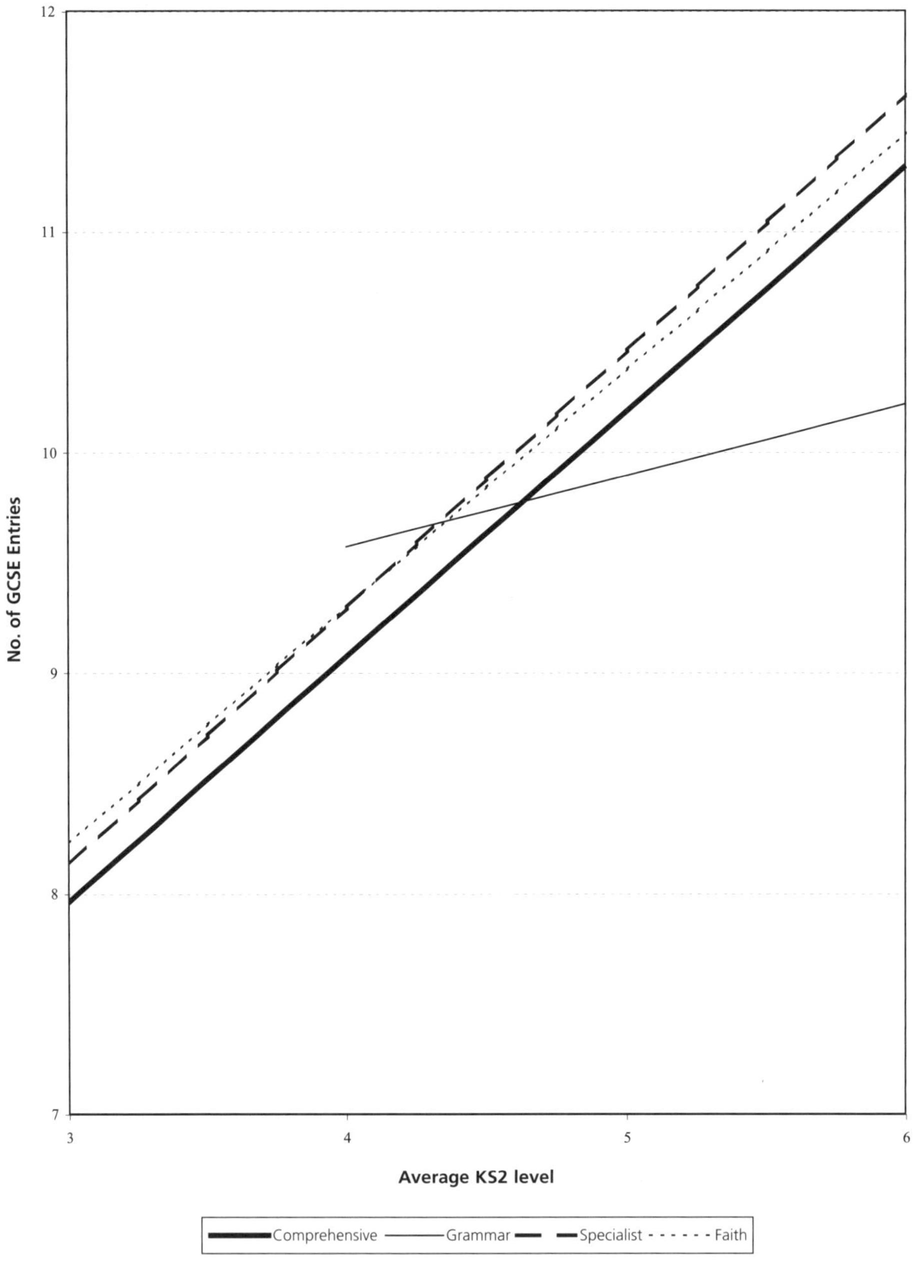

10 PERFORMANCE OF PUPILS AND SCHOOLS IN SELECTIVE AND NON-SELECTIVE LOCAL AUTHORITIES

David Jesson, Centre for Performance Evaluation, University of York

'...The selective system failed to meet the needs of all children and the talents of many were not recognised. Comprehensive schools overcame the ill effects of rigid selection and have done a great deal to improve opportunity...'
(2001 White Paper Schools: Achieving Success Chapter 2 paragraph 34)

Comparisons of performance between grammar and comprehensive schools have, in the past, generated considerable heat but not a great deal of light. The 2001 DfES White Paper's statement, therefore, brought this issue back into sharp focus (DfES, 2001). This paper provides a new investigation of the issue, using data made available via the Data Access Board.

In the mid-80's John Gray and I (Gray, Jesson and Jones, 1984) worked on this issue and felt that we had probably laid it to rest. There appeared little strong evidence to swing the debate one way or the other; although some in entrenched positions continued to claim that 'their' system produced better results. The issues were well reviewed in a special edition of the Oxford Education of Review in 1984 (Gray, Jesson and Jones, op.cit.). However, since then a number of things have changed which may both help to throw light on the issues and provide clarity for new policy decisions that may need to be made. Some of these important changes are listed below:

- Comprehensive data is now available showing the progress made by *individual pupils* across most phases of their educational lives using national curriculum test scores;
- Recognition that 'Value-added' methods are essential to evaluate 'how well schools perform';
- Development of more appropriate statistical methods for handling hierarchical data (pupils in schools in LEAs of different types; see, for example, Aitkin & Longford (1986) and Goldstein (1999). These methods are not used in this paper).
- Rather surprisingly, the number of LEAs described as 'fully selective' has **doubled** from 8 (in 1996) to 15 today (see Ofsted, 2001 National Summary Data Report for Secondary Schools).

There are now <u>fifteen</u> 'fully selective' areas. They are:
Bexley, <u>Bournemouth,</u> Buckinghamshire, Kent, Kingston-on-Thames, Lincolnshire, <u>Medway, Poole, Reading, Slough, Southend-on-Sea,</u> Sutton,

<u>Torquay</u>, Trafford and Wirral. Note that these are all relatively socio-economically advantaged areas.

(Unitary LEAs are underlined; Buckinghamshire, Kent and Lincolnshire whilst retaining the name of the original shire county are now also unitary authorities serving more restricted areas than their earlier namesakes.)

There are around 570,000 pupils nationally, in each Year 11 cohort. Total numbers of pupils educated in the fifteen selective areas identified above account for about one in ten of all pupils nationally. Selective local authorities therefore continue to play a significant role in the English educational scene, but there has been to date, little analysis of how well *pupils* in these areas, with their distinctive style of schooling, perform in comparison with *similar pupils* in the rest of the country where comprehensive systems of school organisation are in place. The purpose of this paper is to develop one such analysis.

Background

Claims are often made by supporters of selective education that these schools provide the 'best' education for pupils, and there is no doubt that the regular appearance of grammar schools at the head of local and national league tables of GCSE performance has done much to re-enforce this contention. However, with the development, and recognition of the fairness, of 'value-added' studies it is becoming much more difficult for these schools (or their vociferous supporters) to claim 'outstanding' performance – and the fact is that many high ability pupils in comprehensive schools outperform their selective school peers. Since, however, grammar schools educate only a *minority* of all the pupils in selective areas it is clearly important to look more broadly at the outcomes for <u>all</u> pupils rather than just at those of the selected minority.

It is in this context that a number of worrying signs emerged in the early 00's, suggesting that all may not be well with schooling in these areas. These provide added emphasis to the need for an appropriate comparative analysis of how well ***all*** pupils in these areas perform.

- Selective areas have, proportionately, more 'failing schools'; (Ofsted, 2001)
- The new category of 'schools facing challenging circumstances' are represented at *double the level* in selective areas compared with those elsewhere (and this in the context that the fifteen areas listed above serve socio-economically advantaged areas; in non-selective areas, 18%, in selective areas: 36%)
- Rates of improvement in performance are, in general, lower in selective areas than they are elsewhere.

Pupils and schools in selective areas: official names may not reveal their character

One of the features of selective systems of education is that a minority of pupils are selected for grammar schools whilst the majority (often 75 percent or more) attend other, non-selective schools. These non-selective schools have, in general, very few high ability pupils (since most of these go to grammar schools) – so it is clearly confusing that some of these non-selective schools are designated 'comprehensive' when they clearly are not. Commenting on this issue, Rhodes Boyson (House of Commons, 1980) clarified their position as follows:

... where there are grammar schools and so-called comprehensive schools serving pupils in a given area, these comprehensive schools are nothing but mis-named secondary modern schools...

In the fifteen selective areas there are around 357 secondary schools in total, 107 of these are selective schools whilst the others, 250 in number, we describe, in this paper, as 'secondary modern' schools – although this may not be their 'official' designation. These secondary modern schools educate around 36,000 pupils annually. Our concern in this paper is to evaluate how well pupils in these schools perform compared to their peers in genuinely comprehensive schools.

Some previous commentators, mainly, it must be said, from the grammar school lobby, have suggested that pupils in secondary modern schools 'do well' in GCSE and other examinations, but there has been, to date, no detailed comparative evaluation – and even the DfES' classification of 'modern' school cannot be relied on to identify similar schools. Many so-called 'comprehensives' in selective areas fit Rhodes Boyson's definition of 'modern' given above.. It is to the associated issues that we now turn.

We look first at the broad picture using LEAs as our first focus, then we look at performance by school, and then, in more detail, at the performance of individual pupils.

Data sources and procedures

There is a strong argument for using data relating to the full five years of secondary education, but DfES have been dilatory in providing official sanction for this. We have therefore adopted the approach of the 'official' value-added methods and compared the outcomes of schools at GCSE utilising their performance at Key Stage 3 two years earlier. GCSE and GNVQ results for around 550,000 pupils (in Year 2002) were matched to their Key Stage 3 levels of performance in 2000. This provided a prior attainment measure for each pupil, and by aggregation, for each of over 3000 schools, and 148 LEAs; similar procedures were adopted to create aggregated outcome measures for schools and LEAs.

Schools in the fifteen selective authorities were identified as either grammar or secondary modern, using the definition supplied by Rhodes Boyson above.

Comparative framework

The most appropriate statistical way to address these issues is to utilise multi-level models of performance reflecting the hierarchical nature of the data – pupils in schools, which are themselves, administratively, grouped into local education authorities (LEAs), see for example, Aitken et al (1986) and Goldstein (1999).

These procedures have not, however, been used for the results reported here. This has been done in an attempt to create a user-friendly interface between researchers and the interested public. It is, of course, important that 'appropriate' means are used to evaluate school and pupil performance issues; differing audiences, however, imply different modes of presentation. Statistical complexity has its place, and the limitations of the analyses presented in this paper are acknowledged; further work is in progress.

LEA 'performance' comparisons – what do they look like?

The first way of looking at this issue was to form an aggregate of all pupils' GCSE and Key Stage 3 results for each of the 148 LEAs with reasonable numbers of secondary schools (we have omitted City of London and Isles of Scilly from the 150 in total). The plot of these results for LEAs with 'comparable' characteristics is shown in **Figure 1**:

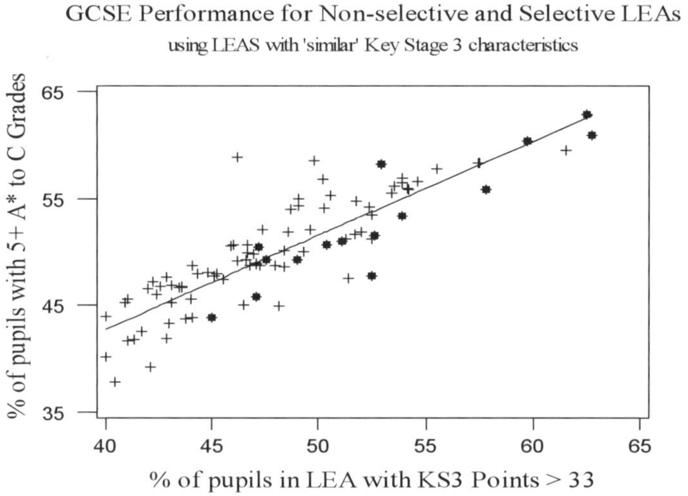

*Selective LEAS are only found amongst more advantaged LEAs.

The straight line in Figure 1 represents the 'predicted' GCSE outcome for LEAs with each prior attainment characteristic. Ten of the fifteen selective LEAs (66%) occur 'below' this line – indicating 'poorer levels of performance than expected'. This visual finding and interpretation is expanded in the analysis reported below:

Statistical comparison was carried out using the Mann-Whitney test, which uses the ranked differences between 'predicted' and actual GCSE outcomes and compares these between selective and non-selective LEAs. The results are reported in **Table 1**:

Table 1

		Median Residual	
Non-selective LEAs	(133)	+ 0.25	
Selective LEAs	(15)	- 1.5	
Pt Estimate of difference		+ 1.4	Range (0.2: 2.8)
Sig. Level for Non-sel > Sel		**~ 0 5%**	

The conclusion (rather weak is must be added!) is that selective LEAs turn in 'worse' performances for their pupils than do others not organised on selective lines.

Comparisons between Schools: Secondary Modern and Comprehensive schools

In recent years The Autumn Package (published annually by DfES, Ofsted and QCA) has provided a convenient way for schools to assess how well they are doing. This is done through the use of Performance Benchmarks, which, typically, indicate where a school's performance places it in comparison with schools serving 'similar' pupil populations.

There are two benchmark frameworks in common use, but it is benchmarks based on *pupils' prior attainments* that have far and away the most powerful impact. These benchmarks compare schools' aggregate performance (using, say, the percentage of pupils gaining 5 or more A* to C passes at GCSE/GNVQ), by grouping schools which had pupils of similar average ('prior attainment') scores at a previous time-point.

The Autumn Package categorises schools into six groups of broadly similar schools, providing benchmark frameworks for each. The 250 secondary modern schools in the fifteen selective LEAs appeared mainly in three of these groups as shown in **Table 2**:

Table 2

School Group	1	2	3	4	5	6
Average KS3 Pts	Lt 27	27 - 30-	30 - 33-	33 – 36-	36 – 39-	39+
All schools	101	584	1128	933	167	167
Secondary Modern	~	62	148	39	1	~

It is possible, therefore, to make comparisons between secondary modern and other schools for those in three of these groups. We have done this in two ways:

Comparison of school performance using benchmark tables
Using the upper (UQ), lower quartiles (LQ) and the median performance for the groupings of secondary modern schools their performance can be compared with the 'parent' distribution; published in the Autumn Package. The results are shown in **Table 3**:

Table 3

School Group	2			3			4		
% with 5+ A* to C	**UQ**	**Md**	**LQ**	**UQ**	**Md**	**LQ**	**UQ**	**Md**	**LQ**
All Schools	30	24	19	46	40	33	64	58	52
Secondary Moderns	**26**	**19**	**13**	**42**	**34**	**26**	66	**55**	**49**

(NB – the **highlighted** figures show where secondary modern performance is **lower**)

Inspection of Table 3 suggests strongly that **secondary modern school** performance *lags well behind that of other schools with similar prior attainments*. The median values are from 3 to 6 percentage points lower for secondary modern schools than for other schools with similar prior attainments. (In groups 2 and 3 the lower quartile differences are even greater. This emphasises, once again, the negative impact of 'selection' on the outcomes of those pupils not selected in these 210 schools.)

There is just one instance where 'secondary modern' schools outperformed their comprehensive peers - at the upper quartile for Group 4. This particular grouping of schools is the smallest (just 39 schools compared with over 800 comprehensives; there is NO statistical evidence of 'higher' outcomes). We address this issue after we have presented a second method for comparing these schools' performances. The overall message is one confirming our previous findings of lower performance for secondary modern schools..

In general secondary modern schools tend to lie in the *lower* part of the figure, indicating lower performance levels than the schools with which they are being compared. This issue is explored statistically in the second method section, which follows.

2. Comparisons of school performance using ranking methods

A second way of comparing schools' performance uses order statistics (Mann-Whitney tests) to test the significance of the relative rankings of comprehensive and secondary modern schools within each of the three Autumn Package groups shown in Tables 1 and 2. We present these results in **Table 4a:**

Table 4a

Autumn Package Group	2		3		4	
	No	Median	No	Median	No	Median
		(%5+A*C)		(%5+A*C)		(%5+A*C)
Comprehensive schools	434	21.7	828	38.0	758	56.1
Secondary Modern schools	62	19.2	148	33.9	39	55.1
Pt Estimate of difference	- 2.5		- 4.0		- 0.2	
Sig. Level for Comp>SecMod	5% (*)		0.1% (***)		ns	

The last line of Table 4a shows that for *the great majority of secondary modern schools GCSE performance is lower or much lower than for comprehensive schools* serving similar pupil populations. In the largest group of secondary moderns, group 3, this difference is very large - amounting to around 4 percentage points better performance for comprehensive schools.

This is clear evidence that many secondary modern schools provide lower GCSE results for their pupils than do comprehensive school serving similar pupils.

Group 4, which has the smallest number of secondary modern schools, is the group where GCSE performance is most akin to that of similar comprehensive schools. It is worth taking a closer look at these 39 schools.

This group is somewhat unusual – almost 60% of the secondary modern schools in this group are either Foundation or Voluntary aided schools, and as such are their own admission authorities. This compares with only around 30% (half the secondary modern school proportion) in comparable comprehensive schools. It will be interesting to follow up this issue in subsequent investigations. The work of Stephen Gorard on **segregation of schools** has shown that in selective areas this is already at relatively high levels. It may be the case that within some selective areas a 'pecking order' has been established in which some secondary modern schools recruit 'better' pupils at the expense of their less fortunate colleagues. (This paper cannot pursue this issue, since one of the conditions of use attached to Data Access is that no school be identified.)

We turn now to the vital issue of *pupils* and their comparative performance.

Comparing _pupils'_ performance in secondary modern and comprehensive schools

Whereas Benchmarks place _schools'_ performance in context it is even more important to evaluate how well _pupils_ perform. There are a number of statistical reasons why comparisons between schools may not be fully revealing – uppermost amongst these are the different sizes of schools and the potentially very different distributions of pupils' prior attainments within them even where the 'averages' are rather similar. So, whilst comparative analysis of different types of schools' performance is *potentially* revealing, it is even more important to estimate the effects on pupils' performance of whether they are educated in comprehensive or secondary modern schools. It is this analysis which is potentially the most informative and which could have greatest impact on future decisions about the structure of secondary education in England.

Comparisons of *schools'* performance always raise numbers of questions, which a simple analysis such as this cannot hope to address. These questions are by no means trivial, but they can easily divert attention from the substantive issue – *is there evidence that pupils in secondary modern schools do better, or worse than similar pupils educated in non-selective schools elsewhere?* Schools are unique entities, and comparisons between schools can, at best, only 'control for' some of the most obvious similarities and differences.

It is appropriate therefore to turn attention to the performance of the approximately 36000 pupils educated in the 250 'secondary modern' schools in the 15 selective LEAs. These pupils are the counterpart to the 14,000 or so educated in these areas' grammar schools.

Questions about the relative performance of selective LEAs should be answered on the basis of the performance of *all* of their pupils. We have already seen that pupils in grammar schools 'do well' (but not necessarily better than similar pupils in comprehensive schools), so the critical issue relates to the performance of those who are educated in secondary modern schools. If it turns out that these pupils *do better* than their counterparts in comprehensive schools, then supporters of selective education will be able to claim that selective education produces 'better' examination results. If, on the other hand, these pupils *do less well* than their peers, the reverse is true, and the comprehensive system of organising educational provision will be shown to produce better performance.

To carry out these comparisons we grouped all pupils in comprehensive and secondary modern schools, into one of the five *pupil prior attainment groups* used in the Autumn Package (DfES, 2002). We then compared the GCSE performances of those who were in non-selective schools (some 493,000 pupils) with those in secondary modern schools in selective areas(almost 36,000 pupils).

The results are shown in **Table 4b:**

Table 4b

School Group	1	2	3	4	5	Pupil No's
2	*Comparison of 'KS3 Prior Attainments'*					
3 KS3 Pts	Up to 25	27 to 30	31 to 33	34 to 37	38 +	
4 % Comp Sch	17	19	22	20	22	493313
5 % Sec Mod	17	22	25	22	13	35836
6	*Performance Comparisons: % pupils with 5+ A* - C*					
7 Comp Sch	**1%**	**9%**	**36%**	**76%**	**92%**	
8 Sec Mod	**0%**	**7%**	**32%**	**70%**	**86%**	

Rows 4 & 5 of Table 4b show that secondary modern schools have, as would be expected, fewer pupils in the highest prior attainment group – since many of these pupils would be in grammar schools. These schools have, however, very similar proportions to those in comprehensive schools in each of the other four groups. This is due to the fact that, as we have seen, selective LEAs are generally located in more socio-economically advantaged areas where the prior attainment profile is well above that of the nation as a whole. It is interesting to note that even when pupils in grammar schools are excluded, the Key Stage 3 attainment profile of secondary moderns is close to that of pupils in non-selective LEAs apart from the incidence of higher ability pupils. This makes comparison between pupils OUTCOMES in the two 'systems' even more relevant and appropriate.

The implications, therefore, of the results in the rows 7 & 8 of Table 4 are profound:

in every grouping of pupils the performance of those in secondary modern schools is lower than those of similar pupils in comprehensive schools.

(Similar results occur for the 'other' GCSE performance indicator, the number of GCSE/GNVQ points scored by each pupil.)

Conclusions from these three sets of comparisons

Thus each of the three levels of comparison between selective and non-selective systems of school organisation point in the same direction – *selective school systems, and in particular, the secondary modern schools which educate the majority of pupils in these systems, underperform substantially compared to the outcomes for comprehensive schools.*

Discussion and policy significance of these results

When the present government was first elected in 1997 one of its prime targets was the raising of standards of performance at all levels in the education system. There have, to date, been a number of well-publicised successes – most notably in standards of literacy and numeracy at Key Stage 2, and in the continuing rise in performance at GCSE and beyond, particularly in specialist schools. One of the key phrases used at the time suggested that the government's interest was with *'standards not structures'*. This was surely the right way to proceed at the start of the reform programme. However, it would seem that, some years into the 'radical reforms' of the education system, the issue of *structures* cannot now be ignored. We have shown in this paper that some of those structures appear to militate against the best interests of pupils in some parts of the country.

Selection is always an emotive concept, since 'selection' of the few always results in the non-selection (or 'rejection' as some would describe it) of others. Government has shown itself willing to tackle some of the 'big' issues which it felt stood in the way of maximising the educational performance of pupils, but has seemed strangely less interested in this particular one. Mainly, it must be said, because there was little convincing evidence available which identified the nature of the problem. Added to which there was a vociferous lobby, which claimed that the situation was actually the reverse of what we have shown in this paper.

However, it is now possible to address this issue with a degree of attention to detail, which was not possible previously.

We have shown that pupils in non-selective schools in areas with fully selective education systems, with a few interesting exceptions, achieve much lower examination results than similar pupils educated in genuinely comprehensive schools. When this finding is linked with earlier work showing that the ablest pupils in comprehensive schools do as well, if not better than, similar pupils in grammar schools, it is clear that there is a very real issue of *underperformance* in these schools to be addressed.

Comprehensive schools had for some years a rather bad press, but the expansion of specialist schools has re-invigorated the comprehensive principle and shown some dramatic innovations and improvements. The fact remains, however, that there are still far too many schools which are not helping their pupils achieve their maximum potential. The clear evidence from this study is that a further barrier to raising national performance (and even more crucially, individual *pupils'* performance) could be removed by moving to end the two-tier system, which exists in selective areas. This, of itself, significantly depresses the GCSE results of far too many pupils in the areas where selection persists.

This is not to claim that all grammar schools should be abolished overnight, rather that all pupils should have access to the widest range of schools in their locality, without arbitrary 'selection rules' being imposed, so that all pupils' performances can be maximised. School organisation must still have a distinctive local flavour, but it must no longer be the case that by serving only the interests of a minority of pupils that substantial disadvantage results for the majority. Social justice requires no less.

The White Paper's assertion and the findings published here agree that:

The selective system failed to meet the needs of all children and the talents of many were not recognised. Comprehensive schools overcame the ill effects of rigid selection and have done a great deal to improve opportunity...(HMSO Para 2.34)

The future for selective systems of secondary school organisation must now be seriously questioned.

Work by Stephen Gorard and colleagues (Gorard & Taylor, 2001) has shown that whilst segregation between schools has been falling over the last ten to twelve years, the absolute levels in selective areas are much higher than those generally found elsewhere. We quote, with permission, from a paper by Gorard & Taylor, from which we have extracted figures for 'segregation' by LEA. This very interesting paper uses a measure of socio-economic segregation between schools, measuring the degree to which schools depart from an even distribution of pupils with free school meals. It would be high where some schools serve mainly 'disadvantaged' communities, whilst others are relatively advantaged; it is lower the greater the homogeneity between schools in this respect.

We report (in **Table 5**) the distribution of these measures by selective and non-selective LEAs and have analysed these using Mann-Whitney analysis. Results in **Table 6.**

Table 5

FSM Segregation Measure	Up to 10	to 20	to 30	to 40	to 50
Lea type	Number of LEAs in each 'segregation' group				
Non-select	9	38	46	5	0
Selective	0	0	5	2	1

Table 6

LEA Type	Median	Range
	of Segregation Index	
Non-selective	21	
Selective	30	
Point Estimate of Difference	- 10	(-16, - 4)
Significance Non-sel < Sel	*** Sig at 0.1% level	

The evidence of differences between selective and non-selective LEAs is clearly indicated by the last line of Table 6: Selective LEAs show much greater levels of socio-economic segregation between their schools than those which are non-selective.

This finding has considerable significance in the context of the organisation of secondary education in this country. If education is to continue to play its historic role in breaking down divisions between different sectors of society, retaining selective systems does not appear a constructive choice. The evidence suggests that selective systems of educational organisation create levels of segregation that run counter to what, elsewhere, is being achieved in the area of inclusion. Gorard & Taylor show that segregation levels have been falling over the last ten years for most LEAs. However, LEAs with selective systems have much higher levels than elsewhere. This may be an obvious consequence of the selection procedures in use, but is, nevertheless, a further reason why the maintenance of such systems into the longer term future should now be seriously questioned.

Changes required to bring about a more effective organisation of secondary schooling cannot come about by leaving admission arrangements as they are: we have shown that to do so is simply a recipe for lower performance in those areas which still organise their schools on selective lines. A government committed to raising standards for all must not exclude from its agenda those currently educated in 'secondary modern' schools – these pupils are currently seriously disadvantaged in GCSE performance by the way that their schooling system operates. Maintaining that disadvantage should not be an option.

We note that, in the 2001 White Paper, Government proposed taking reserve powers ('in exceptional circumstances') to *direct a local authority to set a budget for expenditure on schools at a level determined by the Secretary of State having regard to all relevant circumstances*. Is it unreasonable to suggest that similar action is needed in respect of the issue that has been the subject of the analysis presented in this paper?

**© 2003 David Jesson: Centre for Performance Evaluation,
Dept of Economics, University of York
dj2@york.ac.uk**

References

AITKIN, M. and LONGFORD, N. (1986) Statistical Modelling issues in school effectiveness studies. Journal of the Royal Statistical Society, Series A, 144, 1.

BOYSON, R. (1969) The essential conditions for the success of comprehensive schools, in Cox, C. and Dyson, A. (eds) Fight for Education: a Black Paper. London, Critical Quarterly Society.

BRYK, A and RAUDENBUSH, S. (1992) Hierarchical Linear Models, Newbury Park, Sage.

COX, C. and MARKS, J. (1980) Real Concern; An Appraisal of the National Children's Bureau Report on Progress in Secondary Schools. London, Centre for Policy Studies.

CROOK, D., POWER, S. and WHITTY, G. (1999) The Grammar School Question: Review of research on comprehensive and selective education, London, Institute of Education.

DEPARTMENT OF EDUCATION AND SCIENCE (1983), School standards and spending; statistical analysis. Statistical Bulletin 16/83. London, DES.

DEPARTMENT OF EDUCATION AND SCIENCE (1984), School standards and spending: Statistical analysis a further appreciation. Statistical Bulletin 13/84. London, DES.

DEPARTMENT FOR EDUCATION AND EMPLOYMENT (1998). <u>Performance Tables for Secondary Schools</u>. London DfEE.

DEPARTMENT FOR EDUCATION AND EMPLOYMENT (1998). <u>Value Added Pilot Study Supplement to Performance Tables for Secondary Schools</u>. London DfEE.

DEPARTMENT FOR EDUCATION AND EMPLOYMENT (1999). Arrangements for Parental Ballots in respective of grammar schools. London, DfEE.

DEPARTMENT FOR EDUCATION AND EMPLOYMENT, QCA & OFSTED (1998, 1999) <u>The Autumn Package</u>, London, DfEE.

FITZ-GIBBON, C. (1997) <u>Value Added National Project; Final Report: Feasibility studies for a national system of Value Added indicators</u>. London, SCAA, COM/97/844

GOLDSTEIN, H. (1987) <u>Multilevel Modelling in educational and social research</u>, London, Griffin.

GOLDSTEIN, H. (1999) quoted in <u>Times Educational Supplement</u>, 26 November

GORARD, S & TAYLOR, C (2001) Investigating the determinants of segregation between schools (mimeo)

GRAY, J., JESSON, D. and JONES, B. (1984) Predicting differences in examination results between local education authorities: does school organisation matter, <u>Oxford Review of Education</u>, 10, 1, 45-68.

GRAY, J., JESSON, D. and JONES, B. (1986) The search for a fairer way of comparing schools' examination results, <u>Research Papers in Education</u>, 1, 2, 91-122.

GRAY, J., HANNON, V., JESSON, D., JONES, B. and RANSON, S. (1986) The Contexts Project: the use and interpretations of examination results as measures of school performance. <u>Final Report</u> to the Economic and Social Research Council, (pp. 52)

GRAY, J. and JESSON, D. (1987) Examination results and local authority league tables, in A. Harrison and J. Gretton (eds.) <u>Education and Training UK 1987</u>, Newbury: Policy Journals, (pp. 33-41).

GRAY, J. and JESSON, D. (1989) The impact of comprehensive reforms, in R. Lowe (ed.) <u>The Changing Secondary School</u>, Lewes: Falmer Press, (pp. 72-98).

GRIGGS, C. (1989)The New Right and English Secondary Education in R.Lowe (ed) <u>The Changing Secondary School</u>. Lewes, The Falmer Press.

JESSON, D. and Taylor, C (2001) Value Added Estimates of GCSE/GNVQ Performance in 2000 for Specialist Schools

JESSON, D (1999) <u>Value Added Estimates of GCSE/GNVQ Performance in 1998 for Schools in the Technology Colleges Network</u>. London, Technology Colleges Trust

JESSON, D. (1997) <u>Value Added Measures of School GCSE Performance: Final Report</u>, London: HMSO (ISBN 0-85-522617-X)

LORD, R. (1984) <u>Value for Money in Education</u>. London, Public Money

MARKS, J., COX. C. and POMIAN-SZREDNICKI, M (1983). <u>Standards in English Schools</u>. London, National Council for Educational Standards.

MARKS, J and POMIAN-SZREDNICKI, M (1985). <u>Standards in English Schools, Second Report</u>. London, National Council for Educational Standards.

MARKS, J., COX,C. and POMIAN-SZREDNICKI, M (1986).<u> Examination Performance of Secondary Schools in the Inner London Education Authority</u>. London, National Council for Educational Standards.

MARKS, J. (1991) <u>Standards in Schools: Assessment, Accountability and the Purposes of Education</u>. London, Social Market Foundation.

MORTIMORE, P. and MORTIMORE, J. (1986). Education and Social Class, in R. Rogers (ed) <u>Education and Social Class</u>, London, The Falmer Press.

OfSTED (1999) Introduction to <u>The New Handbook for the Inspection of Schools</u>. London, OfSTED

SCAA <u>Value Added Performance Indicators for Schools</u>, The School Curriculum and Assessment Authority, London: SCAA Publications (Ref: COM/94/151), ISBN 1 85838 045 6

11 SELECTION, DIVERSITY AND INEQUALITY IN SECONDARY EDUCATION

Tony Edwards and Sally Tomlinson

This chapter takes issue with current political pressures to increase selection in secondary education, overtly or covertly or through appeals to a modernising diversity. The evidence we review indicates that:

- the private sector is the main source of selective, unequal, opportunity;
- the remaining state grammar schools do not provide better for able children;
- selective systems depress standards overall;
- parental choice has intensified resource differences between schools;
- government promotion of distinct tiers of schooling threatens new inequalities.

When 'secondary education for all' was introduced in 1945, it was still assumed that most children would not need much of it. It was also widely assumed that a differentiated (tripartite) system offered working-class children the best prospects of advancement. Yet by the end of that century, over half the age-group in a largely comprehensive system were achieving results previously believed to be 'naturally' restricted to the small minority identified as having 'grammar school ability'. This has not ended support for dividing children between schools differing markedly in intake, resources, and esteem.

Tony Blair has repeatedly affirmed his belief in a 'meritocracy', even though that word's creator had intended not to praise it but to warn against the social divisions created when those 'judged to have merit of a particular kind harden into a new social class without room in it for others'.[1] Yet it was in meritocratic terms that the leading theorist of the 'Third Way' argued that the old 'egalitarianism at all costs' should be replaced by a 'dynamic life-chances approach... placing the prime stress upon equality of opportunity', even if this risked even larger inequalities of outcome.[2] The Secretary of State for Education rebuked the Left for its old egalitarian' obsession with grammar and private schools, and outlined a five-tier hierarchy in secondary education which openly renounced the 'common school' model of comprehensive education.[3]

In this chapter we argue that research supports neither the Government's acquiescence in the survival of grammar schools, nor its headlong pursuit of greater diversity. When the previous Secretary of State declared himself committed to evidence-based policy, and invited researchers to contribute to 'the real debates which affect people's life chances', he accepted an obligation on government to 'give serious consideration to "difficult" findings' even when these were politically inconvenient.[4] The evidence reviewed here includes difficult findings of that kind.

1. Overt selection

It was an Old Labour view of grammar schools that 'if it is wrong to select and segregate children, it must be wrong everywhere'.[5] Selection then was seen as inefficient because it discarded the talents of too many children too early, and as unfair because it favoured children from socially advantaged families. Although the incoming Conservative Government in 1970 freed local authorities from any obligation to abandon selection, its Secretary of State later recalled in her memoirs her inability to slow down the 'roller coaster' of comprehensive reform. By the time she became Prime Minister in 1979, 87 per cent of secondary-age pupils in the state system were in schools at least nominally comprehensive. Her Government promptly reasserted support for grammar schools, and introduced the Assisted Places Scheme to enable 'clever children from less well-off homes' to escape the low standards attributed to many comprehensive schools by entering 'academically excellent' selective schools in the private sector.

In opposition, Tony Blair had dismissed the 'grammar school model' as a response to a vanished society which needed only its future leaders to be well educated. During the 1997 election, he attacked a 'creeping return' to selection. There was nothing stealthy however about Conservative pledges to create new grammar schools, and allow any 'comprehensive' school to select up to 20 per cent of its intake with that threshold raised for specialist and grant-maintained schools as high as 30 per cent and 50 per cent respectively.[6] During the election, the Conservative Secretary of State (Gillian Shephard) claimed that old arguments for and against grammar schools had been made obsolete by rising numbers of partially-selective state schools. Grammar schools threatened with re-organisation could then avoid it by opting-out of local authority control, while grant-maintained schools generally could use their relative autonomy (if they wished) to manage admissions to their own advantage. Having promised no new 'selection by ability', the Labour Government has not regarded the surviving grammar schools as sufficiently objectionable to justify over-riding the right of local parents to decide for or against their retention. They therefore introduced complex balloting procedures which might have been designed to preserve the status quo, even parents with children at private schools being allowed a vote. Although partial selection has increased far less than if the Conservatives had won in 1997, a hugely expanded Specialist Schools Programme represents a very significant potential source. So, less directly, does increasing competition for entry to the 'best' schools.

1.1 Private selection

The main source of openly selective secondary education is of course the private sector, enlarged during the late 1970s by those direct-grant grammar schools which opted to lose public funding rather than become comprehensive. The sector's significance is highly disproportionate to its size because of a continuing, even increasing, association with privileged access to the 'best' universities and the 'best' jobs, an influential study concluding that a 'Super-Class' of top professionals and managers is now 'an almost entirely privately-schooled elite'.[7] Although only 8 per cent of secondary-age pupils in England are in private schools, the aggregate figure is misleading. In 25 local authorities in 1998, 14 of them in and around London, that proportion was over 15 per cent. The range was from none or almost none in 28 local authorities to about one in five in Manchester, Newcastle, Merton, Croydon and Oxfordshire; about one in four in Harrow, Southwark, Surrey and Bristol; and one in three in Richmond-on-Thames.[8] In these areas especially, private schooling constitutes a large diversion of able children from a still predominantly comprehensive state system.

Although the incoming Labour Government announced in 1997 that the Assisted Places Scheme would be phased out, the main providers of places are raising money to replace it. The Girls Schools Trust has a target of £70 million for its 25 schools, Manchester Grammar School's fund-raising exemplifies what its headmaster claimed was merely a return to its tradition of access on merit, and the Sutton Trust's substantial sponsorship of means-tested entry has included enabling the Belvedere Girls School in Liverpool to open all its places on that basis. Although these ventures have been encouraged by the Government, it is unlikely to support the proposed 'Open Access to Schools in the Independent Sector' (Oasis) whereby each pupil should bring annually up to £3000 of public money, a figure which represents about half the average tuition fee.[9]

1.2 State selection

Within the state sector, 164 grammar schools remain of the 1000 existing in 1965. They contain about 4 per cent of pupils of secondary school age, to whom should be added another 12 per cent in schools nominally or for practical purposes 'secondary modern'. Labour Ministers have tended to treat arguments for their abolition as irrelevant. There is evidence however that admissions to grammar schools increased by nearly 20 per cent between 1992 and 2000, with a corresponding increase of over 15 per cent in admissions to secondary modern schools. That research also indicated an increased demand for apparently high performing selective schools, which tended both to expand and to take in disproportionately more middle-class children.[10]

Grammar schools have a huge influence on education in Kent and Medway, where they constitute almost a third of all secondary schools, and in fourteen more local authorities where they account for at least 20 per cent of pupils of secondary age. Although other secondary schools in those areas should not be called comprehensive, they are consistently labelled 'secondary modern' only in Bournemouth, Buckinghamshire, Kingston-on-Thames, and Trafford. In many other parts of the country, surviving grammar schools adversely affect nearby comprehensives, which may thereby fall below that threshold entry of academically able children (at least 15 per cent) widely regarded as necessary for anything like a balanced intake.

Church schools have been exempt from the ban on selection by interview providing the interviewing is only to confirm a relevant religious commitment. That interviews can be used as cover for selection by ability or social background may partly explain why a 1994 survey found that more Church of England comprehensive schools had predominantly middle-class intakes than comprehensives generally.[11] To date only a small minority of specialist schools, mainly ex-grammar and grant-maintained, have acted on their right to select up to 10 per cent of their intake by aptitude.[12] The possibility of doing so, however, becomes available to many more schools as the Programme expands. Popular schools have to choose somehow from a surfeit of applicants where demand for places exceeds supply. What is evident is that voluntary-aided and foundation schools, able to act as their own admissions authorities, are significantly more likely to engage in some kind of selection by ability or aptitude.[13] Support in the 2001 White Paper for more vocational courses in Key Stage 4, special provision for 'gifted and talented' children, more specialist schools and city academies, led a politically well-connected commentator to conclude that 'selection is back as a centrepiece of education policy'.[14]

2. Selection and 'standards'.

On one side of what is wrongly described as a dead debate about grammar schools were claims that identifying around 20 per cent of the age-group as academically able drew far too thinly on the nation's pool of talent, thereby creating widespread perceptions of educational failure. On the other side were claims that clever children needed to be in the company of their intellectual peers, and that standards would decline if grammar schools were no longer there to exemplify academic excellence.

The concept of 'standards' is elusive, especially when a rise or fall over time is claimed without taking account of changes in what is taught and how learning is assessed.[15] With this necessary qualification, the attribution of a crisis in standards to the spread of comprehensive schools requires a resolute nostalgia for an age when a small minority of selected pupils were tested on 'academic' subjects. The most widely cited 'measure' of individual and school performance is five or more A*-C passes at GCSE, the grade a direct replacement for O-level. The prominence given to five such grades is a remarkable echo of the School Certificate abandoned in 1951. Yet only 16 per cent achieved that 'standard' in the mid-1960s, when grammar schools were at their peak. In an overwhelmingly comprehensive state system, that figure is now over 50 per cent. The proportion of unqualified school leavers, a system indicator by which England has compared particularly badly with other countries, a figure of 47 per cent in 1970 had fallen to 10 per cent by the end of the 1990s. At that earlier date, when fewer than 30 per cent had attended a comprehensive, the proportion of state school leavers with two or more A levels was 10 per cent; in 1998, when 87 per cent were in comprehensives, that figure was 16 per cent. When the year 2000 brought the eighteenth successive rise in A level passes, girls gaining more A-grades than boys for the first time, the proportion of the age group going on to university was double the 17 per cent which the Robbins Committee in 1963 set as an optimistic target. Such figures do not demonstrate an 'experiment which has failed', yet politicians have been remarkably reluctant to claim even its partial success.

2.1 Standards and selection in the private sector.

The conspicuous success of private schools in local league tables and annual lists of the country's 'top' secondary schools is regularly highlighted, sometimes being taken as grounds for restoring grammar schools both to retain middle-class custom in the state system and to restore working-class opportunity.[16]   For example, there were only two state schools, both grammar schools, in the Financial Times list of the 'top 50' A level performers in 2001.   Such lists are entirely misleading.   They take no account of intake or of value-added by the schools.   They also tend to count total A level points per student, to the obvious advantage of those (mainly private) schools whose students take four subjects. Although analysis of examination results in England during the 1990s suggested that state schools were closing the performance gap[17], the private sector still produces 30 per cent of those gaining three or more A-grades, and over 40 per cent of passes in the 'hard' subjects of physics, mathematics and economics. Great care is needed in interpreting that apparent achievement.

Substantial within-sector variation means that the performance of different types of secondary school overlaps considerably.[18]   The 'raw' results of leading schools, and high rates of entry to prestigious universities, obscure the existence of the many private schools which are not academically selective.[19]   Even among those independent schools which applied for an allocation of assisted places, many had to be rejected as unsuitable for that Scheme's explicitly academic purposes.[20]   About one in four of the schools assessed by the Independent Schools Inspectorate in 2001 were rated as less than 'good'. Although differences in criteria and procedures rule out straight comparisons, that proportion is not so obviously superior to the 32 per cent of state schools similarly graded that year as to justify the over-generalised association of private schooling with educational excellence.[21]   Yet the sector continues to benefit from the halo effect thrown by its leading schools, the performance of which reflects highly selected intakes and superior resources.   At the top end of the continuum, the resource advantage is huge.   In 2001, at least nine boarding schools had total incomes (including gifts and endowments) of over £10 million; in some cases it was well over that figure, with Eton's £30 million an unsurprising market leader.   Average private school tuition fees for secondary education were then about two-and-a-half times average per capita funding in the state sector, where the funding range was from £2500-£3800, Even in the traditionally less expensive members of the Girls Schools Association, average annual fees in 2002 were £7599; in boys' schools represented in the Headmasters and Headmistresses Conference, the average was £8877.[22]

2.2 *Standards and selection in state schools.*

Within the state system, the survival of grammar schools raises critical empirical questions. Given so many years of contradictory claims, it might be expected that each of the following statements could either be sustained, or rejected as untrue, or treated as at best unproven.

- academically able children do better in academically-selective schools;
- academically-selective schools are more effective in value-added terms;
- academically-selective local and national systems are more effective than non-selective.

Yet arguments continue about the relevant facts and how to interpret them. The most familiar conclusions are that able children do slightly better in selective schools, but children of average and below average ability do better without selection. In other words, the advantage of being at a comprehensive school appears to diminish as ability levels rise. A consequent trading of advantages for the 'greatest good of the greatest number' might then be placed in the context of evidence that schooling has less effect on realising the potential of 'gifted and talented' children than of pupils of more average ability.[23]

Recent research, however, has questioned the benefits of academic selection even for able children. In line with other large-scale studies which have taken prior achievement into account, an NFER analysis of pupils' progress from GCSE to A level showed no average difference between grammar and comprehensive schools, though students with poorer GCSE performance appeared to have done slightly better in independent schools. A governmental comparison of the GCSE and GNVQ results of 'top ability' pupils in grammar and comprehensive schools indicated that it was the latter had done slightly better overall. That conclusion supported by David Jesson's subsequent analysis of successive national GCSE results which also found that even the very ablest pupils had done better in comprehensive schools.[24]

At local authority level, Jesson's conclusion is that selection depresses overall standards by polarising high and low performing schools. By the criterion of value-added between Key Stage 3 and GCSE, he found none of the 'wholly selective' local authorities to be in the top ten nationally; four were in the bottom ten. These findings are highlighted by his recent report on standards in Kent and Medway, where a quarter of all remaining state grammar schools are located. 'Excellent' outcomes for some were 'gained at the expense of others, particularly of those in less advantaged circumstances', so that there were more high performing and more low performing schools than in comparable authorities and a greater polarising of pupil attainment than anywhere in south-east England.[25] Although an NFER analysis showed a 'slight but significant overall advantage' for low selection Authorities (with fewer than 25 per cent in grammar schools) when prior attainment and eligibility for free school meals were taken into account, pupils in high-selection authorities did worse than those where all secondary-age pupils were in comprehensive schools.[26]

It is reasonable to conclude from this research that not taking intake characteristics into account allows some selective schools to benefit from a reputation they do not deserve, and that the costs of selection for standards generally outweigh benefits for those selected.

2.3 International comparisons

Comparison of system-level performance can usefully begin with a United Kingdom which is considerably disunited in the practice of selection. Northern Ireland is currently considering how to replace a selective bi-partite system, one in which the proportion of pupils in grammar schools has risen to around 40 per cent in response to demand from a growing middle-class. As would be predicted from the evidence just cited, examination results have been rather better than in England at the top end, but at the expense of a longer tail and relatively low rates of participation in post-compulsory education.[27]   Wales has a much smaller, less influential, private sector than England, and no state grammar schools. Performance at GCSE and A level has been somewhat poorer, although no more so than would be predicted from higher levels of poverty, but is rapidly catching up.[28] In sharp contrast to the 2001 White Paper in England, the Welsh National Assembly's equivalent 'Paving' Document included a firm commitment, not to increasing diversity but to maintaining community comprehensive schools. Scotland went comprehensive earlier and far more thoroughly than did England, with the all-through 12-18 school the dominant model, free from the disadvantage of co-existing with grammar schools and with few private schools outside Edinburgh and Glasgow to divert able children.   It has had, by comparison with England, consistently higher average attainment, less variation in attainment between schools, smaller differences in attainment between social classes, and higher rates of participation in post-compulsory and higher education.[29]

Wider comparisons are even more difficult because different ways of assessing different curricula give scope for presenting selectively and out-of-context those results which appear to predict a relatively well-schooled future workforce.[30] For what they are worth, they also point in different directions.   Some traditionally high performing countries have selective, and some non-selective, school systems. Germany has been a favourite example for supporters of wholly-selective systems, although different regions (Lander) have varied in that respect. After re-unification, the mainly comprehensive East German system prompted moves towards comprehensive schools (Gesantschule) which have affected even conservative Bavaria. Even before this, direct comparisons with West Germany were undermined because the placement of children aged 10-11 was made with parental consent, it was followed by a two-year guidance stage, and the main 'choice' was between the more 'academic' Gymnasium and Realschule which represented a relatively well-resourced and esteemed technical/vocational traditional which England has lacked and from which higher education was readily accessible. The third 'part' of the system, the Hauptschule had become by the 1980s residual provision for migrant and minority children and those with learning difficulties.[31]

Germany also came significantly below England, (as did France, Italy and the United States, for example) in the most recent OECD comparison of the performance of 15-year olds from thirty-two countries in reading, science and mathematics.   Only those from South Korea did better than their English contemporaries in all three areas, a result which does not support cries of a crisis in standards and which prompted the *Times Educational Supplement* to the headline - 'Shock news - we're doing OK' (7 December, 2001). But the survey also showed a wider range of achievement between the 'haves' and the 'have nots' than in most comparable countries.[32]

3. Selection and opportunity

Defenders of grammar schools have typically emphasized the unique opportunities they offered clever children from disadvantaged backgrounds. Thus the careers of many thousands of men whose education spanned the period from the early 1920s to the early 1970s indicated that working-class boys who went to grammar schools had had much better chances of 'middle-class' employment than middle-class boys who had failed the 11-plus, many of the former having embarked on an 'extraordinary ascent'.[33]

Such facts explain the Labour Party's prolonged ambivalence about grammar schools. They may also help to explain why a Government which promptly announced the end of the Assisted Places Scheme has appeared to favour privately-funded replacements which have the declared objective of restoring 'lost' opportunities. A report from the Sutton Trust for example, having described Britain (England would have been more appropriate) as unique in the extent to which 'the most successful schools are closed to the vast majority of its citizens', proposed that all places at the 'top hundred independent schools' should be government-funded so as to break the tightening 'link between wealth and opportunity'.[34]

Claims about the irreplaceable contribution of state grammar schools to upward mobility need to be placed in context. The majority of pupils in their 'golden age' in the 1950s and 1960s were undoubtedly working-class, but this could hardly have been otherwise when three-quarters of the male working population (compared with less than 30 per cent now) were in manual occupations. Even so, middle-class children were significantly over-represented when and where competition for grammar school places was most severe.[35] They were also over-represented in the most prestigious schools. Although some of the direct-grant grammar schools, often applauded as the 'the pride of the meritocracy', were less selective academically and socially than maintained grammar schools nearby, those most closely associated with academic excellence had predominantly middle-class intakes drawn mainly from within the top 5 per cent of the ability range. References to their unique social mix relied heavily on highlighting the presence of individual children from poor homes without establishing how typical these were. The safest evidence-based generalisation is that the more academically selective the school, the wider its geographical catchment and the more socially selective its intake.[36]

It is also claimed that working-class chances of university education were relatively better when large numbers of grammar schools were there to foster ability. Again, simple comparisons between past and present are invalid because there is now a very much smaller working-class from which to recruit. Evidence that the proportion of working-class entrants declined after the simultaneous introduction of tuition fees and withdrawal of maintenance grants has drawn government attention increasingly to problems of access. But matters are complicated by large status differences within a system transformed remarkably rapidly from 'elite' to 'mass' form. The boundary between such systems is conventionally set at a participation rate of about 15 per cent of the age-group. By the early 1990s, that overall rate had risen to a third. Among young people from professional and managerial families, it has risen since to over 70 per cent but with a very uneven distribution across the system. In 1998-9 for example, a middle-class entry of over 70 per cent in the most prestigious universities was in sharp contrast to less than a third at a number of 'new' universities. In the following year, and for obviously connected reasons, students from private schools constituted almost 40 per cent of all entrants to the thirteen universities ranked highest for research and teaching in newspaper tables, and almost half the entry to the 'top five'. In the 'top five', it averaged almost half the entry.[37]

4. Covert social selection

Selection by ability is often portrayed as more efficient and fairer than selection by parents' capacity to pay fees, or selection by mortgage or post-code. From that perspective, residential segregation produces socially segregated 'neighbourhood' comprehensives, whereas entry on merit is said to produce intakes much less stratified by social class, race, and family income. This argument concentrates on those who are selected, routinely ignoring effects on those who fail to be so and on schools with consequently very unbalanced intakes. John Major's 1997 call for 'a grammar school in every town' typically omitted to add 'and two or more secondary moderns'.

A Conservative Government committed to empowering the consumers of education could hardly fail to recognise that grammar schools offered choice only to children able to meet their entry criteria. It therefore justified replacing geographically-defined catchment areas by 'open enrolment' on the grounds that this would greatly extend opportunities to avoid, or escape from, poor schools. But enrolment is not open when schools are over-subscribed. The 'quasi-market' created in urban areas marked a deliberate shift from secondary schools as local (community) institutions to schools as competing providers, proximity to a child's home being least relevant for those parents inclined to seek the 'best buy' and able to meet consequent costs.

Studies of secondary school entry found that choice other than of the local school ranged from below 30 per cent to 73 per cent, to be greatest in inner-cities, and to be least in middle-class areas with 'good' schools and rural areas with no accessible alternatives. It included significant movement across local authority borders, notably in London.[38] A main finding of the second study cited was that parental choice was potentially most damaging to 'the average inner-city school', which was likely to lose children from higher socio-economic families to other comprehensives and to local grammar schools.

The Labour Government has taken steps to make admissions 'clear and fair', lack of clarity being especially unfair on parents unfamiliar with the applications 'game' or lacking confidence to play it hard. A Code of Practice was introduced, with adjudicators appointed to settle local disputes. Both mechanisms were also intended to restrain schools from acting without regard for the effects of their admission policy on other institutions. Appeals in the first year of the new system were most frequent where the local market contained numbers of directly competing schools. Potentially unfair practices, which could be used to screen applicants to the benefit of league table position, included interviewing parents, referring to the academic records of both applicants and their siblings, and criteria which were employed but were not made explicit.[39] Evidence of substantial informal or covert selection suggests that the Government should intervene more positively to secure 'fairness' than relying on local petitions and individual complaints where potentially unfair practices exist.

Some poor families have undoubtedly been enabled to avoid what they saw as poor schools. But the 'active choosers' who make the difference to whether or not a school is 'full', and particularly to whether or not its intake is likely to bring high raw-score school performance, tend to be middle-class, and to give priority to academic results.[40] Of course, parents in all social classes have other priorities too. But the political and media prominence given to five or more good GCSE passes and average A level points scores, has intensified competition for entry to schools highly placed in local league tables, and between schools for pupils likely to sustain that placing.

In these conditions, it remains unclear whether or not the overall effect of parental choice of school has been to increase social segregation. Researchers differ in how they 'measure' socio-economic status and poverty, and in how they define a 'fair' distribution of socially disadvantaged children between schools so as to assess the extent of departures from it.[41] There is disagreement about whether and how far the gap between market winners and losers is widening, with consequences for cumulative advantage and disadvantage. The most socially skewed intakes do appear to be in the most and in the least popular schools, a finding explained largely by marked social class differences in which schools are applied for.[42] This suggests that the Government is rightly concerned to avoid a concentration of 'the most disadvantaged children in the least popular schools', especially given the fact that the proportion of people living in poor households doubled to almost 20 per cent between 1980 and 1999 and that those households contain a third of all children of school age.[43]

There are especially strong grounds for concern in relation to schools perceived as failing. It is true, as David Blunkett remarked when he attacked 'cynics who say that school performance is all about socio-economics and the areas that these schools are located in', that no child is 'preordained to fail by class, or by gender, or by ethnic group or by their home life'.[44] No reputable research would use aggregated data to predict the fate of individuals in that rigidly determinist way. Nevertheless it is important to examine the relationship between social disadvantage and school performance. The evidence we cite is at school level. A study of the results of over 300 secondary schools between 1991 and 1998 found a low level of social disadvantage to be a prime factor in improved performance, and that schools with high levels of social disadvantage tended to become even more disadvantaged. Analysis of the examination performance of 3000 secondary schools from 1992 onwards demonstrated very high correlations with the socio-economic mix of their intakes. Although exceptions are likely to be publicised energetically, very few schools with high proportions of children eligible for free school meals - the most widely used measure of poverty - had achieved 'good' examination performance.[45] Such evidence does not show that 'schools don't matter'; but it does show that their power to overcome 'challenging circumstances' should not be exaggerated. It may also suggest the potential educational effectiveness of redistributive policies to reduce poverty. In particular, if most of the variance in school results is predictable from the composition of their intakes, then comparisons of the performance of different types of school which fail to take into account their circumstances, whether 'challenging' or favourable, deserve to be treated sceptically.[46]

5. Diversity, standards and opportunity.

In opposition, future Labour Ministers and their advisers argued that the 'standard' comprehensive school had outlived its usefulness. In office, a Government pledged to no new selection by ability also declared itself determined to challenge the mediocre 'sameness' it attributed to unreformed comprehensive education. In the words of its first Education White Paper, 'modernising the comprehensive principle' demanded that comprehensive schools should be enabled to develop and promote their own distinctive identities and expertise. 'How much diversity is compatible with equality?' is then a relevant question for a reforming Government.[47]

The 'one size fits all' model which Ministers continue to dismantle bears no relation even to how things were. Comprehensive schools vary 'naturally' in their ethos and priorities; that is, they do so without government prompting. They have always provided curriculum options, usually on some basis of ability and interest and prospective occupational futures. Indeed, among the justifications offered for imposing in England and Wales the world's most extensively prescriptive national curriculum was that by setting a high threshold of common knowledge to which children everywhere would have access, it would curb schools' inclination to experiment with their pupils' education. Subsequent paring down of its demands was mainly to give scope for differentiation within rather than between schools.

In status, governance, control over admissions, funding, and brand name, there is considerably more diversity now than when Labour took office in 1997. Most grant-maintained schools chose foundation, not community, status. New schools 'with a religious character' have joined the state system, the 2001 White Paper promising many more provided 'there is clear local agreement' that they are wanted and that they 'serve the whole community'. Alongside steeply rising numbers of specialist comprehensives have been advanced specialist schools, beacon schools, training schools, and city academies Even wider funding differences between secondary schools of comparable size reflect the continuing historical vagaries of standard spending assessments, but they also result from the rising ratio of total spending which now comes from the Standards Fund and which is distributed directly to those schools willing and able to meet government conditions for receiving it.

Greater variety of status, mission and curriculum has been promoted politically as the appropriate response to the cultural diversity of modern society. That this has not happened in Scotland or Wales suggests that the benefits are less obvious than Ministers seem to assume. Indeed, as cited earlier, research in England indicates that school intakes are more socially segregated in areas with relatively high proportions of selective, foundation, church and specialist schools, while evidence from Scotland indicates that choice without diversity is more equitable than choice with diversity. Our focus here is therefore on possible implications of distinct 'tiers' of schooling for educational standards and for unequal opportunity.

There is substantial evidence that schools tend to gain market appeal from being formally recognised as different. City technology colleges, for example, were widely seen as better, certainly as better resourced, by parents and children who were largely unaffected by their image as a new, high-technology, version of secondary education.[48] 'Foundation' status has traditional connotations which may attract some parents, as may the 'college' label adopted by many specialist schools. Terms like 'beacon', 'advanced', 'specialist' and 'city academy' have marketing attractions. With amendments to the entrepreneurial language, it is tempting to quote the comment that 'image and brand name count for far more in generating profit than efficiency of manufacture'![49]

Church schools are far more successful at attracting pupils than the churches are in attracting worshippers. Constituting about 15 per cent of state secondary schools, their undoubted popularity rests on parental perceptions of orderliness, a clear moral code, and higher standards. Most are not exclusive on religious grounds, and admit children 'of other faiths or none'. The great majority are however voluntary-aided, and so act as their own admissions authorities. The Secretary of State has described it as 'reasonable' for those which are considerably over-subscribed, as many are, to give preference to applicants of their particular faith. Some schools already make regular, attested, church attendance a condition of entry and so are openly exclusive in practice. Overall, faith schools are over-represented statistically among high-performing and improving secondary schools as judged in 'raw' terms. Value-added evidence is slight. What there is suggests that they tend to do slightly better, but without pointing clearly to a cause.[50]

We now concentrate on specialist schools, because these are the Government's principal mechanism both for modernising secondary education and for raising standards. Inheriting over 200 of them in 1997, its initial target of 500 by the end of its first term was already exceeded by the summer of 2000. Now over 700, in March 2003 they made up about a quarter of all state secondary schools. It is the Government's intention that every comprehensive school should have achieved or be working towards specialist status by the end of 2006.

5.1 Specialist schools, standards and sources of advantage.

Greatly expanding the Specialist School Programme reduces the risk of an elite sector. Extending the list of specialisms may help to disperse choice over a wider range of alternatives, thereby further enabling parental and child 'interest' to cut across boundaries of race and social class. This would help to overcome that concentration of demand on a single dominant model of 'good' typically traditional-academic schooling which cross-national research has shown makes educational opportunity even more unequal by limiting the chances of children from poor homes being accepted by, or even applying to, its most prominent exemplars.[51] On the evidence so far, however, choice has increased differences between schools in intake and resources, but has done more to encourage them to play safe than to engage in conspicuous innovation in curriculum or pedagogy.[52]

Nor is there evidence of much parental demand for curriculum specialization. The private sector, often taken as exemplifying the benefits of a direct cash relationship between providers and consumers, is noted mainly for adherence to traditional 'academic subjects'. Within the state system, beginning with the

Conservatives' introduction of city technology colleges, specialization has been vigorously encouraged from above. A high proportion of the first specialist schools admitted to having sought specialist status 'for the money', while a majority either claimed no particular strength in their designated specialism or admitted to being stronger in other subjects.[53]

Ministers have tended to play down the extent of specialization, partly perhaps in response to continuing objections to premature and invalid assessment of aptitude for particular subjects[54], and to emphasize that it occurs within a balanced curriculum and is often delayed until Key Stage 3. Regretting that 'a lot of nonsense' has been written about specialist schools, the Secretary of State insisted that they are 'in fact' only 'modern comprehensive schools' which set more challenging goals, are supported financially in doing so, and gain better results.[55] Ministerial claims that they had shown relatively greater improvement in GCSE performance 2000-2001 were initially over-stated by underestimating what had happened in non-specialist comprehensives. The comparison was then corrected to take into account differences which could reasonably be attributed to differences in resources. Research by David Jesson, however, showed not only that pupils in specialist comprehensives had made greater progress between Key Stage 3 and GCSE than those in non-specialist schools, but also that it was those in areas of high social disadvantage who had made the greatest improvement. His explanation for these findings was not in terms of preferential funding or privileged intakes, but because the specialist schools had used 'creative and innovative ideas to transform the delivery of the curriculum'.[56] The funding advantage is under-estimated when presented as a very small fraction (typically 3-4 per cent) of a school's total budget; most of which will be committed to ongoing expenditure; this new capital and extra recurrent money therefore enables schools to pay for new facilities not possible otherwise. Although these resources have to be shared with other schools and with the local community, they still constitute a significant advantage.

As argued earlier, claiming superior performance for types of school has to take into account the close association of results with intake characteristics, for example, the 'better' results of grant-maintained schools were inseparable from having less than their 'share' of socially-disadvantaged children. That they then showed apparently faster rates of improvement could be explained by their 'success' in further reducing the numbers of pupils from poor families through open and covert selection.[57] Grant-maintained schools were considerably over-represented among pre-1997 specialist comprehensives. Since then, the Government has actively encouraged specialist schools in disadvantaged areas, where some 40 per cent are now located. The current total is therefore more representative of comprehensive schools generally. Nevertheless, Jesson's findings have been questioned because they were based on school-level and not individual pupil data, because his value-added analysis did not remove the level-of-poverty factor, and because he did not allow for what remains a significantly higher proportion of former grammar schools, single-sex and foundation schools than among comprehensives generally.[58] Nor did he differentiate between specialisms, an NFER study showing that only the performance of technology and language colleges was better, and only slightly, than that of non-specialist comprehensives.[59]

Even if the entitlement to select not more than 10 per cent of the intake on aptitude has not been acted on except for a small minority of specialist schools, the temptation to do so may increase as more such schools compete for 'promising' pupils in their local market. Fears that self-selection and covert selection will increase, and will bring new inequalities of opportunity, were not allayed by the blunt assertion in the 2001 White Paper (with no reference to any evidence-base) that specialist schools 'will not' constitute a new hierarchy.

5.2. Parity of esteem.

Underlying fears of increasing unfair selectiveness is the traditional incapacity of the English system of secondary education to develop types of school which are 'simply' different without being unequal in esteem, resources, and so in the prospects available to their pupils. The Conservatives' 1992 White Paper Choice and Diversity, its title capturing the main themes of secondary education policy ever since, defined that Government's objective as 'diversity without hierarchy'. It then made a sharp but untenable distinction between 'selection', when it was schools which did the choosing, and 'specialization' when it was parents who did the choosing. Where schools specialized by faith or by curriculum are over-subscribed, then in some way or other it is they who do the choosing.

In so far as diversity tends towards more selection and more social segregation, then the greater the diversity the greater the selectiveness. Although history is not bound to repeat itself, Ministers surely have an obligation to explain why things really will be different this time. A Government committed to 'high achievement for the many', and to avoiding a high concentration 'of the most disadvantaged children in the least popular schools', must surely confront evidence that the endemic weaknesses of the English system continue to be a wider difference of attainment between 'high' and 'low' attainers, a higher proportion of unqualified leavers, and lower participation rates in post-compulsory education (outside the universities) than in comparable countries.

6. Policy alternatives

David Blunkett's invitation to researchers to contribute to 'improving government' included a warning against unconstructive criticisms, or proposals which however desirable were politically or otherwise impractical. We believe that the recommendations which follow are practical. They are consistent with the Government's belief in not 'leaving things to the market', in the beneficial effects of government interventions such as Sure Start and Excellence in Cities, in generally higher public spending on education, and in positive discrimination in favour of schools where around 40 per cent of pupils are on free school meals and/or have special educational needs or 'challenging circumstances'. They are not consistent, however, with apparently uncritical admiration of the private sector, the lack of a clear policy on academic selection, excessive reliance on the 'information' provided by school performance tables, and excessive deference to parental choice at whatever cost to a wider public interest.

1. Leaving grammar schools to survive if local ballots seem to support them encourages the view that comprehensive schools are inherently second-best. So do privately-funded escape routes into a private sector deemed uncritically to be a sure source of academic excellence. Both are matters of public interest, on which Government policy should be much clearer than it is.

2. Closer co-operation between the public and private sectors should not rest on assumptions either that all potential benefits flow one way, or that schools with highly selective intakes and relatively rich resources can simply transfer some of their 'quality' to schools in severely 'challenging' circumstances.

3. As aptitude for a particular form of curriculum cannot be reliably identified at the age of 11, there is no logic in even 10 per cent selection on that basis; entry to specialist schools should be entirely by 'interest'.

4. The range of specializations should be extended to comprehensives with a strong record of social inclusion, which are unlikely to show well on tables of aggregate performance. It should also be extended to schools (especially in rural areas, where a division of labour between differently specialized schools makes no sense) which offer 'all-round excellence'. Better still, the Government should accept the view of one of its own advisers that 'there are many ways to be a good comprehensive school'. It should enable schools to construct their own case for additional funding, no longer treat specialist status as a self-evident badge of quality and capacity for innovation, and accept that 'meeting the needs of individual children' points to diversity within rather than between schools.

5. League tables should be abandoned. As a mechanism for raising standards, they are not used in Scotland, have been given up in Wales, and their disappearance has been recommended by both the Secondary Heads Association and the Headmasters and Headmistresses Conference. As consumer information, they are both narrow and seriously misleading. Despite the introduction of bench-mark targets and measures of value-added pupil progress, 'raw' results continue to be taken as hard evidence of the relative merits of non-comparable schools. Among the destructive effects is the dominance of selective fee-paying (and some state) schools in annual lists of 'best schools', thereby reinforcing belief that private and selective are best, and the view that a good school is, simply, a school with good results.

6. The prominence of A*-C passes as the prime measure both of individual pupil achievement and school performance is a particularly destructive survival from the past, entirely inappropriate for assessing performance across a school's range of ability.

7. Current experiments with consortia of schools should be encouraged. But the anxieties and disappointments caused by severe competition for popular schools are inherent in a system too deferential to parental choice. Much greater priority should be given to enabling parents to regard their local school as satisfactory than to enabling some parents to take their custom elsewhere, and thereby crowd out less 'promising' local children. The Government should extend its search for useful 'lessons from abroad' to efforts being made in other countries to avoid academically and socially unbalanced intakes for example through banding systems and forms of 'controlled' parental choice.

Acknowledgements

We are very grateful to Margaret Tulloch, former Chair of CASE (Campaign for State Education), for helpful advice and information, and for commenting on earlier drafts of the paper. Patrick Eavis, former head of a Northumberland community comprehensive school, also commented helpfully on the last-but-final draft.

This chapter was originally published under the heading 'School admissions and selection in comprehensive schools: policy and practice' in the Oxford Review of Education (2004) 30:3 pp 347-369; www.tandf.co.uk/Journals/titles/03054985.asp.

References

1. Michael (Lord) Young, 'Down with the meritocracy', *Guardian 29 June 2001*; his satire *The Rise of the Meritocracy*, reprinted many times, was first published in 1958.
2. Anthony Giddens, *The Third Way and its Critics*, Polity Press 2000, pp 85-6.
3. Estelle Morris, speech to the Social Market Foundation, June 2002.
4. David Blunkett's opening address to the Economic and Social Research Council's annual conference, February 2000; its title was 'Influence or irrelevance: can social science improve Government?'
5. Ted Short, Secretary of State for Education in 1970, quoted in A Kerckhoff, K Fogelman, D Crook and D Reeder, *Going Comprehensive in England and Wales*, Woburn Press 1996, p 34.
6. In the 1996 Education White Paper, *Self-Government for Schools*.
7. Andrew Adonis and Stephen Pollard, *A Class Act: the myth of Britain's classless society*, Penguin Books 1998.
8. Written Parliamentary reply to Lord Preston, 20 May 1999.
9. *Financial Times* 9-10 June 2001.
10. J Bradley and J Taylor, *The Report Card on Competition in Schools*, Adam Smith Institute 2002, p11.
11. Caroline Benn and Clyde Chitty, *Thirty Years On*, David Fulton 1996, p 133.
12. A West, P Noden, M Kleinman and C Whitehead, *Examining the Impact of the Specialist Schools Programme*, Centre for Educational Research, London School of Economics and Political Science, 2000: D Jesson, *Value-Added and the Benefits of Specialism*, Technology Colleges Trust 2002.
13. S Gorard and C Taylor, *Specialist Schools in England: track record and future prospects*, Occasional Paper, Cardiff University School of Social Sciences, 2001.
14. Stephen Pollard, 'Selection is back', *Guardian Education*, 5 September 2001.
15. H Goldstein, 'Using pupil performance data for judging schools and teachers: scope and limitations', J Gray, H Goldstein and S Thomas, 'Predicting the future: the role of past performance in determining trends in institutional effectiveness at A level'; both papers in *British Educational Research Journal*, 27, 2001, pp 433-42 and 391-405.
16. G Walden, *We Should Know Better: Solving the Education Crisis*, Fourth Estate 1996; W Hutton, *The State We're In*, Jonathan Cape 2000; C Woodhead, 'Bring back grammar schools', *Reader's Digest* no 592, 2002, pp 91-94.
17. S Gorard and C Taylor, 'Market forces and standards in education' *British Journal of Sociology of Education*, 23, 2002, pp 5-18.
18. S Powers, T Edwards, G Whitty and V Wigfall, 'Destined for success? Educational biographies of academically able pupils. *Research Papers in Education 14*, 1999, pp 321-339.
19. G Walford, *Private Schooling: Tradition, Change and Diversity*, Chapman 1991.
20. T Edwards, J Fitz and G Whitty, *The State and Private Education: An Evaluation of the Assisted Places Scheme*, Falmer Press 1989, pp43-46.
21. *Times Educational Supplement* 3 May 2002.
22. C Canovan, 'School wealth divide as big as ever', *Times Educational Supplement*, 9 August 2002.
23. D Crook, S Power and G Whitty, *The Grammar School Question: a review of research on comprehensive and selective education*, London: Institute of Education Publications, 1999; Joan Freeman, *Educating the Very Able: current international research*, HMSO, 1998.

24. This DfEE study was reported in a Parliamentary Answer, House of Lords, 6 April 2000. David Jesson reported his research in *Evaluating Performance at GCSE in LEAs and Schools of Differing Types*, University of York Centre for Performance Evaluation, February 2001.
25. D Jesson, 'Selective systems of education – blueprint for lower standards?' *Education Review* 15, 2001, pp 8-14; D Jesson, *A Review of structure and performance of secondary education on Kent and Medway*, commissioned by Kent Labour MP Dr Stephen Ladyman, June 2002.
26. Ian and Sandie Schagen, *The impact of selection on pupil performance*, NFER website: www.nfer.ac.uk.
27. T Gallagher and A Smith (2001), 'The effects of selective education in Northern Ireland', *Education Review* 15, pp 74-81.
28. S Gorard, 'A re-examination of the effectiveness of schools in Wales', in R Daugherty, R Phillips and G Rees (eds) *Education Policy-making in Wales*, University of Wales Press, 2000.
29. L Croxford, 'School differences and social segregation', *Education Review* 15, 2001, pp68-73.
30. Margaret Brown, 'The tyranny of the international horse race', in R Slee and G Weiner, with S Tomlinson (eds), *School Effectiveness for Whom?* Falmer Press 1998. R Alexander, P Broadfoot and D Reynolds, *Learning from Comparing, Volume 1*, Symposium Books 1999; S Gorard, 'International comparisons of school effectiveness: the second component of the "crisis account" in England' *Comparative Education*, 37, 2001, pp 279-96.
31. A Green and H Steedman, *Educational provision, Educational Attainment and the Needs of Industry*, London Institute of Education, 2000.
32. OECD (2001) Knowledge and Skills for Life (Programme for International Student Assessment).
33. A Halsey, A Heath and J Ridge, *Origins and Destinations: Family, Class and Education in Modern Britain*, Oxford, Clarendon Press, 1980.
34. Sutton Trust, *Educational Apartheid: a practical way forward*, Sutton Trust, 2001.
35. R Blackburn and C Marsh, 'Education and social class: revisiting the 1944 Act with fixed marginals', *British Journal of Sociology* 42, 1991, pp 507-536.
36. H Glennerster and G Wilson, *Paying for Private Schools*, Allen Lan, Penguin Press 1970; H Glennerster, 'Quasi-markets for education?', *Economic Journal* 101, 1991, pp 1268-1276.
37. *Times Educational Supplement*, 5 March 1999; *Times Higher Educational Supplement*, 3 December 1999.
38. C Taylor, 'Hierarchies and "local" markets: the geography of the "lived" marketplace in secondary education provision', *Journal of Education Policy* 16, 2001, pp 197-214; E Parsons, B Chalkley and A Jones, 'School catchments and pupil movements: a case study in parental choice', *Educational Studies* 26, 2000, pp 33-48.
39. A West and D Ingram, *School Admissions in England since 1997: Is the system fairer?* London: Research and Information on State Education, 2002; A West and A Hind, 2002; West and Ingram, 2001; West and Hind, 2002.
40. J Adnett and P Davies, 'Competition and curriculum diversity in local schooling markets: theory and evidence', *Journal of Educational Policy* 15, 2000, pp 157-67; S Bradley and J Taylor, 'The effect of the quasi-market on the efficiency-equity trade-off in the secondary school sector', *Bulleting of Economic Research* 54, pp 295-314.
41. S Gorard, 'Questioning the crisis account: a review of evidence for increasing polarisation in schools', *Educational Research* 42, 2001, pp 309-321; P Noden, 'Rediscovering the impact of marketisation: dimensions of social segregation in England's secondary schools', *British Journal of Sociology of Education* 21, 2000, pp371-85. Gorard used an 'index of even distribution' to assess schools' representative share of children eligible for free school meals, whereas Noden calculated the probability that a pupil on free school meals would have fellow pupils like him, thereby (he claimed) identifying individual schools with higher concentrations of such pupils and therefore a higher probability of being a 'failing' school.
42. P Noden, A West, M David and A Edge, 'Choice and destinations at transfer to secondary school in London', *Journal of Education Policy* 13, 1998, pp 221-236.
43. *Social Trends*, Stationery Office, 2000, p 93.
44. David Blunkett was addressing a conference on secondary education, reported in the *Times Educational Supplement*, 3 March 2000.
45. J Bradley and J Taylor, *The Report Card on Competition in Schools*, Adam Smith Institute 2002.

46. Stephen Gorard, *Education and Social Justice*, University of Wales Press, 2000, p 128; R Levacic and P Woods, Raising school performance in the league tables: disentangling the effects of social disadvantage' *British Educational Research Journal* 28, 2002, pp 207-226.

47. The question was raised by Michael Barber, 'Power and control in education 1944-2004, *British Journal of Educational Studies* 42, 1994, pp 348-362.

48. Anne Wes, G Whitty, T Edwards and S Gewirtz, *Spcialization and Choice in Urban Education; the city technology college experiment*, Routledge, 1993.

49. A Giddens, 'The Third Way and Its Critics, 2000, Policy Press, p70.

50. S Schagen, D Davies, P Rudd and I Schagen, *The Impact of Specialist and Faith Schools on Performance*, LGA Report 28, 2002, NFER.

51. OECD, *School: A Matter of Choice*, Centre for Educational Research and Innovation, 1994; G Whitty, 'Creating quasi-markets in education: a review of recent research on parental choice and school autonomy in three countries', *Review of Research in Education*, 22, 1997, pp 3-47.

52. Adnett and Davies, 2000, see note 40.

53. West, Noden, Kleinman, Whitehead, 2000, see note 12.

54. J Freeman *Educating the Very Able*, 1998, HMSO p43.

55. Estelle Morris 'We need your help to make a difference' *Education Review* 15.1, 2001, p4.

56. D Jesson, *Value-added and the benefits of Specialism*, Technology Colleges Trust, 2002.

57. R Levacic and J Hardman 'The performance of grant maintained schools: an experiment in autonomy *Journal of Education Policy* 14, 1999, pp 185-212.

58. S Schagen, D Davies, P Rudd and I Schagen, *The Impact of Specialist and Faith Schools on Performance*, LGA Report 28, 2002, NFER.

59. The advice was from Sir Cyril Taylor, interviewed in the Guardian 29 January 2002; he was and remains chairman of the Specialist Schools Trust.

12 ARE CHILDREN BEING SET UP TO FAIL?

Discrimination against racial minorities

In theory the education system now has a legal duty to promote race equality, and yet the Department for Education's 'Five Year Strategy' doesn't make a single reference to racism. Meanwhile new reforms may recreate the problems of the past by condemning Black pupils to a second rate education.

David Gillborn, Institute of Education, University of London

'The publication of today's report on the killing of Stephen Lawrence is a very important moment in the life of our country. It is a moment to reflect, to learn and to change. It will certainly lead to new laws but, more than that, it must lead to new attitudes, to a new era in race relations, and to a new more tolerant and more inclusive Britain'.
(Tony Blair, 24 February 1999)

Speaking in the House of Commons on the day that *the Stephen Lawrence Inquiry Report* was published, the Prime Minister acknowledged the scale of the changes necessary to address the deep seated problem of institutional racism. The report made it clear that **education has a vital role to play in helping *all* children attain their potential and in combating racism in society**, but how far have things changed?

Education 14-19: new developments, old problems?

There is widespread agreement that the education system needs reform between the ages of 14 and 19 years and it seems likely that these reforms will include more scope for separating pupils into different routes or pathways. If this is true, then there is a very real possibility that things will become even harder for aspiring Black (African-Caribbean) youngsters. This is because research in Britain and the US overwhelmingly suggests that **the use of selective pupil grouping (in sets, streams, tracks and bands) does *not* bring about any net improvement in overall achievement but it *does* operate as a means by which a disproportionate number of Black young people are given a second class education in the lowest ranked groups.**

Although pupils in higher ranked groups may benefit from increased teacher expectations and peer support, any gains are often balanced, or even outweighed, by the losses endured by those in the lower groups who face teachers with low expectations and work solely with peers who feel labelled as second-rate and destined for failure. There are particular dangers for minority ethnic pupils because selection gives institutional force to teachers' expectations and entrenches inequalities of opportunity. Research in London, for example, shows how setting and other forms of selective pupil grouping restrict opportunities for certain pupils (especially Black pupils). In addition there are **problems at the heart of the exam system itself.**

The dangers of tiering

Most GCSE (General Certificate of Secondary Education) subjects are now 'tiered'. Tiering means that entrants are separated into different papers, depending on their teachers' assessment, instead of sitting a single common examination paper. The most frequently used approach is the two-tier model. Here, pupils in the 'Higher' tier can be awarded grades A*-D. Those in the lower ('Foundation') tier can only be awarded grades C-G. In this way, **before a young person has answered a single exam question, the exam system effectively places a ceiling and floor on their attainments**.

In most cases a pupil entered in the Higher tier who fails to earn a grade D will fall through the tier floor and be 'ungraded'. Similarly, pupils placed in the Foundation tier know that the highest grades (A*-B) are literally beyond them - this can rule out the possibility of further studies at 'A' level. Additionally, the risk of Higher tier pupils falling through the grade-floor, and being 'ungraded', prompts many teachers to play safe by entering greater numbers for the lower tier. In this way some teachers are treating the Higher tier in a very selective manner so that only those viewed as 'the most able' are permitted entry (see figure 1).

Figure 1: Tiering and the grades available in GCSE examinations

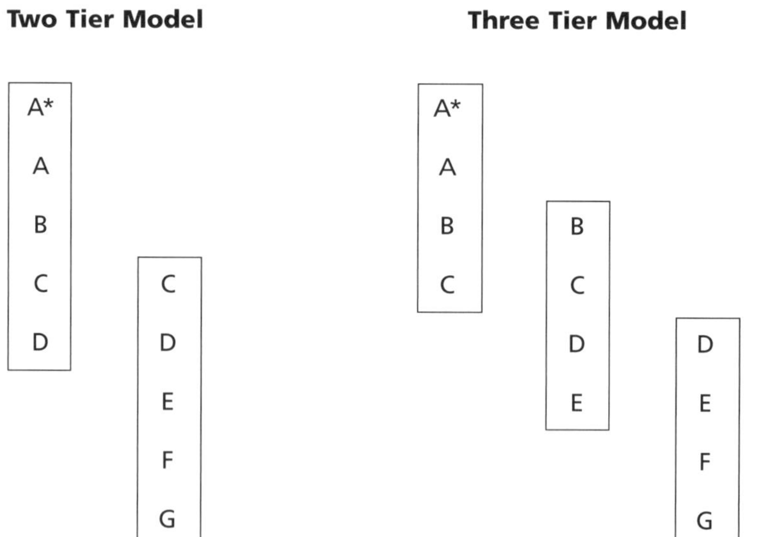

The system in mathematics is even worse; here a three-tier model applies. Pupils in the Higher tier can be awarded grades A*-C; those in the middle ('Intermediate') tier can win grades B-E; those in the Foundation tier can only attain grades D-G. That means that as pupils enter the examination room those in the Foundation tier know that they *cannot* attain the all-important grade C (commonly accepted as a minimum cut off by many selectors in education and job markets).

Destined for failure

Some indication of the devastating effects of such approaches can be gained from the fact that, in two London schools that I studied with my colleague Deborah Youdell, Black pupils were under-represented in Higher tiers and over-represented in Foundation tiers: two-thirds of the Black pupils were entered for maths in the foundation tier. That means that **two in every three Black kids knew they could not possibly achieve a 'C' grade, simply because of the exam that their teachers had entered them for.**

How is ability determined?

Research shows that Black pupils are usually over-represented in the lowest status groups, which receive the worst resources. This means that **whenever there is talk about different 'abilities' we should be very cautious** because 'ability' is very often another word for what teachers *think* kids can do. One simple fact is vitally important: there is no test of potential: *all* tests measure *learned* competencies. Even leading researchers in intelligence testing (a field with an appallingly racist track record) now agree that tests cannot measure innate potential. The racist outcomes that result from supposedly colour-blind selection in setting and tiering procedures suggest a wider lesson. **Although reforms might be conceived (and presented) in colour-blind terms, their effects are frequently anything but blind to 'race'. Colour-blind policies often have racist effects.**

Words and deeds

This summer the Department for Education published its *'Five Year Strategy'*. Running to more than 100 pages the strategy sets out the future priorities and policies for education, yet the word 'racism' does not appear at all. In contrast, 'business' and 'businesses' appear 36 times, and 'standards' warrant 65 appearances – prompting the question, standards for whom?

This remarkable absence is all the more worrying because one of the key lessons of *the Stephen Lawrence Inquiry* was the importance of facing up to racism and challenging it openly and honestly.

'There must be an unequivocal acceptance of the problem of institutional racism and its nature before it can be addressed, as it needs to be, in full partnership with members of minority ethnic communities.' (*The Stephen Lawrence Inquiry*, p. 31)

It is difficult to overstate the importance of the fact that the education system's five year strategy has nothing to say about anti-racism nor the need to challenge institutional racism. It is true, of course, that schools now face a tough set of expectations on race equality, arising from the Race Relations (Amendment) Act 2000 – which was a direct result of the courage and tenacity shown by Stephen's parents and their supporters in finally winning a public inquiry. As a result of this new legislation *every* state-funded school in England, Scotland and Wales must:

- have a written policy on race equality;
- monitor their activities for signs of bias (especially focusing on pupil achievement); &
- they must actively plan to eradicate race inequality.

These new duties are mandatory and require schools to be pro-active in their pursuit of race equality. This is a major step forward and is among the most radical equalities legislation on Earth. **Unfortunately, early indications are that the education sector in general, and schools in particular, are lagging behind other public authorities.**

Too busy to care?

The Commission for Racial Equality recently published an initial report on compliance with the new laws - it paints a discouraging picture in relation to the education sector. First, in a survey of more than 3,000 public authorities, schools were the least likely to reply: only 20% of schools replied, compared with an overall rate of almost 50%. Of course, nothing substantial can be read into a return rate alone. For example, among countless possible explanations, it might be thought that schools were not interested in race equality, or that they were more fearful of responding to a survey sponsored by the authority that polices the legislation. The most obvious explanation, in the eyes of teachers with whom I've discussed this, is simply that schools are too busy to fill in questionnaires. Any or all of these might have a grain of truth.

Looking ahead, however, we might assume that since so few schools responded, then at least the ones that *did* participate would be among the most committed. If that is true then the rest of their responses make even gloomier reading. More than half of respondents in the education sector had not identified clear 'goals' or 'targets' for improvement. In relation to differences in attainment, which is especially prominent in the legislation, **only one in three schools had set any clear goals for change.**

Furthermore, **schools were among the least positive about the effects of the changes** that they had made: 65% of respondents in schools believed their race equality work had produced positive benefits, compared with 74% of those in criminal justice and policing, 80% in Further & Higher Education, and 89% in Central Government. Perhaps most worrying of all, despite the relatively poor response so far, **people working in education were the least likely to express a need for further guidance.**

Put simply, **early indications suggest that many schools are inactive on race equality: at best they are too busy, at worst, they appear to be complacent about their duties and uninterested in further progress**.

Institutional Racism: if we can't discuss it, how will we defeat it?

No gains in wider social justice could ever compensate for the loss of a child. Nevertheless, Stephen's death and the tireless efforts of Doreen and Neville Lawrence have led to enormous changes. The scope and potential power of the new race relations legislation is beyond what many would have believed possible just a few years ago. Without action, however, the legislation is worthless. **The fact that *the Stephen Lawrence Inquiry* made headlines around the world, and that the law has been changed, means nothing if lessons have not been learned by the powers that be.** It is worth reminding ourselves of the Inquiry's definition of Institutional Racism.

'The collective failure of an organisation to provide an appropriate and professional service to people because of their colour, culture, or ethnic origin. It can be seen or detected in processes, attitudes and behaviour which amount to discrimination through unwitting prejudice, ignorance, thoughtlessness and racist stereotyping which disadvantage minority ethnic people.

It persists because of the failure of the organisation openly and adequately to recognise and address its existence and causes by policy, example and leadership.' (*The Stephen Lawrence Inquiry*, p. 28)

This definition requires that we examine the *effects* of actions and policies, not their intent. Education reforms do not automatically benefit all groups equally – indeed, Black children have usually drawn *less* benefit from the changes. Notice, in particular, the last sentence of the quotation (which is rarely included when people quote the definition). Institutional racism 'persists because of the failure of the organisation openly and adequately to recognise and address its existence and causes by policy, example and leadership'.

Current evidence suggests that the education system has failed to learn from the tragedy of Stephen's murder and the resultant inquiry. Schools have been slow to respond to their new duties and most appear content to take no further action. At a national level, in the Education Department's '*Five Year Strategy*' for radical educational change, institutional racism is notable by its total absence.

The Stephen Lawrence Charitable Trust is pursuing a range of projects to raise the achievements of disadvantaged young people and to tackle racism in education. It is a fitting tribute to Stephen and is making a real impact: but it is increasingly swimming against the tide. Five years after *the Stephen Lawrence Inquiry Report* delivered its damning verdict, it is time that the Trust's energy was matched by the most influential players in education (from the corridors of Whitehall to the staffrooms of every school). Some important victories have been won in the battle for greater racial justice, but the struggle is far from over.

Acknowledgements & Addendum

This paper was originally produced for the Stephen Lawrence Charitable Trust and is reproduced with acknowledgement of the incredible contribution made by the Trust, and especially Doreen Lawrence OBE. Since its first publication the Department for Education has announced that the three tier GCSE model will be phased out in the coming years: unfortunately the two tier system will remain and there have been no moves to address the race inequality in tier entry. Worse still, official statistics released in 2005, as part of the Youth Cohort Study, suggest that inequalities in attainment at the age of 16 are widening.

David Gillborn is Professor of Education at the Institute of Education, University of London. He is an award-winning author and founding editor of the international journal, *Race Ethnicity & Education*. His recent publications include the book *'Rationing Education'* (with Deborah Youdell) published by the Open University Press. He is editor, with Gloria Ladson-Billings, of *the RoutledgeFalmer Reader in Multicultural Education*.

13 GRAMMAR SCHOOLS – CAN PARENTS DECIDE? HOW THE GOVERNMENT IS PROTECTING SELECTIVE EDUCATION

Margaret Tulloch

Before 1997 many people hoped that the election of a Labour government might mean an immediate end to selection in the areas where 166 English grammar schools remained. The publication in 1995 of *Diversity and Excellence*, the policy paper produced by the then Labour education team should have indicated that this dream might not be realised quite as quickly as we hoped.

It said:

> *'We are implacably opposed to a return to selection by 11 plus. Labour's commitment to lifelong learning and comprehensive education means ensuring that every child in every school has available to them the highest possible quality of education, thus avoiding the division which segregation inevitably brings for education and for society as a whole. Parental preference is denied where selection by examination is employed. Our opposition to academic selection has always been clear. But while we have never supported grammar schools in their exclusion of children by examination change can only come through local agreement. Such a change in the character of the school would only follow a clear demonstration of support from the parents affected by such decisions.*

Diversity and Excellence 1995

A 'demonstration of clear support' was taken by many to mean that a new Labour government would bring about change to a fully comprehensive system, but that final plans would need the ultimate endorsement of local parents. With hindsight, the phrase 'parents affected by such decisions' also needed closer analysis.

By early 1997 when the Labour education team published one of its bulletins, the extent to which policy had changed became clear. It became apparent that it had shifted almost to that of neutrality.

'Any change in the character of a particular (grammar) school should only be agreed by a ballot of all parents affected by such a decision. It will be for parents who are anxious about the admission policies of a grammar school to initiate by means of a petition to the Secretary of State, any ballot seeking a change in the admission policies of an individual school. If there is no desire among local parents for a change in the admission policies, there will be no ballot and no

change… the ballot will focus on parents of primary age children within the school's catchment area, whose children will be those who would have the opportunity of attending the grammar school under an open admissions system. Where an entire LEA has a selective system - and change is sought - the ballot could be open to all parents of school age children in the authority.'
(March/April 1997 Labour Education Bulletin 1997)

It was clear that if elected a new Labour government would take the legal right to bring in comprehensive education out of local authority hands and give it to parents. Why the policy had hardened to such an extent can only be the subject of speculation. It is possible that it was thought that since parental ballots were involved in the procedures whereby schools opted out of local authority control, the same mechanism could be used for grammar schools. The situations however are very different.

It is likely that promises made in selective Wirral during the bye-election played a big part. Tony Blair, as we learnt (see Hattersley p26) was seemingly sympathetic to the notion that grammar schools are the route out of poverty. A quick glance at the free school meals data could have corrected that impression. He may have listened to influential advisers such as Adonis and Pollard, both sympathetic to selection. It is difficult to believe that Labour politicians thought there were enough votes over selection to lose them the forthcoming election, had they taken a principled stand against it.

As the law stood before the election of a Labour government LEAs with grammar schools could have proposed a change to comprehensive education. Very few grammar schools remained as county schools for which the LEAs would have been the admission authority as most had opted out to become grant maintained. Proposals would have been subject to public consultation and the agreement of the Secretary of State. Any Labour LEA which had grammar schools, Wirral for example, which might have wanted to introduce comprehensive education before 1997 would have been making proposals to be ratified by a Tory government which, latterly at least, believed in a grammar school in every town. Grammar schools are mostly in Conservative LEAs whose councillors support selection. These LEAs were hardly likely to get the support of councillors to submit plans for change to a new Labour government. So, perhaps it was thought parental petitions stood more chance of bringing about change.

However for whatever reason that period between 1995 and 1997 seems to have been crucial in the formulation of Labour policy over grammar schools.

Nonetheless the manifesto upon which the Labour Government was elected in May 97 did not spell out the detail over the mechanism of change. It gave the following commitment on comprehensive education -

In education we reject both the idea of a return to the 11 plus and monolithic comprehensive schools that take no account of children's differing abilities. Instead we favour all-in schooling which identifies the distinct abilities of individual pupils and organises them into classes to maximise their progress in individual subjects. In this way we modernise the comprehensive principle, learning from the experience of its 30 years of application…

And on grammar schools it said:

Any changes in the admission policies of grammar schools will be decided by local parents

In August 1997 the then DfEE invited comments on the mechanism for parental ballots. Significantly it was decided that the letter about this 'consultation' which was sent during the summer holidays should go only to LEAs with grammar schools and to grammar schools. Following protest the then Minister of State Stephen Byers wrote to the Campaign for State Education in September 1997.

'We considered carefully the distribution of the consultation letter on grammar school admissions. We decided that the letter should be sent automatically to those most directly affected, but that we should also draw its existence to the attention of a much wider audience... **(23 September 1997 Stephen Byers, letter to the Campaign for State Education)**

The short sighted official attitude that selection only affects those selected, not also the majority rejected, has been a significant feature of the government policy over grammar schools.

Following consultation the rules governing an end to selection in areas where there are grammar schools was put in primary legislation in the School Standards and Framework Act 1998. The arrangements about grammar schools were debated, although the full implications of the ballot regulations were discussed most in the Lords.

The Act required that there should be no more selection on ability and introduced the possibility of ending selection into grammar schools in the 36 English LEAs, where it still exists, in one of two ways. The governing bodies of the 164 grammar schools could decide to change the admission policy of the school. This would be an alteration which would be subject to a public consultation and a decision by the school organisation committee. **(Section 109 SSFA)** Unsurprisingly this has not happened.

Or, change could come and grammar schools required to admit children of all abilities if there were 47 successful parental ballots. But crucially, before such ballots could take place, petitions would have to be signed by one in five of the parental electorate. All these signatures would have to be collected during a petition year starting in September and ending in the following July. **(Sections 104 - 109 SSFA)**

There would have to be 10 area ballots where all parents would be able to vote and 37 ballots relating to groups of grammar schools or single (stand alone) grammar schools, where only parents whose children attend primary 'feeder' schools are entitled to vote. Again the attitude that selection is of interest only to those selected seems to have been influential. There were many protests about the feeder school eligibility, as it was pointed out that many local parents would be denied a vote were a ballot to take place. In November 1998 the then Minister of State Estelle Morris wrote to CASE.

'I am sorry you do not agree with the definition of those parents who will be eligible to petition or vote in non-selective areas. When we said in the Manifesto that we meant 'local parents' to have a vote, we meant that in contrast to national government. Grammar schools draw pupils from large areas. We had originally thought in terms of feeder schools ballots for all grammar schools, as

the parents of schools with traditional links with the grammar schools would be those whose children are most likely to have their children considered (or rejected) as possible pupils for the grammar schools.' **(26th November 1998 Estelle Morris, letter to Campaign for State Education)**

One LEA, the newly unitary Bristol managed to end selection in its two grammar schools in the narrow window when it as an LEA still had powers to propose and consult on change and the new Labour government agree it, before the School Standards and Framework Act became law. A public consultation brought no objections and change was brought in, agreed by David Blunkett.

The regulations on parental ballots came into force in December 1998. During 1999 campaigns were set up in Ripon, Kent, Trafford, Sutton, Barnet, Birmingham, and Buckinghamshire. Campaigners were not encouraged by the legislation but believed that they had to try to end selection, and if this was the only way, they were going to have a go.

CASE set up a specific campaign – *Say NO to Selection* - to campaign nationally for an end to selection and to support campaigners who wanted to set up local campaigns. An email newsletter was part of this campaign. CASE put campaigners in touch with each other and with the media and tried to bring about an informed debate.

In only one place, Ripon, were sufficient signatures gathered to trigger a ballot in March 2000. The campaign succeeded in showing up the bizarre effect of the feeder school ballot regulations. Private school parents were hugely over-represented making up a quarter of the electorate, although a parliamentary question at the time revealed that only 4.6% of primary children in North Yorkshire were in private education **(Written reply, House of Lords, 22 February 2000, Baroness Blackstone)** the second largest group were parents in a school 10 miles away, while some Ripon parents could not vote. The idea that these parents in the area of the schools do not have an interest in whether the school were to admit children of all abilities is bizarre.

Both in Ripon and in the other campaigns selection has been raised as an important local issue and all the campaigns have illustrated the huge difficulties of using the legislation to end selection. This experience has shown it is impossible to achieve an end to selection by means of parental petitions and ballots.

So after two Labour Governments with massive majorities, in Labour's third term more children face the 11 plus or selective entry tests for secondary education as when Labour took office.

It is clear under present arrangements parents cannot decide.

Why parents cannot decide - the practical difficulties

There are many practical difficulties and absurdities which mean that, unless there is a drastic change in the legislation, parents will never again get the chance to decide about the admission policies of their local grammar schools, simply because it is clear there will be no more campaigns under the present law.

- All campaigns need people willing to devote a great deal of their time. This is difficult in any circumstances but campaigners to end selection have found they need the hide of a rhinoceros to cope with vilification of local and national press. The vitriol of some grammar school supporters has to be experienced to be believed. Members of Ripon CASE, people whose values they thought the Labour Government shared, were left to take the full force of the tabloid press while Government looked the other way. Local press are very influential.

- At the start campaigners need to know how many signatures are needed to trigger a ballot (the threshold number) and additionally feeder school campaigners need to know which schools are feeder schools. This information is collected by the Electoral Reform Services. Amazingly, only 10 signatures are needed to trigger the requirement that the Electoral Reform Services start to contact the schools to collect the information to assemble the list of feeder schools and establish the threshold number. In contrast thousands of signatures are required just to trigger a ballot.

- The collection of threshold figures and lists of feeder schools costs a great deal of public money. A recent parliamentary answer has revealed since 1998 £1,102,945 has been paid to Electoral Reform Services to collect this information as campaigners trigger their collection in order to work on gathering petition signatures. These costs include £1780.07 on the Ripon ballot itself. ***(Written parliamentary answer David Miliband to David Chaytor MP 8 April 2003)*** So over a million pounds of public money has been spent, which could have paid for proper research into selection, a genuine public consultation and perhaps some financial assistance to schools to bring about the change to a comprehensive system.

- The process of collecting this information takes a long time. For example it took 5 months for the threshold number for the Buckinghamshire campaign (18,453 signatures) to be calculated.

- Campaigners have first to get the parental lists for the names and addresses of parents so they are able to go and collect signatures. Campaigners find it difficult to get the parental lists as only parents from the particular school can ask for them. Many parents are frightened of putting their head above the parapet in this way. When the lists are obtained they may be inaccurate as parents may move without telling the school. Trafford campaigners found some addresses were those of the children's grandparents.

- The petition takes a long time to fill in. It takes even longer to collect signatures door to door. Some campaigners have not been allowed to collect signatures in the playground. Signatures may be difficult for the Electoral Reform Services to validate because people are unsure of the name of their children's schools and fill the petition in inaccurately.

- In feeder school ballots many local parents cannot vote or sign a petition even though if the schools in question were comprehensive they would be their local schools. For example parents whose children attend infant schools or small schools do not get a vote. Parents whose children attend a nursery unit attached to primary school do get a vote while those who attend stand alone nursery units do not. Private school parents (as in Ripon) are inevitably over represented as prep schools often coach children to get to grammar schools. In Barnet, which has three grammar schools, a third of Barnet primary school parents would be ineligible to vote, some of them with children in primary schools next door to the grammar schools in question. Meanwhile parents with children in primary schools further afield across North London are eligible.

- Petition signatures cannot be carried over from one petition period to another despite that fact that only one cohort of parents becomes ineligible each year and a new one eligible. In other words the legislation assumes parents will change their minds about wanting a ballot from one year to the next.
- There is no limit on spending on campaigns – Ripon pro-selectionists could afford to send a video to every home.
- The system seems designed to ensure there is no proper debate. Several campaigns became heavily immersed in correspondence with the DfES about the interpretation of Section 107 of the School Standards and Framework Act and the Ballot Information Code.

Extract from the Ballot Information Code, from Schedule 4 to the Education (Grammar School Ballots) Regulations 1998

1. *The principles specified in paragraph 2 shall apply to providing materials for parents relating to a petition or a ballot.*

2. *Material provided:*

    a) *should provide information which is as factual and accurate as possible, with a view to helping parents reach a soundly-based decision about whether grammar schools should or should not retain selective admission arrangements;*

    b) *insofar as it offers opinions, predictions or view, it should do so on the basis of fact or a reasonable interpretation of fact; and should clearly distinguish between what is a fact and what is opinion or prediction;*

    c) *should be objective or explanatory, seeking to clarify the issues without omitting important facts or arguments, and without selecting facts or arguments in such a way as to distort or mislead;*

    d) *should not be likely to cause alarm, concern or offence;*

    e) *should not in content, tone or presentation be party political;*

    f) *should not attack the view of individuals or of groups taking a different view of the future of selective arrangements at grammar schools.*

Extract from Section 107 of the School Standards and Framework Act

(1) An authority to which this section applies shall not occur any expenditure for the purpose of -

(a) publishing any material which, in whole or in part, appears designed to influence:

    (i) eligible parents in deciding whether to request a ballot under section 105, or

    (ii) the outcome of such a ballot;

(b) assisting any person to publish any such material; or

(c) influencing, or assisting any person to influence, by any other means

    (i) eligible parents in deciding whether or not to request such a ballot, or

    (ii) the outcome of such a ballot;

(2) This section applies to:

(a) any local education authority, and

(b) the governing body of any school maintained by a local education authority.

- It is unfortunate that the interpretation of these rules was never subject to the scrutiny of the courts. Their effect seems to have been that headteachers and teachers were discouraged from speaking out in favour of change or about issues surrounding the testing for fear of offending Section 107 or the Ballot Information Code. Teachers in Ripon, although they were advised by the LEA that the DfES line was that they could 'give an opinion based on fact' (whatever that means) were also advised that they should err on the side of caution. Only two headteachers in Ripon gave an opinion - the head of the secondary modern and the head of the grammar school (both supported the status quo). Parents in Ripon must have assumed that silence from primary teachers meant support for selection. Primary headteachers may not want to make their views public in case local parents think they will not help their child pass the 11 plus. Petitions cannot be sent out through pupil post as the DfES rules that this might be interpreted that the school is taking sides. There is a lack of clarity in the process about the issue of whether or not a governing body, PTAs, school staff for example can make clear that it would support or would not support an end to selection, as this would inform local parents. For example in a letter to CASE in November 1999 the DfES said *'a school may incur expense in presenting factual information, and may state their position as long as it is clear that it is their opinion. '* When asked for the definition of a 'school' for this purpose CASE were told *'Anyone who issues information using a schools' resources ... is acting on behalf of the school'.*

- So, a 'neutral stance' from the professionals means in practice support for the status quo. This line seems to have the support of the DfES. This means parents are not informed by professionals and there is no real local debate.

- Campaigns are long drawn out and complicated. Campaigns have to focus on getting signatures on the petitions although the real issue is selection. Once a ballot has been triggered, the DfES would allow a two sides of A4 leaflet to be sent out via schools providing its content is agreed with the DfES. But this, which was a later concession, following the Ripon ballot, entirely misses the point that it is as soon as signatures are sought that unfair practices emerge and misinformation begins. In Ripon once the petition threshold was reached ballot papers were sent out very quickly. Exhausted by the time the ballot came campaigners found that parents returned the ballot papers almost immediately and no real debate happened. There was then a long wait for the result, ten weeks after the valid petition.

- Apart from the cost to the public purse of collection of information on the basis of ten signatures there are other anomalies. For example there are seemingly arbitrary and great differences in the number of signatures to get a ballot ie about 600 to get a vote on one grammar school in Ripon whereas, Buckinghamshire need about 1500 signatures and the Barnet campaign would need about 2000 for one grammar school. CASE organised a meeting of campaigners with the DfES officials from the grammar school ballots team. It was clear from those conversations that there had been no modelling of the procedures.

Why parents cannot decide - the main stumbling block

Perhaps these many anomalies and drawbacks are evidence for the persistent rumours that it was always intended that no ballot would succeed. But there is a further crucial flaw. The most important factor is that although Government policy is that parents must decide, the parents given this power have no official encouragement to end selection. Campaigns run by local campaigners cannot replace officially supported plans for change.

Even before signing a petition parents want to know what a local comprehensive system would look like, a question campaigners cannot answer. So pro-selectionists get away with defending the status quo. The talk is of abolition, excellence and choice and 'better the devil you know'. Children and their rights and the effects of selection on children and their educational opportunities do not get the consideration they deserve. Discouraged by the Ballot Information Code, teachers and LEAs do not make their views clear.

In practice parents have to vote on a principle. In Ripon there are two schools, the grammar and a secondary modern on opposite sides of the road. It was easy for pro-selectionists in Ripon to criticise the campaign to bring in comprehensive education on the basis no plans had been put forward. A leaflet produced at the time by pro-selectionists in Ripon said *'The ballot paper does not specify what school(s) we will have in the future, therefore voters can only speculate. Those who want to end academic selection have not produced a clear costed alternative.'* But a parent-led campaign is in no position to put forward plans. Campaigners were not in the position to answer a legitimate question from parents as to whether change to an all ability intake would mean one school or two, a junior school and a senior school or two competing comprehensives. So in fact it is encouraging that as many as a third of Ripon parents who were eligible to vote, voted yes to the question - *Are you in favour of Ripon Grammar school introducing admission arrangements which admit children of all abilities?* without knowing what the consequences of their vote might mean.

So what is by far the worst feature of the whole of this flawed legislation is that parents do not get any proper information upon which to decide. There are no plans for parents to decide about, so debate is stifled and parents have to vote in a vacuum. It is irresponsible of Government to say parents should decide and then set up a system which makes sure there is no informed debate and no plans to decide about. What a contrast this is with Northern Ireland where an elected local government has consulted local people (at public expense), encouraged an informed local debate and taken a decision to end the 11 plus.

In the past Government has tried to give the impression that ending selection is not part of the big picture - it is a side issue involving only a few schools - not relevant to the Government's agenda of raising standards and promoting social inclusion. This claim does not hold up to scrutiny. One grammar school creates 3 de-facto secondary moderns. So the effect of 164 grammars added together makes almost 20% of English secondary schools affected by selection. Benn and Chitty's survey showed 14% of 'comprehensive schools' across the country reporting that their intakes were directly affected by selection into nearby grammar schools. *(Benn and Chitty. Thirty Years On. 1996)*

Surely selection affects the Government's policy of raising standards and creating a more inclusive education system? Concern about the effect of testing at 7.11.14 and 16 seems to be growing. For many children in the 36 LEAs which retain grammar schools entry tests to these schools are additional to their other tests at 7 and 11.

Research seems to show comprehensive systems do just as well overall as selective ones. This is a compelling argument for ending a system which demotivates three quarters of ten year olds by telling them they have failed.

How could parents decide?

Assuming the manifesto commitment that parents decide remains there could be a better system. Primary legislation would be required. But crucially Government policy must change from a neutral stance to a clear policy that for the sake of the children selection should end. Tinkering with the regulations is not the answer. Government has to make the decision that it wants to see change. Official information about the educational and social reasons for bringing about an end selection must come from Government. This will require a policy shift from that which has been adopted so far. An extract from a letter to CASE from Estelle Morris in 1998 illustrates how much of a policy shift is needed - *'We think it important that the Department should be impartial on the issue of whether or not parents should petition or indeed how they should vote if a ballot is triggered.* **(10th November 1998 Estelle Morris, Minister of State letter to CASE)**

- The Government must make sure as much information as possible is available to parents and assure LEAs and parents that funds will be available to implement a comprehensive system, were they to vote for it.
- Government could require LEAs to bring forward plans for a comprehensive system and only leave much reduced parental petition facility if LEAs were unwilling to do so. LEAs would be required to bring forward proposals for discussion about ending school admission by selection by ability test at 11. Parents must be clear about what a vote for change might mean. There should be consultation on a local comprehensive <u>plan</u> following an informed local discussion encouraging professionals to give their views over a defined period leading to a ballot.
- The feeder school parental eligibility should go. Ballots should be an area parental ballot either the whole LEA or within LEA in a designated area to include all parents affected by selection. The 'relevant areas' regulations might be of use here. The law (105(2)(a)) allows the Secretary of State to declare areas within an LEA for an area ballot so regulations could be changed so that all grammar schools could be subject to area ballots which would involve parents within the local area.
- Only primary and preschool parents should be eligible to vote in a ballot as changes would be most likely to affect them and their children.

Should parents decide?

Many observers have expressed a view that parental interest in schools is too short term and too closely allied to the interests of their own children to look at the big picture. They argue that the whole community should ballot. Under current arrangements of course this argument cannot be tested as parents are not given a big picture.

Parents are perhaps better placed than the general public to know the effects of selection on children. Another argument in favour of giving parents the ultimate decision is that it would be politically very difficult for another government, local or national to come along and override that decision. But teachers in particular must be allowed to express an opinion and influence the decision the parents finally make. Parents could decide. But they need proper information and there has to be a Government wanting to bring about change. Neither of these conditions is being met at the moment.

14 NORTHERN IRELAND: HOW COMPREHENSIVE EDUCATION HAS BEEN OPPOSED

Niall McCafferty

Except for a short interlude of devolved government, Westminster has been directly responsible for education in Northern Ireland since 1972. Throughout these 33 years the socio-economically powerful grammar school lobby and the Department of Education (DE) have been allowed to continue unhindered disseminating carefully selected examination statistics that mislead the public into believing that our selective system is the most successful academically in the UK.

OECD rankings on reading, mathematical, and scientific literacy show that there is no significant difference between Northern Ireland and England (PISA Report, Dec. 2001) or between Northern Ireland and Scotland (PISA Report, Dec. 2004). These reports also show that Northern Ireland has one of the longest ranges in the scores of individuals, and an above-average gap between the mean scores of the advantaged and disadvantaged sections of society. While Northern Ireland does better than England at 5+ GCSE Grades A*-C level, England does better than Northern Ireland on 5+ GCSE A*-G. The Scottish comprehensive system consistently outscores Northern Ireland at the 5+ A*-C level (5+ Standard Grades 13).

The grammar lobby also asserts that the grammar school provides a route out of poverty for the working class. The truth is that the present system provides privileged education for children from professional backgrounds and for a **very small minority** from manual backgrounds. 80 per cent of grammar school places go to the children of parents in professional occupations, and only 20 per cent go to the children of parents in manual occupations. Only 8 per cent of grammar school places go to the children in the two bottom categories (4 and 5) in the Registrar General's scale. In some disadvantaged areas, even fewer; for example, only 2 per cent of the children in the Greater Shankill area of Belfast are selected for grammar school. Northern Ireland confirms OECD (PISA) findings (2001 and 2004) which show that in all differentiated systems there is a socio-economic divide between so-called privileged, middle-class, academic schools and the working-class, underprivileged, vocational schools.

A short history of events since 1997

- 1998 Westminster Government commissions research by Gallagher and Smith
- 2000 Research published. Martin McGuiness establishes group led by Gerry Burns to carry out independent review
- 2001 Burns report published for consultation

- 2002 Consultation ends. Martin McGuiness announces end of transfer tests in 2004. Northern Ireland assembly suspended. New Westminster minister Jane Kennedy establishes Post Primary Review working group chaired by Steve Costello
- 2003 Costello report submitted to Government
- 2004 Costello report published and Government responds. New arrangements announced. Transfer tests to end in 2008.
- 2005 New admission arrangements to be announced in November

Westminster has been responsible during the current 7-year review for accepting the failure of the Department of Education (DE) and the official review groups to seriously research comprehensive education - the most widely employed, academically successful, and socially just system worldwide (ref PISA data). In fact the Burns Group actually misled the public into believing that comprehensive education is unsuitable through invalid and erroneous inferences from three documents that are methodologically inadequate (Burns Report, pp 100 – 103).

Continuing support for the present system by the Catholic grammar schools is illustrative of the intransigence of the grammar lobby as the Northern Ireland Catholic bishops have described the system in their response to Burns as 'no longer tenable on ethical or educational grounds'.

In a Westminster Parliamentary debate on Northern Ireland education (02/03/05) DUP and UUP MPs stated the Protestant Voluntary grammar schools' case. An English Conservative MP, whom representatives of the Catholic grammar schools had met the previous day, stated the Catholic grammar schools' case against changing the present selective system.

But the Labour governments refused to move to the introduction of a comprehensive education system. Seeking a solution which would avoid criticism from the right-wing press, the easiest policy was to appease Middle Northern Ireland by rejecting a fair comprehensive system and giving them what they have designed themselves and defended obstinately for 57 years - a privileged elite education for their children free of charge.

The proposed new system

The following is a brief summary of the proposals of the new system:

1. The existing grammar and secondary schools will continue as "academic" and "vocational/occupational" schools, free to become a specialist school if they choose.
2. Transfer at age 11 by parent selection, informed by a Pupil Profile compiled by the primary school.
3. Oversubscribed schools will select their pupils on basis of non-academic criteria not yet agreed.
4. Every school will enable each pupil to choose from a curriculum Entitlement Framework of 24 courses at KS4 and from 27 at post-16. One-third must be academic and one-third vocational. Within these general guidelines, each school will determine its curricular type either "academic" or "vocational".

5. Finance will be allocated on the basis of the number of pupils enrolled in the school.

It is hoped that this new system will reconcile the demands of those who want a fair comprehensive system and the grammar school lobby. The hope seems unrealistic, indeed naïve.

New Curricular and School Systems

The "new" **curriculum** is essentially the same as the present curriculum – in separate so-called academic and vocational tracks. And the "new" **system** is essentially the same as the present one - differentiated between so-called academic (grammar) and vocational (secondary) schools. The Burns-Costello division of the curriculum into separate tracks and the schools into differentiated institutions is based on the English National Qualifications Framework devised by Sir Ron Dearing (1996) which puts the John Major Government's White Paper (1991) policies into effect. Burns rejected the corresponding proposals for Northern Ireland (which had been produced jointly by the Training and Employment Agency and the DE) recommending a much more coherent education and training curriculum, closer to international norms which provide curriculum unification through modular courses accessible to all pupils in a single school. This gives variety, choice, and flexibility; the Burns-Costello model precludes this.

The Burns-Costello specialist schools will not alter the current division of schools into academic, ie high status, and vocational, ie low status, schools. It will greatly increase the hierarchy of schools in parents' minds and, therefore, the gap between the top and bottom schools, the latter becoming even more deprived of resources, human and material, with consequent effects on pupils: those in the most deprived schools will suffer even more.

The proposed new curriculum and school system are based on the same false premises as the present curriculum and system, that children have qualitatively different types of mind (academic and vocational) and that schools must be either academic or vocational to accommodate this.

The speculative opinion of Burns-Costello regarding what should be provided in the way of vocational courses and how these will prepare children for opportunities of the workplace ignores evidence from England. The evidence from the Nuffield Review Study, currently being conducted in England, has many lessons for Northern Ireland's Burns-Costello system.

It shows that curriculum participation from 14-19 declines with age, and that this relates to social disadvantage. Post-16 selection, like selection at 11, feeds on social division. And there are lower achievement rates in vocational than in academic courses of the same level.

It shows that decisions about which pathway to follow post-16 are driven by the maxim that if you have the GCSEs needed to take AS or A-levels you should do so. Teachers see the AS/A-level route as the preferred option for their pupils, with the vocational and work-based routes seen as an option primarily for the less able. Thus the evidence from England indicates that in the education and training system chosen by Burns-Costello and adopted by the government for

Northern Ireland, parity of esteem between vocational and academic pathways is a remote prospect.

The Nuffield Study has also found that even the Curriculum 2000 reforms to the Dearing system, representing a move towards a more linked system, have not increased the proportion of young people studying for vocational qualifications at Level 3. Currently three-quarters of those in England working towards Level 3 qualifications are taking AS/A-levels. The work-based pathway is also seen to be quite marginal, of low quality, and has not succeeded in gaining genuine employer engagement and commitment. Even the Modern Apprenticeships have not been a success. Right across the Foundation Modern Apprenticeships, 6 out of 10 apprentices leave without achieving any qualifications at all, worse than in its predecessor, the YTS. Across all the Advanced Modern Apprenticeships, less than half of the learners achieved either the full framework or the Level 3 NVQ.

Pupil Profile

Chapter 1 of the Consultation Document on the admission arrangements in the new system states: "The new Pupil Profile will provide parents with clear and objective information on their child's progress and achievements and an assessment of their attitudes, aptitudes and interests, as well as identifying areas for development and future learning". In Appendix 1, which provides an outline of the Pupil Profile, it is claimed, "For each of these skills (i.e. talking and listening, reading, writing, numeracy, information and communication technology) each pupil would be assessed and assigned a level". In the five other areas (i.e. thinking, attitudes, aptitudes, interest, further developments) "teacher comment" would be provided.

This account of the Pupil Profile is misleading. First, there are simply no tests, nor will there be any tests, of sufficient objectivity, validity, reliability, accuracy, and relevance on which to determine the future education, career, and life opportunities of an individual at age 11 or 14. Second, in five of the six areas of the Pupil Profile it is wholly dependent on the "comments" of the teacher, which, while professional, are still subjective. Besides, they are based on past experience and cannot foresee future changes in the child, or in her/his future opportunities.

The Pupil Profile, therefore, amounts to the 11-Plus with teachers' comments. The parents will use the document to select a school for the child. This constitutes a parentocracy. This means that (1) parents as a group have greater power in educational decision-making than the whole society of which they are only a part, and (2) since all parents are not equal, in terms of knowledge and ability to manipulate the education system to their advantage, it also means that the more powerful parents are in a position to enforce their views on society and cause the children of the less powerful to receive inferior educational provision. Further, while most parents are good, love their children, know their personality and character better than anyone else and have an all-important role to play in their educational guidance, they do not necessarily know them better than anyone else academically, nor will they be the best qualified to advise on available courses for their children or to provide educational and careers counselling.

There is much research evidence from around the world (for example, OECD countries, especially Germany and France) to show that differential provision such as is envisaged in the Burns-Costello proposals results in academic schools being predominantly middle class, vocational schools predominantly working class, and half the children in second-level education ending up in the wrong type of school.

How will schools select their pupils? They will do it by means of the Pupil Profile at the transfer interview. The Burns-Costello proposal was that the second-level school should not see the Pupil Profile before the pupil had been placed in the school. However, in the Consultation Document it is now proposed that parents bring the Profile to the interview with the second-level principal, who will effectively select or reject the pupil on the basis of the Profile. OECD research shows that parents from the disadvantaged section of society who have managed to screw up the courage to go to an interview in the academic school are comparatively easily talked out of it. Hamburg University research in Baden-Wurttenberg state in 2004 showed that in such circumstances the children of professional parents are four times as likely to be recommended for the academic school as their working class peers, even if both have the same marks.

Specialist Schools

The most significant difference of all between the English and Northern Ireland conceptions of the specialist school is that in England the specialism was a subject, but in Northern Ireland it could be a "mainly academic" or a "mainly vocational " approach. This originated in the Burns Report and has been re-articulated by the Permanent Secretary of the DE at a conference in Belfast on 16/11/04. Specialist schools, he said, will offer their distinctive curricular strengths. "This will range from a mainly academic approach, a mainly vocational approach, a balance between academic and vocational, which will vary from school to school". In other words, a variation on the English specialist school has been introduced here. It means that the grammar schools will adopt "a mainly academic approach", that is, they will remain grammar schools.

References

Department of Education Northern Ireland (2001) A report by the post primary review body (Burns report)

Department of Education, Northern Ireland (2004) Future post primary arrangements in Northern Ireland; Advice from the Post primary review working group (Costello report)

Gallagher,T and Smith,A (2000) The effects of the selective system of secondary education in Northern Ireland: main report. Department of Education, Northern Ireland

OECD (PISA) reports 2001 and 2004. Paris

15 DEFINING COMPREHENSIVE EDUCATION

Mark Hewlett, Director of CSCS,
Centre for the Study of Comprehensive Schools

Introduction

There is an extensive literature on the ideology of comprehensive education running back to the formative book, *Comprehensive Values*, by Pat Daunt, who promoted the equal value principle: all young people are worthy of equal attention and provision. The ideology focuses on goals of inclusion, social justice, equal opportunities and maximising provision for **all** learners: these are the foundations of the comprehensive debate. In earlier chapters of this book evidence is produced to suggest that comprehensive systems provide more effective and efficient means of achieving these goals including raising educational standards even when narrowly defined by examination results. I will argue strongly for comprehensive schools in a system carefully managed to ensure that every school has that critical mass of ability and parental support which appear vital for success.

But the notion of 'comprehensive' has been limited to thinking in terms of a certain type of school which takes all secondary age students of all abilities from its locality. The comprehensive (versus selective) debate has addressed issues within a too limited frame of consideration. **We need to think beyond the comprehensive school to comprehensive education which is more than schooling**. Note that Brighouse, Chapter 16, says, 'It was clear that no secondary school alone could meet all the educational needs of all their pupils'. Few writers have seriously addressed the full meaning of comprehensive in the sense of all-embracing. Perhaps this is because it has seemed politically risky (see Hattersley p25).

Despite the emergence of federations – in a rather haphazard way –almost nothing has been written about delivery systems harnessing all available resources to provide comprehensively and effectively for the needs of all learners in a locality. This paper seeks to address this issue by reviewing the essence of the comprehensive ideology and outlining a locality-based, theoretical model of comprehensive education described as a Comprehensive Learning Community.

It seems possible that consideration of education within a broader context might offer a way to help reconcile and absorb issues of continuing conflict, eg comprehensive versus (a degree of) differentiation, vocational versus academic, general versus specialist – by offering a wide range of quality experiences for young people with their very different abilities, interests and aspirations; it may even be possible to start to break down the apparently insoluble (politically) issue of **public** versus **private** by bringing about a different way of thinking about (comprehensive) education and who actually provides it.

This chapter argues for the word 'comprehensive' to be considered more broadly, in particular to rethink the optimum unit for managing the provision of education for young people. A school is too small, an LEA too large. Something in between - an accessible locality-based unit is what is needed, using the whole (viz comprehensive) range of providers available within the locality.

Values and ideals

Richard Pring's eloquent paper delivered to the conference series refers to three important characteristics of comprehensive schooling:

(i)   the importance of equality of esteem and respect for all types of school, to ensure that students are not stigmatised as a result of attending a particular type of school;

(ii) the importance of seeing education as equally important to students of every ability;

(iii) the importance of common cultural experience of citizenship, which can be promoted by bringing together (young) people of different social, ethnic and cultural backgrounds to share a common experience and acquire commitment to essential shared values, an idea which resonates loudly in the UK as I write this in July 2005.

This third characteristic relates closely to the opening paragraph of *The Comprehensive School* Robin Pedley, 1963 in which he quotes from a Times leader of that year:

'In spite of the virtual abolition of poverty; in spite of the rise in rewards of labour, Britain is still a jealous and divided nation.'

The idea of the comprehensive school attended by all secondary age students in a locality regardless of class, wealth, religion and ability - seemed, and still seems – to be a sensible, practical and civilised arrangement for bringing up the next generation of children in what will hopefully be a prosperous and harmonious society in which people understand and respect each other. It is the norm across Europe, North America and much of the rest of the developed world where selective schooling is seen as socially damaging and academically pointless. Selection is arguably an English disease.

It is interesting that Tony Blair said in 2000, 'We can't afford to write off children after six years of schooling. The worst start any child can have in life is to be branded as a failure.' We surely all know this – in our various roles, for example as parent, teacher, coach. If you tell people they're no good they will fulfil the prophecy and underachieve.

The Government's desire to retain electoral popularity and create an impression of dynamic reform by creating different types of schools and offering 'choice' (however spurious in practice) has however deflected it from worthy principles it publicly avows. Also in a democracy we are unable to prevent people purchasing advantage directly or indirectly at the expense of the common good. Having said this I shall take the literature of comprehensive ideology as read, so I shall not expand on the rationale for 'comprehensive' beyond summarising the essence of CSCS's policy and practice based on two concepts:

1. INCLUSION rooted in ideas of equity, social justice, and social unity and, in particular, an aversion to any system which unnecessarily and institutionally stigmatises and demoralises (young) people.

2. MAXIMUM ACCESS TO OPPORTUNITIES TO ENABLE EVERY INDIVIDUAL TO ACHIEVE HIS/HER POTENTIAL acknowledging that different people have different talents and needs.

If there has been any shift in thinking from the 1990s it is in regard to the second aspect – access to wider opportunities for all. Notions of differentiation, excellence, indeed elite, performance in all aspects of education – sports, arts and academic – fit more comfortably within comprehensive thinking than might once have been the case. The DfES publication 'Excellence in Cities: Modernising the Comprehensive Principle (2000)' contains reference to target-grouping, fast-tracking, accelerated learning, multiple intelligences and so on - now mainstream concepts throughout the comprehensive system.

The (New Labour) Government has demonstrated awareness of the need to enrich provision for all students and introduced some positive policies, eg Excellence in Cities, SureStart, Every Child Matters, Extended Schooling, Gifted and Talented Initiative designed to embrace different needs, ie to provide a more comprehensive service. But in order to achieve electoral advantage it has emphasised peripheral notions of choice and competition and distanced itself from the label of comprehensive schools for fear this might suggest to the floating (Conservative) voter it wishes to woo, that it is too closely associated with unreconstructed socialism. However, there is no question that the Government does want an enriched comprehensive service. At the same time the pro-comprehensive lobby has perhaps been a little too conservative, appearing more ideologically entrenched and negative than it actually is and lacking imagination in presenting its case.

My argument is that focussing on the following vital question will produce what everyone wants, namely: HOW CAN WE PROVIDE AN EDUCATIONAL SYSTEM WHICH IS COMPREHENSIVE IN EVERY SENSE: **a system which gives every learner maximum opportunity to succeed** (within a context of agreed social, ethical principles as outlined above).

Specialisation for all

In re-examining the meaning of comprehensive education I make the assumption that, as every individual is different, and as we are endeavouring to unlock the talents of the whole population as effectively as possible, we need a differentiated system which caters for each individual: a genuinely child-centred approach (which colleagues will say reflects practice in all good comprehensive schools).

P E Daunt's comprehensive concept of the 'equal value - of every learner' (in 'Comprehensive Values' 1975) may be translated into 'every individual is different and special and therefore has different and special needs' (applying across the whole spectrum from disabled to gifted). A system which makes comprehensive provision for every learner ideally does so on an individual basis. The comprehensive key is **maximum differentiation but without stigmatisation**. Of course, scarce resources mean that practice will inevitably fall short of the ideal.

How can we achieve the best solution? The answer lies in how we can make best use of all educational agents in providing education which effectively meets the needs of all learners. The solution lies in looking more thoroughly and comprehensively at how and where people learn – through a range of experiences in their homes and communities as well as schools.

Comprehensive Learning Communities

If we are seriously committed to raising educational standards, the purpose of which is to improve our social, economic, and cultural life, it is important to move more radically and energetically towards a system designed to elicit the whole range of educational agents in the population – different types of schools/colleges and other agents not part of the formal education system.

CSCS put forward its model of comprehensive education through (federal) learning communities to Downing Street in early 2001, since when – whether as a result of that discussion or not – the idea of federations/consortia/collegiates has become popular.

The purpose and characteristics of Comprehensive Learning Communities

The purpose is to implement an educational system which enhances and accelerates development of all learners by making available maximum support, expertise, and specialist provision for every learner. I believe that current inadequate practice arises from failure to ask simple questions, eg 'What is learning, how do we learn, from whom and where?'.

Education is the assimilation of knowledge, ideas, skills, judgement, common sense and attitudes from a range of sources, eg home/family, neighbours, experiences in the local and wider environment, the media and formal schooling - and note that a child in 'full-time' education spends only fifteen per cent of her/his waking hours at school; secondary (comprehensive) schooling is a small proportion of a young person's total educational experiences. Research suggests the obvious, viz that most of what people know – even science – was not learnt at school. The Kenyan aphorism 'It takes a whole village to educate a child' is appropriate. Today we might translate village into the multifarious factors that influence young people as listed in Diagram 1.

In order to make accessible the degree of specialisation and expertise we all want, we must plan in terms of units (localities/communities) **large enough to provide a wide range of specialisation** (eg to take sport, the whole range of Olympic sports; to take music, a youth orchestra, an early music group, jazz and quality provision for other minority interests) at the same time **small enough to be accessible to all potential users**. The catchment of **a single secondary school/family of schools is too small to provide the specialisation we need. We need to use the resources of larger units**, carefully planned and co-ordinated, which would, typically, include two or three secondary schools and their families of feeder primary, infant, nursery, playgroup and pre-school provision, also further education, with a direct link to an institute of higher education.

Planned provision should go far beyond formal educational programmes - to pre-school family support groups, health and social services. The years 0-5 are absolutely vital for all children, especially for the many who are educationally and socially impaired – some irreparably – by the time they are five – contributing to an underclass of people unable to provide for themselves and a burden to society. Trying to improve education through current statutory schooling provision alone is not enough.

I include sports clubs, arts organisations, faith communities, libraries, museums and resource centres, businesses of every type, independent providers of educational services including independent schools whose charitable status should be dependent on their contribution to the comprehensive community. There are in our communities huge, and as yet only partly used, resources; they are partly used mainly because most organisations, businesses, in many cases even parents do not see themselves as having an educational function and thus do not realise their abilities as educators.

This locality-based learning community would be part of a national hierarchy of specialist provision with higher order specialist providers at regional and national levels providing, for example, for the special needs of the unusually gifted and talented and those with special learning, physical and behavioural, difficulties.

The components of the comprehensive learning community listed overleaf is an outline summary of potential agents in the learning process. Note that the list includes both existing organisations and some that are not yet in existence, eg the Ideas Bureau/Patent Office/Creation Shop, Science and Technology Development Centre, Craft and Enterprise Centre, Business and Social Entrepreneurs Centre, for people of all ages who would meet, interact and exchange ideas in a vibrant, creative environment designed to identify and solve problems in the local community and in the wider regional, national and international contexts. These centres and the work of the Health, Social, and Police services and Neighbourhood Regeneration Units would ideally link into a more relevant and useful school curriculum; at the same time making the knowledge and skills of teachers more accessible to the whole community. The interrelationship between school and community is a key dynamic in the Comprehensive Learning Community – enabling families to more fully appreciate the value of education and encouraging schools to play a more significant role in improving the quality of life in neighbourhoods and communities, in particular to engage in educating parents who have probably the key role to play in developing appropriate attitudes in the young.

Diagram 1

COMPONENTS OF A 'LEARNING COMMUNITY'

PROVIDERS OF EDUCATIONAL EXPERIENCES IN THE FULLEST SENSE. We would suggest that all these providers should, if they wished, become formally accredited educational providers, subject to appropriate inspection	Offering provision	**directly**, e.g. a business or health centre offering its facilities to learners for work experience or as a base for a club or **indirectly** via school based activities
Families, including those in 'Education Otherwise' **Early years, family support groups**, Sure Start, HELP (Home Early Learning Project), FEC (Family Education Centre) etc Neighbourhood provision – **play areas, toy libraries, workshops**	supporting the vital foundations of learning based in nursery schools and giving help, support, and advice to parents and extended families: bearing in mind that many children are seriously educationally impaired by the time they reach nursery school	
Social services **Health centres**, hospitals, clinics **Housing services** **Neighbourhood Regeneration Unit Office**	potentially vital in providing support for young children, including providing parenting skills to help parents provide a safe disciplined and stimulating environment during the critical years, 0-4	

Formal educational organisations
    play groups
    nursery, infants, primary
    secondary (including community education functions)
    extended schooling
    independent providers
    tertiary centre
    further education/sixth form colleges including evening class provision
    neighbourhood academies linked with higher education
    special education
    Education Extra/Schools Plus
	offering the full range of curricular, extra-curricular and specialist provision in conjunction with sports clubs, arts, special interest, public services and all the other providers.
	
	each secondary school offering a degree of specialisation.	

Learning support units Pupil referral unit, City Learning Centre, Neighbourhood Support Centre, learning support units, family support centre	for young people with particular learning and behavioural needs	
Personal **mentors**	recruited from the widest possible range of occupations	
Youth clubs of **every** type including guides, scouts, Duke of Edinburgh military cadets, religion based etc etc	important in developing social skills, interests and a broad education	
Community Education Development Centre (CEDC) **Campaign for Learning** **Princes Trust**	incorporating a co-ordinating and developmental function for extended educational opportunities	
Libraries/resource centres/cybercafes **Museums, art galleries** **Craft centres** **Theatres, cinemas** **Citizens Advice Bureau**	providing educational functions, linked to school curricula	
Faith groups	offering a wide range of social, moral and intellectual education directly and through schools	
Sports clubs, centres: public and private	planned integrated provision, not just of main popular sports but the whole range of Olympic and minor sports	
Arts: performing arts/music/dance/visual arts - providers both public and private (dance schools etc), craft centre	whole range of arts activities linked with schools	
Scientific and special interest groups science clubs, maths clubs, writers clubs, horticultural, debating, political, philosophical etc etc	wide range of clubs, societies, as might be found in an exemplary list of 'extra-curricular' activities supported by community and education	
Police	operating pro-actively in educational activities	

Business   manufacturing industry
    offices   professional services, legal, financial etc
    shops   restaurants/pubs (and not just the major firms with high educational profile such as WH Smith, Sainsburys, Boots etc)
    Ideas Bureau, Creation Shop, Science and Technology Development Centre, Craft Enterprise Centre
    Business and Social Entrepreneurs Centre
	Every shop, office, and public service, however small, already offers some form of education, but with imagination and support could offer so much more, especially to the very young, conveying the idea that learning is everywhere, not just an artificial activity that occurs in school. Pub quiz league organisation could be put to excellent use by pursuing non-trivial as well as trivial pursuits.	

Public utilities **Local government** **Political parties**	(as for business) offering direct experience and incorporating useful educational ideas as part of their publicity	
Environment Centre	including nature reserve and active conservation activities	
The Media	nationally and locally, to assume an enhanced role	

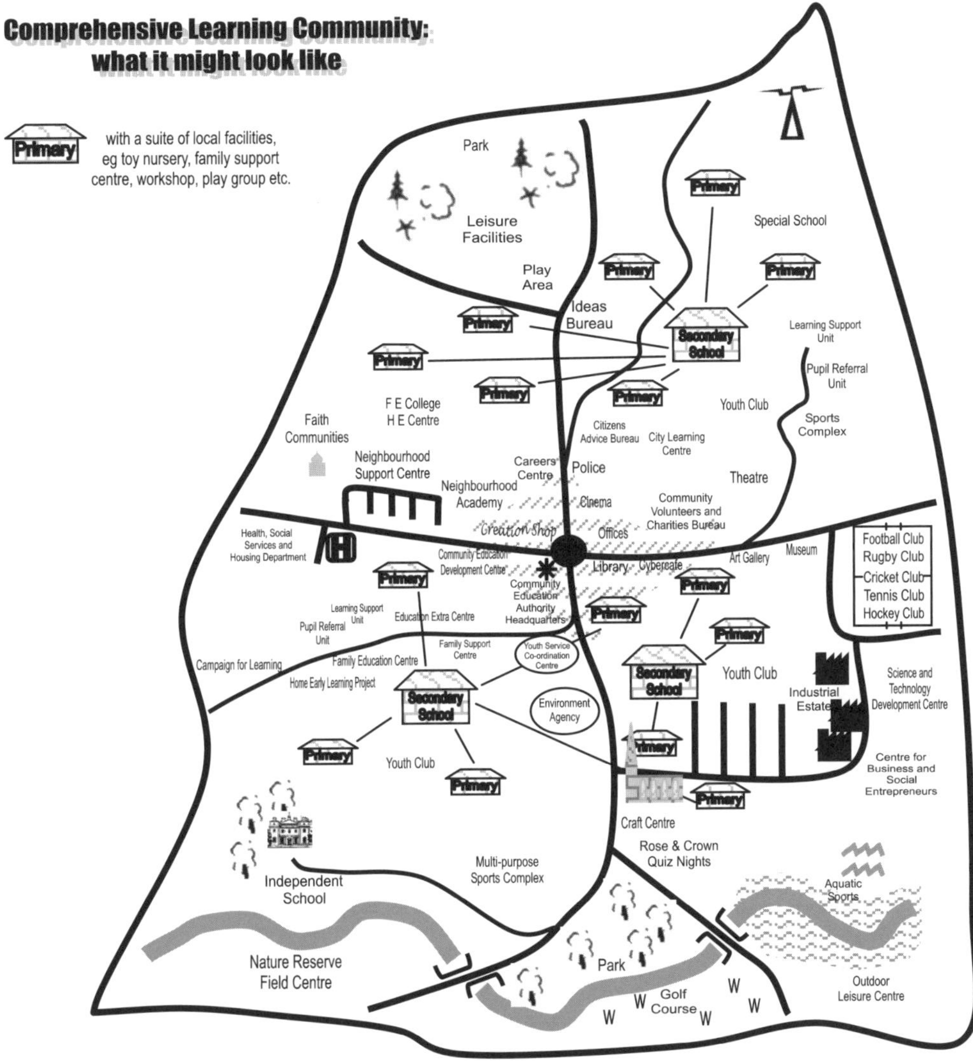

Joined-up thinking and action co-ordinating all agencies

Implicit in the ideas of the holistic Comprehensive Learning Community is that learning pervades all aspects of life, or put the other way: life is learning. But this requires planning and co-ordination of a very high level. The current jargon of 'joined-up thinking' is a precondition of success. This is one reason for defining manageable geographical areas – very much smaller than LEAs which are too large as units for the management and co-ordination of a multiplicity of functions. To get the various agencies in Diagram 3 working actively together in a small locality is complex and demanding enough.

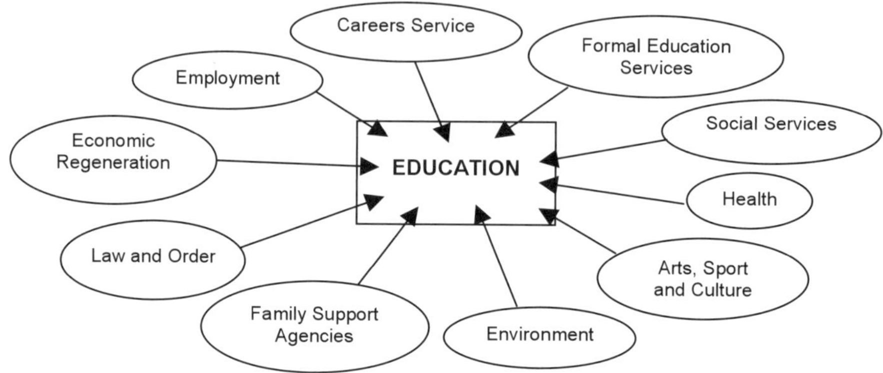

Government and management of the Comprehensive Learning Community would require representation of all agents, both at governing and management levels. I would not underestimate the complexity of co-ordinating, say, sixteen departments in a learning community.

Diagram 4

Illustrating the practical complexity of managing and co-ordinating diverse functions with representatives of 1. Pre-school education; 2. Primary education; 3. Secondary education; 4. Further and higher education; 5. Business; 6. Family support; 7. Health; 8. Social services; 9. Housing and environment; 10. Youth affairs; 11. Learning support and mentoring service; 12. Faith communities; 13. Arts; 14. Sports; 15. Cultural/scientific/technological; 16. Police, law and order

The number of support staff and resourcing will vary according to different needs: some managers would be operating in areas where there already exists a well staffed organisation and clear structure (eg schools, police) in contrast to other areas where the leadership and structure will need to be provided more or less in toto, eg learning support and mentoring, the mobilisation of businesses and faith communities, family support and a host of non-statutory but vital activities for children such as Home Early Learning Programmes, providing non-standard sports activities, Outward Bound, Community Volunteers programmes.

The task may seem daunting. However there are precedents, if only in embryo, in some Excellence in Cities initiatives; small EAZs; community colleges, eg in Cambridgeshire and Leicestershire which have offered what is now termed 'full service' provision under the Extended Schooling Policy for many years; initiatives developed under CEDC, now 'ContinYou'; and Education 2000 (now the Twenty-first Century Learning Initiative), and in work emerging from the Neighbourhood Regeneration Unit related to the Social Exclusion Unit calling for integrated and sustainable approaches to housing, crime, unemployment, community welfare, and education.

But however daunting, if we believe in **comprehensive** (sic) strategies to improve education in our country for the benefit of everyone in all their life's roles, while we obviously have to consider schools, we must look more deeply and more radically at what education really is. I would argue that the formal education system has been tinkering partially and superficially with a limited quasi-academic concept of education. A truly comprehensive educational revolution has hardly begun.

For readers who wish to pursue these ideas in depth and consult background documentation contact Mark Hewlett: cscs@rmplc.co.uk.

16 COLLEGIALITY: THE WAY FORWARD

Tim Brighouse

I first want to pay tribute to Richard Pring. His lifetime's work has been an inspiration not just to me, but to many. His time in Oxford has been exceptional in sustaining the department's close links with secondary schools and in extending its reputation for research to new and very high levels of distinction. Above all, he is a delightful colleague who has that uncanny but enviable knack of making those he meets not only better for meeting him, but always stimulated to think more deeply and clearly about whatever they have discussed. The background to this paper is to be found in a paper presented in honour of Caroline Benn and Brian Simon in September 2002.

In that paper I firstly analysed the development of the comprehensive school in three broadly defined contexts – the suburban and rural; the conurbations with their large inner city areas; and the small city or large town surrounded by a rural environment. My argument was that however defined, whether by a representative spread of abilities or by reference to the 'common' school for the local community or some combination of these two, the comprehensive ideal had not been realised save in the suburban, rural and country areas. Moreover, in the large conurbations it was clear that far from the ideal being realised, there was a sharp differentiated pecking order of schools ranging from what Peter Newsam has called the 'super selective' at one extreme, through to comprehensive plus to comprehensive minus – in effect secondary modern at the other. Substantial differences exist between these schools in terms of results, quality of student intake, parental support, equipment and staffing: a serious problem for less favoured schools which find it more difficult to recruit and retain staff than more favourably regarded schools. Such schools, de facto secondary modern schools, are in no sense comprehensive and they have existed for thirty years or more in Birmingham, Manchester, Leeds, Newcastle, London and other cities.

I then argued that the time had come to stop chasing a comprehensive school mirage but instead to think again about what we mean by secondary education. It was clear that no secondary school alone could meet **all** the educational needs of **all** their pupils and that some found it very difficult indeed to meet **most** of the needs of **most** of their pupils. Was it time, I speculated, to encourage teachers, parents and pupils to think of secondary education as consisting of belonging to a secondary school plus something extra? This 'something extra' might be a 'junior university' either as a separate body which operates independently but in collaboration with groups of secondary schools, colleges and a university. Or it might be – my preference – a 'collegiate' consisting of say a group of four or five schools which combine together so that their collective expertise can offer more than the individual school can offer independently. In my original paper I expounded the thesis as follows:

We must strike out boldly for an ideal where young people, whatever their 'home-base' school, whether in the state or private sector, take substantial periods of their education together. This would be within a collegiate framework which acknowledges that secondary education involves belonging to at least two institutions – the school and the collegiate to which it is attached. In urban areas this has become essential for a variety of reasons in order to:

- *overcome the huge and unfair divergence of experiences for pupils according to whether they have had access to a school near the top or the bottom of the pecking order;*
- *match the diversity of provision of schooling to the diverse needs of individual children;*
- *give all pupils equal access to the separate specialisms and expertise designated specialist schools have earned;*
- *give pupils from all schools the best possible access to high quality staff in shortage areas;*
- *ensure that gifted pupils on the one hand and youngsters with barriers to learning on the other, come together and gain from the scarce expertise of specialist staff;*
- *increase the intellectual curiosity and knowledge which comes from teaching with other staff from different schools in the same discipline, sharing opportunities for continual professional development;*
- *take advantage of the transformational progress now occurring in the learning technologies and avoid losing time in doing so during the present pioneering phase;*
- *increase the chances of a good fit for any pupil in their individualised 14-19 learning pathway;*
- *mix and bring together, at least for a time, pupils of both genders from different social, ethnic and religious backgrounds to learn, to engage in sport and the expressive arts, to undertake citizenship tasks and to debate their future as international as well as national citizens.*

If schools are left stranded in a 'devil take the hindmost' competition of 'beggar thy neighbour', we shall achieve none of this. We shall not win the race between 'education and catastrophe' for many of our disadvantaged youngsters.

For me the comprehensive ideal will be the 'collegiate' academy. The purpose of the collegiate, beyond that of the individual school, will be to consider 'school plus' – ie the part which when added to school creates a secondary education experience. Why collegiate? Bring to mind Oxbridge or the Durham Colleges and University. A group of several, say four or five, schools would comprise at least a comprehensive plus or selective school and a range of others, including a faith school and a special school, together with a major FE/HE provider. For some purposes and in some places an independent school also perhaps. These schools would be either loosely or tightly coupled. The spectrum from loose to tight would start with agreements about ensuring heads of department are off timetable at the same time across the collegiate so that ideas can be shared and curriculum and professional development organised. To avoid unnecessary competition between schools, results for the collegiate should be published, eg at key stage 4 and key stage 5.

As the model becomes more tightly coupled, the advantages increase for the pupils and for the realisation of the new comprehensive ideal. This would be one where youngsters from all backgrounds (and in urban areas this background frequently has an international or global dimension to it) have experience of learning together, whether in the classroom, the workshop, the music suite, the debating chamber, the workplace, the theatre, the laboratory, or in sport. They also will learn and meet each other 'virtually' using the full range of the new learning technologies which will help bind the collegiate together and enlarge its capacity. Such collegiates and their constituent schools may have 'associate members' – those who come from other collegiates for short or long courses that are offered there, or from those educated 'otherwise' by individuals or groups of parents.

The issue is how we shall move from the very divided present to a future where diversity and equality can coexist – even reinforce one another. This should be the mission of the collegiate academy where young people, while experiencing and enjoying independence, experience the more profound learning advantages of interdependence.

How shall we move from here to there? Is there a way of harnessing the agenda of 'city academies', 'beacons', 'extended', 'training', 'advanced' and 'specialist schools' which our government has provided as the building blocks for the future? Is there a way of tempting Head Teachers and governors to join in? (For make no mistake about it, the pleasures and powers of independence and autonomy are considerable, especially when in living memory they were preceded by the shackles of dependence.)

We must explore possible scenarios. What if the city academy (and perhaps the independent schools in the urban areas) have only one cross-collegiate entry admission form and where the resource centre of the collegiate of which it is a member and/or the location of most post-16 study? What if the beacon status were adjusted to reflect departmental or phase 'leading edge practice' in different schools within the one collegiate? What if each collegiate had its own residential centre? What if each collegiate were the lead agency for looked-after children and secured the foster parents necessary? What if the specialist structure of each school were to be seen as complementary to its partners in the collegiate? Could the collegiate contribute to the broader social agenda by being the point of focus for inter-agency services for the most vulnerable families?

Why should incomers in Year 7 not deal with the admissions office of the collegiate and be placed in any one of the constituent schools? Parents should be confident that the collegiate programme is so extensive that wherever their youngster were placed she or he would have full access to the best that several schools could offer between them. Programmes of study should be published by collegiates and by their individual constituent schools.

At this point, I would like to add a new dimension to the notion of the collegiate: an international dimension through which collegiates were linked with sister schools in countries in the other continents of the world? And surely the collegiate could run international baccalaureates or equally rich variants alongside or instead of the mediocre, largely irrelevant diet of examinations we now require young people in our country to digest.

What does collegiality mean?

My purpose today is to explore 'collegiality' and what it means for practice both **within** schools and **between** schools so far as curriculum and timetabling are concerned. When I came to speculate about it however, I found it is difficult to separate 'curriculum', 'timetabling', 'teaching and assessment policy and practice' and 'professional development'. So what follows touches on all four of these.

First a definition. By collegiality I mean people behaving interdependently (often as a team) rather than either independently or as dependents unable to exercise their judgement consistently but deferring to a superior. Moreover I am using 'collegial' to imply a regular and permanent habit of behaviour where people share an identity. I draw a distinction between collegial on the one hand and collaborative on the other. Collaboration is working together for a given period to solve an identified often loosely defined and shared problem. Collegial is more than that although it does not preclude collaboration with others. Collegial is part of the way we behave. We are aware that 'collegially' we have a broadly similar value system, a common purpose and most importantly an identity.

There are innumerable opportunities **within** schools to develop a collegiality of common purpose, through deliberate attempts to foster team (as opposed to individual) success. The professional development of staff and their teaching and learning practices is a key to developing a conscious and focussed collegial approach. The following summary of Little's work in the 1980s makes the point. She observes that schools improve where:
- teachers **talk** about teaching;
- teachers **observe** each other's practice;
- teachers plan, organise, monitor and evaluate **together**;
- teachers **teach** each other things.

The emphasis of her work implies collegiality. In struggling schools - or struggling departments within schools - it is easy to see the reverse, where teaching has fallen back into an isolated and independent fight against the odds.

If Little's conditions are to be met there are implications for school practices. Questions with a collegial intent crowd in: Is there a staff library? Do staff have an entitlement to watch each other teach? Does the timetable allow departments time together? Does the timetable provide for the senior team to be off timetable on one day in the week or in such a way that they can take over the teaching of a substantial part of a department so that teachers are released to observe another department's work in their own or another school and subsequently debate what they saw with colleagues? Is that followed up by the senior team's review of what **they** saw in teaching in a department for a day? Do teachers plan lessons together and then while one teaches, another observes and they subsequently debate practice? Are residentials organised with collegial intent both for staff and pupils? Is professional development organised in such a way as to encourage collegiality?

Two Case Studies of Collegiates

I have referred to collegiality **within** schools to emphasise the point that where there is a commonality of purpose and an active exchange of good practice everybody benefits. I return to collegiality between institutions.

There are four collegiates in Birmingham. I focus on two – the Catholic partnership, a collegiate of nine catholic schools which have worked together for a dozen years. The other ('The Oaks') a group of five comprehensive schools and a special school have been working together for nine months.

The Catholic partnership has a shared off-site pupil refuge – The Zaccheus centre which takes children with behavioural issues for brief periods and reintegrates them either in their original or another school in the partnership. The leader is acknowledged as an expert coach with many connections to other local and national coaches in the matter of behaviour. The example illustrates how within the field of special educational needs such a collegiate might acknowledge the expertise of each participating school. So we might imagine the collegiate's growing expertise and confidence in its capacity to be inclusive – especially since timetabling is marginally less of a problem for such youngsters since they usually have special individually timetabled arrangements anyway.

So far as timetabling is concerned the Catholic partnership timetablers accept various 'givens' in the timetable. For example there is agreement about collegiate professional development days including a two-day annual conference of senior management teams to compare notes as they revise school development plans. But it also includes fixed mornings or afternoons when heads of departments are off-timetable so that twice termly (or more often) conferences of subject heads of department to compare notes is easily organised without disruption to the home school.

So it is not inconceivable to imagine that the same accumulation of greater collective experience witnessed in SEN might develop in different aspects of the learning opportunities in, for example, history and science. The rich diversity of medieval, European, economic and social etc history would combine to offer, at key stage 4 and beyond, something akin to the faculty of Modern History at the collegiate University of Oxford. Perhaps too, the GATSBY further maths project whereby in an acknowledged shrinking shortage area one school takes a lead and widens the learning opportunities of all youngsters within the collegiate.

So in terms of curriculum offered, it is easy to see how the collegiate dimension could be significantly richer than any single school can provide by itself.

Whether that offer significantly changes the experience of any youngster in the collegiate depends on three other factors one of which, professional development, I've already touched on. Indeed the area of professional development is the one most immediately welcomed by participating staff and the resources of the Catholic partnership over the years have been orchestrated to improve middle management, enrich induction to role (eg Head of Department, NQT), subject knowledge and bring to the staff the best available national and international expertise. The professionals in the collegiate are quite simply more knowledgeable than they would have been had they operated separately. But the other two prerequisites of youngsters accessing something of more significance through a collegiate curriculum deserve further mention. They are the timetable and ICT.

It seems to me unlikely that timetables, except post-16, can or should be aligned on the expectation of pupil movement within the 25 period week or 50 period fortnight which after all is the usual pattern of the school timetable. Legitimate objections to what in effect would be a complicated split-site school would arise – and be justified. But if every timetable within the collegiate were to agree to modular components to be taken in collegiate weeks or days when the normal timetable is suspended then those particular objections would be overcome. So a prerequisite to a full collegiate working in smooth harmony is some agreement (covering perhaps a very modest amount of time at first) in agreeing collegiate 'days' or 'weeks' where the joint collective programme can be agreed.

But when one turns to the imminent possibilities of the learning and communication technologies more timetabling possibilities occur. Period zero and period zero plus involving live video interactive lessons before and after school are being actively piloted by 'The Oaks' collegiate. (Some rural schools have been trying out this technique.) The technological capabilities to develop a new way of teaching and learning are now improving with expanding band-width and other 'distance-learning' technological developments. When this is coupled with personal e-tutoring, exploiting the full expertise of all the members of a collegiate subject faculty it is easy to see considerable possibilities which before the advances in technology would not have been possible.

'The Oaks' collegiate is creating its own intranet while the other two Birmingham collegiates are piggy-backing on the local manifestation of an enhanced national grid. In both cases their intranets are infinitely richer as a result of shared work and ideas while preserving the pride of local creation and originality.

In short, what is needed now is for there to be a serious study of how the creation of a collegiate is beginning to extend the professional skill resources and curricula of say a five or six school collegiate. It can lead to a situation where each school is the secure base where the student knows their tutor helps them to make their learning coherent and provides himself or herself expert coaching or secures it from others. But the tutor and the learner know too, and make full use of, the supplementary and complementary enrichment provided by the collegiate. For the very first time in urban areas, we shall realise, through the collegiate, our dream of enabling young people from different backgrounds and across the full range of ability to be educated together within an enhanced and more truly comprehensive environment.

17 FAITH SCHOOLS: HAVE THEY A PLACE IN THE COMPREHENSIVE SYSTEM?

Richard Pring, former Director of Oxford Department of Educational Studies

Church Schools have been funded by the state since the 1870 Education Act. Following the 1944 Education Act, Jewish schools were established within the state system. More recently, Muslim and Sikh schools have been added. Hence, the now preferred title of 'Faith Schools'. With the onset of comprehensive schools in the 1950s and 1960s, the compatibility of church or faith schools with such a system was hardly questioned. In the main, Catholic and Church of England schools became comprehensive, just like the rest (except of course, where a grammar school system remained).

There were inevitably some who would question whether membership of (and thus exclusion from) schools on the basis of beliefs could be genuinely comprehensive, in the same way that people questioned that single sex schools could be comprehensive. Comprehensive would seem to be just that – inclusive of all young people irrespective of gender, race, ability or social class. But, generally speaking, even the strong advocates of a comprehensive system were prepared to accept the distinction within the system between 'community', 'voluntary aided' and 'voluntary controlled' schools – each with different admissions and governance arrangements.

The climate has now changed. And division between schools on the grounds of religious beliefs is being seriously questioned for reasons which are partly based on an extension of the comprehensive ideal and partly for more fundamental reasons concerned with the funding of schools, at taxpayers' expense, the aim of which is to nurture pupils in a particular faith.

This paper sets out the arguments and the possible responses to them. It argues that faith schools are compatible with the comprehensive ideal – but only under certain conditions.

Arguments for faith-based schools

The main interconnected justifications for the maintenance of such schools within any system, whether comprehensive or not, are, first, historical, and, second, the rights of parents to have their children educated according to their religious beliefs.

Historically, in England and Wales, the churches (especially the Anglican Church) preceded the State in the provision of education. To this day the land on which so many village primary schools are located is owned by the Church. The entry of the state into educational provision after 1870 (apart from the subsidies from the Privy Council from 1833 onwards) was essentially to fill the gaps, arising from the growth of towns as people migrated from the countryside. The State as somehow responsible for education – for what should be taught and for the principles which should underlie the teaching – is a comparatively recent phenomenon. The State instead was there not mainly to provide directly (that is not the role of the State) but to make sure that there are conditions for universal education – and therefore to plug the gaps where those conditions did not prevail. At the heart of the education are values, reflected in the aims of the education on offer. And, in a society which is, to a great degree pluralist in belief, there will be different values and different aims. Not to respect the historic roots of the diversity of educational provision, arising in many cases from considerable sacrifice and dedication on the part of those who paid for the building of those schools, would be to presuppose a unity of aims and thus of values which in fact does not prevail. Diversity of aim should be reflected in diversity of provision, essential if individuals and families are to be protected from the Leviathan of the State.

The second, connected argument appeals to human rights, in particular to the Human Rights Act (1998, Article 9.1):

> Everyone has the right to freedom of thought, conscience and religion; this right includes freedom to change his (or her) religion or belief, and freedom either alone or in community with others and in public or private, to manifest his (or her) religion or belief, in worship, teaching, practice or observation.

Of course, such a declaration supports both the rights of parents and the rights of the child, and there are explicit interpretations of this which assert the right of the child to an education which is not simply the product of the parents' beliefs. On the other hand, it also supports the parents who, in being responsible for the upbringing of their children, have a right not to have their values negated by a set of educational values to which they do not subscribe. It continues:

> In the exercise of any functions which it assumes in relation to education, and to teaching, the state shall respect the rights of parents to ensure such education and teaching in conformity with their own religious and philosophical convictions.

Thus, if education is concerned with the development of the human person, then there is a need to foster, rather than subvert, within the educational system different understandings of what it means to be a person – and to be one more fully. Parents, who are concerned about what they see to be the 'secular culture' permeating society and hence schools, may well wish for a school which embodies different values, reflected in a religious tradition. Indeed, the responsibility for them to do so is reflected powerfully in the Chief Rabbi's reference in *The Politics of Hope* to Jacob Neusmer.

> Civilization hangs suspended, from generation to generation, by the gossamer strand of memory. If only one cohort of mothers and fathers fails to convey to its children what *it* has learnt from its parents, then the great chain of learning

and wisdom snaps. If the guardians of human knowledge stumble only one time, in their fall collapses the whole edifice of knowledge and understanding.

However, tucked within such defences – brought in as supplementary support, as it were - are other arguments. First, faith schools are claimed to obtain better examination results and thus raise standards generally. It is also claimed that their ethos is more congenial with a greater sense of purpose and discipline. Furthermore, they are perceived to provide a necessary element in a system which espouses choice – itself providing the comparisons and competition necessary for the raising of standards. But these are subsidiary arguments, and ones which should carry little weight even if they were proven to be true.

There is a third argument, however, which is rarely heard but which deserves close examination. To many, faith schools are divisive, especially where faith is strongly identified with a minority ethnic group. Such divisiveness, so it is argued, is both nurtured by and further promotes the racial divisions and attitudes which education should be overcoming. However, history may have lessons to teach us here. The development of Catholic schools in the late part of the 19th century and the early years of the 20th enabled the often immigrant Catholic population to maintain a sense of cultural identity and self-esteem which otherwise might not have been possible. It was a similar story in Australia where the Christian Brothers established schools for the poor Irish and Italian immigrants, providing an education of quality, thereby enabling the Catholic population to be integrated much more easily into national life. It may well be the case that separate Muslim schools would ensure the kind of education and self esteem which would enable them to enter public life in a more effective way.

Arguments against faith schools within a comprehensive system

Certainly the voices against division on the basis of religious beliefs are now strong and growing stronger – from the British Humanist Society, from members of parliament and from those who are concerned about the contribution of schools to a more divisive society. There are two sorts of argument. The first concerns the incompatibility of having such schools with the comprehensive ideal. The stronger argument is that, irrespective of the system (comprehensive or selective), it simply is not acceptable that the taxpayer, often someone who has no religious beliefs, should pay taxes to nurture such beliefs in young people.

The incompatibility argument has several elements. The first is that schools within a comprehensive system ought to be all playing on a level playing field, with the same admissions and governance arrangements. But quite clearly the Faith schools, especially those that were voluntary aided, need not have – and for the most part have not had - equitable admissions arrangements. The trustees, namely, the respective Churches, in setting their own admissions arrangements, are able to be selective – and, until recently, use interviews for this purpose. Ostensibly, such selectivity is based on religious faith, but it would seem, in the light of the evidence, that such selection is thereby skewed to families more likely to be supportive of the educational programme, thereby upsetting the balance in neighbourhood schools. Furthermore, in areas where the neighbourhood school is a Church school, local young people have had to be bussed to other schools whilst those of the right faith have been bussed in from more distant parts. This quite clearly ought to be a matter of concern where shifting populations may create a local population of a very different faith from that of the neighbourhood school.

Second, and following from the above, there is a need to revisit the idea of the neighbourhood school, once a central element in the comprehensive ideal. Indeed, for John Dewey, in his contribution to the idea of the American High School, relations to the local community were crucial. The school was the place where people from different religious, social and ethnic traditions would come together, and thereby come, not simply to tolerate, but to learn from, each other – part of the enriching 'experiential continuum', made possible by the school. The importance of this in Britain was emphasised by Lord Ousley, who emphasised in his report following the Oldham riots of 1998, that 'there are signs that communities are fragmenting along racial, cultural and faith lines' – and that schools have a key role in preventing this fragmentation. Perhaps this issues is brought to prominence by the growth of Muslim schools – few within the national system at the moment, but likely to grow quickly. If Catholics, Anglicans and Jews can have their own schools, so, in fairness, so ought Muslims and Sikhs and other faith groups to be able to have theirs. But then warnings of Ousley emerge, and, perhaps, as society changes, one needs to re-examine the compatibility of an ever more fragmented system, increasingly on ethnic lines, when schools within a comprehensive system should see as part of their mission to heal divisions, foster mutual understanding and see 'dignity in difference'.

The more powerful set of arguments against faith schools arises not from some comprehensive ideal but from an idea of education and its aims which, of course, should be part of that comprehensive ideal, but which are not confined to it. Those arguments spell out the aims of education in terms of the increasing autonomy of the learner, the development of the capacity to develop his or her own beliefs in the light of experience, evidence and argument. The aim of education lies in the development of the mind and thus of the capacities to think, to enquire and to question in its different forms. The school therefore should not promote one set of beliefs rather than another, where such beliefs are not open to proof – where society is divided on them. The nurturing of a particular ideological view of the world is seen as a form of indoctrination, the very antithesis of education. Rather should education aim to provide the tools whereby the young person is able to enter into the ethical and social discourses about the life worth living – through the humanities, the arts, and the sciences. Having acquired the appropriate concepts and ways of testing the truth of claims made, then he or she is able to decide on the kinds of belief and the form of life to be followed.

Evaluating the argument

These philosophical arguments are at the heart of the debate on Faith Schools. Can publicly funded schools have the right to nurture particular religious points of view and forms of life, which not only are not generally shared within society but are positively opposed by many within that society? Ensure the teaching about religion, certainly, but not the teaching of religion.

The key issues seem to be: the idea of autonomy as an aim of education, the accusation that the teaching of religion is a form of indoctrination, and the belief that one can understand a religious practice 'from outside', as it were, without engagement with it as a 'practice'. Let us take each of these in turn.

First, the importance of autonomy as an aim of education (and its incompatibility with the deliberate formation of a religious outlook and character) reflects a particular philosophical and liberal outlook. Growth as a person requires the increasing power of the mind to understand the physical, social and moral worlds we inhabit. Having acquired the capacities so to understand, the young person is freed from dependence on the views of others, able to make up his or her own mind, empowered to reflect and to decide – a truly rational individual who does not appeal to authority to find the truth or the best way to live.

However, autonomy is not a straightforward idea. It is difficult to see what that rational development could consist of outside a social world which gives meaning to the utterances one makes. Reasoning and reflection depend upon participation in a social form of life with its inbuilt modes of understanding embodied in the language which is shared by members of society. The next generation is initiated into those modes of understanding, one of which is religious understanding with its distinctive concepts and ideas. Defenders of autonomy are themselves both empowered and constrained by the philosophical traditions they belong to – by, if you like, a particular secular ideology. Hence, the defenders of Faith Schools will argue that their views are but one set of beliefs to be nurtured within the wide spectrum of beliefs within a multicultural society – not to be dismissed or subverted by a school system which feels little respect for them or which ignores the religious dimension to human flourishing.

But, so it is then argued, any initiation into a powerful set of ideas – powerful in the sense of shaping peoples' lives and engaging their emotions – is a form of indoctrination. Beliefs should be so taught that the initiate is able and encouraged to question and to criticise, and that possibility is lessened where those beliefs are taught in a relatively enclosed community, not exposed to the alternative points of view, especially in areas (e.g. religious belief) where those beliefs are strongly disputed.

Accusations of indoctrination are easier to make than are explanations of what indoctrination means. Indoctrination would seem to apply where 'doctrines' or beliefs are taught as true where their truth is disputed – and disputed because there is no consensus as to what would count as a verification of those beliefs. Religious beliefs would seem to share this character with political, moral and aesthetic beliefs. But that would be drastic indeed, for it would cut out of education the promotion of a moral form of life and an initiation into forms of literary and artistic criticism. Finally, therefore, indoctrination would seem to refer to the teaching of beliefs in such a way that the learner was prevented (mainly emotionally) from questioning those beliefs or from seeing them from a different point of view.   But that refers to a mode of teaching rather than to an initiation into a particular form of life. There is no incompatibility between such an initiation and an openness to alternative ways of seeing things and to a critical appreciation of those beliefs – a foundation for further development in lifelong learning.

Finally, the defenders of Faith Schools would argue that, for their particular traditions to be understood, there has to be an understanding 'from the inside', as it were – a sharing in a set of practices with their own inbuilt ways of seeing and understanding the world. They would accuse the ways in which young people are taught about other religions – a quick Cook's Tour through the belief systems of the world – as too superficial to warrant being called education. Only those who have been initiated into a religious form of life are able to engage in the perennial 'conversation' between religions on what they see to be the most important questions to be asked.

Conclusion

Whether or not there should be Faith Schools is central to the debate on the future of a comprehensive system of education. Selection by any means entails exclusion, and that would seem to be unacceptable to the supporters of comprehensive schools. And that argument is receiving greater support as anxieties are expressed about the fragmentation of the system increasingly along ethnic grounds. On the other hand, people understandably worry about the increasing power of the State in shaping the minds of young people through a National Curriculum within an increasingly secular society. Faith Schools become a defence of particular values which would otherwise be undermined.

None the less, those who support such schools within the comprehensive system must be aware of many of the legitimate concerns. Schools do need to provide the opportunity where young people can come to see, in Jonathan Sachs' words, 'the dignity of difference'. They must, in their selection procedures, have a regard for the wider distribution of students, aware of the impact which such selection can have on neighbourhood schools and neighbourhoods themselves. But this may require looking much more closely at the idea of a comprehensive system rather than comprehensive schools as meeting all the requirements of young people – a point developed in the chapter on 14-19.

18 A COMPREHENSIVE CURRICULUM

Mark Hewlett

Introduction

The comprehensive debate has focused on the nature of the intake populations of schools. Perhaps if the debate had focused equally on what young people learn in school (the curriculum) we might have made more progress.

*In Chapter 15, Defining Comprehensive Education, I argue that while we should hold to certain important principles, we need to re-examine the meaning of 'comprehensive' which has generally been used in a limited way; I argue for clearer thought about the purpose of education, where it takes place – in a wide range of contexts of which school is just one – and about the meaning of the term comprehensive. This chapter pursues this idea by considering the idea of a **comprehensive** curriculum. As practitioner – head of two comprehensive schools – I was always aware of the disservice our students were done by having to follow a narrow and largely irrelevant curriculum ill-designed to draw out the range of their talents and engage their enthusiasms including those of the gifted and talented (who by virtue of good examination results ostensibly succeeded). If we had paid more attention to the meaning of the terms 'comprehensive' and 'curriculum' we would have served the best interests of **all** our students very much better.*

Comprehensive means all-embracing. A comprehensive curriculum is one which provides a broad, balanced coverage of elements relevant to achieving aims for all students. The current secondary school curriculum is neither broad nor balanced and arguably omits or treats peripherally priorities set out by Government and schools. Why? - because the curriculum has never been designed systematically to meet educational aims.

This paper puts forward a definition of the term curriculum, summarises how a curriculum should be designed, provides a set of criteria by which a (comprehensive) curriculum should be judged, sets out a model which meets these criteria incorporating a 'map' of the elements of a comprehensive curriculum in their correct relationship (ie correct according to generally accepted aims and assumptions) and discusses some key questions and likely challenges.

1: What is a curriculum?
Having surveyed the literature I selected two definitions which appeared to represent generally acceptable definitions; standard 'common denominators'.

(A) 'We shall take the term curriculum to be the label for a programme or course
    of activities which is explicitly organised as the means whereby pupils may
    obtain the desired objectives, whatever they may be. The planning of the
    curriculum, or any part of it, is a logical nonsense until the objectives being
    aimed at are made clear.' P H Hirst and R S Peters *The Logic of Education*
    1970.
(B) In 1979, HMI in *Curriculum 11-16 Towards a Statement of Entitlement* wrote,
    'The work of our enquiry led to the conclusion that any adequate
    specification of the curriculum to which all pupils are entitled should include:
    (i)   a statement of aims related to the education of the individuals;
    (ii) a statement of objectives in terms of skills, attitudes, concepts and
          knowledge.'

I accept these two specifications as minimum criteria for an acceptable
curriculum.

The above might be taken as self-evident and thus not worth stating; in
essence before you start on your educational journey make sure you are clear
about your destination – surely a statement of the obvious. But the patent fact
is that, though schools and governments state educational aims, when it comes
to implementing a curriculum, the aims are set aside because the framework of
the curriculum is pre-determined by examination boards rendering schools'
stated aims irrelevant, at least marginal. It may be noted for example that the
DfES recently expounds apparently unexceptionable aims, in '14-19: Extending
Opportunities, Raising Standards' (2004). It refers to 'developing young people's
key skills, to helping energise our economy, to building a healthy – democratic –
society' but then proceeds to ignore these aims in recommending a superficial
tinkering with the subject-based curriculum which bears little relationship to
these aims.

The curriculum DfES de facto prescribes via QCA makes a 'logical nonsense' of
its aims.

2: Starting point for designing a curriculum: educational aims

If one is to construct a curriculum, according to Hirst and Peters and HMI, not to
mention common sense, it is necessary to state some aims. Scrutiny of aims
expressed by Government ministers, DfES, LEAs, and schools produce repeating
patterns. I sought the most frequently stated aims, 'common denominators' of
what LEA advisers and headteachers were saying across the country; these were
no different from those expressed by DfES and other national bodies. For
example (from the eleven aims I quote in CSCS Broadsheet Number 72), David
Blunkett said, 'We need the creativity, enterprise and scholarship of all our
people. As well as securing our economic future, learning helps make ours a
civilised society, develops the spiritual side of our lives and promotes active
citizenship. It strengthens the family, the neighbourhood and consequently the
nation.' This is an admirable and useful statement but it bears no obvious direct
relation to the school curriculum.

What is common in statements of aims is the idea of

(i)   preparing **(all young) people** for their future lives;
(ii) serving the needs of **society** and **all** its stakeholders.

Other priorities emerge:

- the importance of personal qualities and attitudes;
- the development of generic key/skills;
- useful knowledge (There are few surprisingly references to academic capacity, conceptual understanding – perhaps taken as read?).

While every statement in our research made reference to the needs of society and preparing young people for their future lives, there was no specification of what the needs of and demands put on young people would actually consist of, ie the nature of the future lives that they were being prepared for, eg for the problems, issues and opportunities they would face. This is a critical defect: without specifying what these future circumstances are, education arguably takes place in a largely pointless vacuum, divorced from the world outside education. To reiterate Hirst and Peter's definition, 'The planning of the curriculum is a logical nonsense unless the objectives are made clear'… and, given the above, this must include a specification of the various aspects of life that education is preparing people for, eg their roles at work, in the community, in home and family and with discretionary time to spend as they wish, eg for personal and spiritual enlargement. It is negligent to set aside these crucially important aspects of the curriculum, for without it, how can one hope to produce a balanced, relevant curriculum for all students. Failure to do this means that the thinking about the curriculum is incomplete, ie not comprehensive.

3: What is a <u>comprehensive</u> curriculum?

A comprehensive curriculum is not a special sort of curriculum for comprehensive schools; it is for pupils and students of **all** abilities; it addresses the needs of the gifted and talented and those with learning difficulties. It takes into consideration all aspects and dimensions of learning.

The existing conventionally accepted (subject-based) curriculum studied by the majority of pupils throughout the UK is designed neither for those currently considered to be of low ability, nor for those of high ability. At CSCS we argue strongly for greater intellectual challenge - to develop talent, imagination and originality - from a firm foundation of basic skills which will equip all young people effectively for their future lives.

4: The process of designing a (comprehensive) curriculum

(i)   **The first step (after Hirst and Peters) is to articulate aims**. The following is a composite aim, an uncontroversial common denominator of aims expressed by Government and schools designed to reflect the requirements of society's stakeholders and the needs of **all** young people: THE CURRICULUM WE PROPOSE IS DESIGNED TO ENABLE STUDENTS TO ACQUIRE AND DEVELOP (I) KNOWLEDGE AND CONCEPTUAL UNDERSTANDING; (II) SKILLS; (III) PERSONAL QUALITIES AND ATTITUDES TO ENABLE THEM TO TAKE ADVANTAGE OF OPPORTUNITIES AND COPE WITH CHALLENGES IN (IV) THE VARIOUS CIRCUMSTANCES OF THEIR FUTURE LIVES; MORE PARTICULARLY TO ENABLE THEM TO CONTRIBUTE CONSTRUCTIVELY AND SUCCESSFULLY TO SOCIETY IN USEFUL OCCUPATIONS, AS RESPONSIBLE CITIZENS AND IN HOME AND FAMILY CONTEXTS AND TO LEAD ENRICHED AND FULFILLED PERSONAL LIVES.

(ii)   **The second step is to set out the whole range of components of a curriculum** (derived from the above aims) in a full and balanced way. The elements which I have identified from analysis of numerous statements of aims are set out in Diagram 1 (Components of a broad, balanced curriculum).

The summarised[1] components in that diagram are a faithful reflection of the general balance of the curriculum as implied by the aims. Instead of taking the aims as a bland and more or less irrelevant statement (which can be safely ignored as teachers uncritically follow established precedent in teaching 'subjects' which never appear in general statements of aims and which are only weakly and indirectly related to aims, I have taken them as a serious starting point for planning the curriculum and carefully identified each set of components, eg

    (i) **Knowledge and conceptual understanding** – what sorts of knowledge? What types of concepts? Pupils leave school woefully ignorant of much basic information and many leave school functionally illiterate. (This includes many who get five higher grades at GCSE.) (ii) **key generic skills**; in the existing curriculum these are treated as peripheral, or at best secondary, elements.

    The development of (iii) **personal qualities and attitudes.** In all statements of aims, these are given high priority, but in the curriculum, they have low priority; they are in effect set aside and ignored. Fine words find no translation into action; unlike subjects, they receive no systematic planning resourcing.

    The other element described as (iv) **Regions of Application is a direct requirement of the statement of aims** (as argued in Section 2 above) **requiring explicit attention to the 'various circumstances of their future lives', ie where they will hopefully apply their knowledge, skills etc**. Without this element, any list of curricular components (derived from aims which refer to preparing people for their future lives) is

---

1 The full list is available from CSCS in Broadsheet 72 and I would refer the reader back to Richard Pring's observations about the humanising functions of the curriculum in Chapter

incomplete. This is where school curricula are most clearly inadequate – **defining where learning is to be applied** and giving learners experience of applying their learning, so it can become meaningful and useful to them outside the school environment.

The general point here is that a comprehensive curriculum must embrace **all** components and that a broad, balanced curriculum is one which devotes resources (of time and materials, professional training etc) equally (pro rata) to all components.

(iii) **The third step is to arrange the components in relationship to each other so as to make sense of the aims**. Derived directly from aims as generally expressed, a curriculum should develop knowledge, skills, personal qualities etc in order that they can be applied to a variety of circumstances (contexts or 'content'). This is primitively represented in the diagram of beams of light representing acquisition of knowledge, skills and personal qualities illuminating the stage of 'real life' action. Learning (of knowledge, skills and personal qualities) is a process of enlightenment to help people understand and be more competent in all aspects of their lives.

A comprehensive approach to curriculum planning requires thorough attention not just to the individual components of the curriculum but how they fit together to make coherent sense to the learners. The arrangement of elements presented in Table 1 is designed to make sense to the learners – giving the curriculum some obvious intrinsic purpose. The Regions of Application is in this respect a pedagogic tool – a means to enhancing learners' understanding of education, of its purpose, and its value to them.

(iv) **The next step is to engage in a process of refinement and selection**. Limited resources (of staffing, material resources etc) requires selection of elements most importantly   identifying those which have maximum 'generality', ie applicable to the widest range of circumstances.

5: Why current subject-based curricula are inadequate

The simple answer is that, after Hirst and Peters, they are largely a 'nonsense'. Only defective logic and incompetent reasoning would translate schools' and DfES's stated aims into the list of subjects that we see in schools' timetables. The curricular subjects do not follow from stated aims: they are derived from another source – an uncritically accepted tradition which originated in the eighteenth century and became set as established practice in the nineteenth century when universities, in association with (elite) schools laid down what was deemed appropriate for boys who might proceed to higher education – and to offer the other pupils some smattering of learning which might help civilise them.

The result is that in schools today we have a seriously unbalanced curriculum which omits much of what is important (according to stated aims), for example, lack of serious attention (reflected in little timetable time and absence of formal qualifications) to development of personal qualities, learning about the world of work, citizenship, managing one's own financial and other affairs, all of which are consequently perceived by pupils and teachers as being of low status and thus unimportant.

If Diagram 1 is taken as a map of the educational territory, as derived from commonly stated aims, it may be seen that the standard, subject-based curriculum focuses on a very small part of that territory (viz Column 1 Section 6 and some of the skills listed in Column 2) and ignores much of the territory almost completely (ignored in terms of ensuring a serious professional planned approach to them). It is no good saying 'Ah but our school promotes values and develops young men and women' - ie their personal qualities - when everything in that area is casually left to chance. We have our priorities wrong.

The perpetuation of our quasi-academic curriculum is a function of cultural inertia, particularly embodied in teacher training in which intending teachers are trained to appreciate the benefits of teaching their subjects – as a result of which process they arguably sink deeper into grooves of academe – instead of the subjects being considered in regard to their **relative** value in the context of overall educational priorities.

'Most people cannot envisage a curriculum organised other than on a traditional subject basis', (RSA Opening Minds). Difficult though it is to get people to change their mind sets, we must try. If we are to close the gap between schooling and what schooling is for, arguably the cause of so much underfunctioning and low motivation in schools, we must make schooling meaningful and significant (**intrinsically** meaningful and significant, not meaningful and significant just for the paper qualifications to be obtained). This is nicely illustrated by Mary Alice White in *Doing School.* ' Imagine yourself on a ship sailing across an unknown sea to an unknown destination. An adult would want to know where they were going. But a child only knows (s)he is going to school. The chart is not available or understandable to him/her. Very soon the daily life on board ship is what becomes all important – the daily chores, the lessons, the inspections become the reality rather than the voyage and the destination.'

The point of this chapter is that if we are to make the curriculum useful – for academic and practical purposes - we need a new paradigm. We need to change the way people think about the curriculum and get them to open their eyes to its possibilities – embodied in the excellent aims and aspirations - expressed at all levels in education – from Government to individual schools whose achievement is blocked by a curriculum (and qualifications system) which has never been designed to achieve them – a conceptual dog's dinner. 'There's nothing so practical as a good theory' and that's what we've lacked; we need a model that **works**.

6: Criteria of an acceptable comprehensive curriculum

Having set out design processes and considered inadequacies of existing subject-based curricula, it is necessary, before presenting an actual model, to confirm the criteria of an acceptable curriculum and check that it meets them.

Table 1 Criteria of an acceptable curriculum

1.	You are working to a coherent, comprehensive definition of the term curriculum.
2.	a) You have a clear detailed explicit statement of aims embodying your aspirations and ideals b) You have a set of objectives derived from aims which describe what it is you want your pupils to leave school with in the way of personal qualities and attitudes, skills, knowledge and understanding.
3.	Your curriculum is directly derived from your specified ideals, aims and objectives (not derived form other sources, eg public examination requirements).
4.	The curriculum reflects the interests of all stakeholders who stand to benefit (business, public services, academe, etc).
5.	Your curriculum is a broad balanced reflection of the whole range of your stated aims, aspirations and objectives (not skewed towards extrinsic demands of, say, an examination system).
6.	a) Your curriculum maximises benefits to pupils (as stated in your aims) in the context of limited resources – schools can't do everything – by ensuring that decisions about what to include faithfully and directly reflect the priorities of your aims. b) In making selections of what to include, your main criteria are relevance (to your stated aims and priorities) and the extent to which a chosen aspect of study offers the widest range of applications – theoretical and practical – to the widest range of circumstances.
7.	Your educational/curricular priorities are matched by their publicly acknowledged value, ie qualifications.
8.	Your curriculum reflects the best practices of personalising learning: it is adapted to the different and special needs of each individual learner.
9.	a) Your aims and curriculum make sense (ie common sense) to your clients – pupils/parents – in that they clearly see the connection between what is to be studied and what they expect as outcomes (useful knowledge, skills, personal qualities, etc) to prepare them for their present and future lives. b) Your aims and curriculum makes sense to professional educationalists making clear your taxonomy of elements (eg knowledge, general concepts, ideas, skills, personal qualities, context/content) and how the elements are to be arranged and delivered (without omissions and without unnecessary overlap and wasteful duplication).
10.	The various elements of the curriculum are organised and taught in a way which directs and focuses them effectively to achieve your specified aims in a coherent and holistic way (ie not as in the current standard subject-based curriculum which is a disparate collection of unconnected elements).
11.	Your curricular structure has been devised as a pedagogic tool to facilitate and promote learning by so arranging the elements of the curriculum that learners are required to engage in activities which are clearly intrinsically worthwhile and valuable (not just a means to getting qualifications) eg to show how skills, qualities and concepts can make a difference to learners' real lives outside the artificial environment of school.
12.	Having carefully devised your ideal curriculum (eg to equip young people with competences appropriate to their future lives) only then do you consider strategies which enable you to accommodate short-term conventions/pressures imposed by the current qualifications system and other political and cultural constraints.

I argue elsewhere that having analysed the following Regions of Application exemplar which we argue is the only general/universal model available, also the rationale for the RSA Opening Minds Competences Curriculum, the rationale of the International Baccalaureate, the Tomlinson curriculum and the ASDAN Youth Award Scheme, people should check that their curriculum is to their intellectual satisfaction, and, if not, produce a more comprehensive general model.

7: A model of a comprehensive curriculum which meets the above criteria of acceptability being designed to meet the potential needs of all learners

The model in Diagram 1 illustrates the components of a broad and balanced curriculum in their correct relationship. **Learners' competences** (iv), ie their understanding of and ability to apply learning in the various aspects of their lives **are illuminated by the development of (i) knowledge; (ii) skills and (iii) personal qualities**.

A curriculum derived from this model could be organised on the basis of groups of key skills, groups of personal qualities (difficult in practice). The 'traditional variant', Table 2, is based on (A) groups of key skills (given conventional subject titles) 'systematic specialisms' and (B) regions of application (also given conventional subject titles) - holistic 'regional' studies in which the separate key skills etc are applied in different contexts.[2]

In producing a model suited to the needs of all learners I have given particular attention to the development of academic skills and general intellectual understanding, arguably ill-served by the fragmented, patchy nature of the conventional curriculum.

Within systematic studies, especially Column 1, Section (vi), conceptual generalisations may be drawn out. The notion of conceptual generality, a key idea in academic understanding, may be reinforced by the deliberate strategy of encouraging learners to think laterally across all potential areas of application rather than within the limited confines of one academic discipline. The force of a general concept is related to the generality of its applications. As currently taught, academic disciplines tend to be introspective and self-contained, examining a body of internally coherent data but not expanded to be applied outside the discipline's domain.

I would argue that it is of paramount importance is to engage learners in understanding how the development of knowledge, concepts, skills and personal qualities, can enhance their understanding of **all** areas of life thus giving the curriculum an overall coherence and purpose that the fragmented, subject-based one lacks.

---

2 The relationship between (A) and (B) is akin to the division in Geography between systematic specialist studies (eg relief, vegetation, population) and regional studies where the specialist components are brought together and applied 'holistically' in the complex reality of regions.

8: Personalising learning

I note in my chapter 'Defining Comprehensive Education' that Pat Daunt's comprehensive concept of equal value – of every learner (in *Comprehensive Values*, 1975) may be translated into 'every individual is different and special and therefore has different and special needs across the whole spectrum - from disabled to gifted'.

Personalising learning is essentially concerned with adapting education to the needs, preferences and aspirations of every individual learner. 'Personalisation may be seen as a version of (post-Fordist) customisation; putting the customer first, recognising their values, needs and preferences' (David Hargreaves, 2002).

Some have been inclined to think that this is an unrealistic aim. While it would be difficult if not logistically impossible to transform a school curriculum overnight from a static pattern to a very flexible one geared to the abilities, characteristics and special talents of groups of learners, it is not impossible, particularly if one takes advantage of:

a) the vast range of courses available through QCA;

b) working collaboratively in federations of schools and colleges;

c) harnessing the educational opportunities of media and other educational agents in a locality (see Chapter 15 pages 166 and 167)

Of course, virtually all responsible educationists would argue that there are common essential elements which should be taught to all young people. I, for one, am strongly of this opinion - though equally strongly of the view that there should be much greater choice and flexibility. In examining the notion of personalising learning the idea of customisation has validity. We are probably most aware of this in regard to purchasing motor vehicles. But when we require, say, automatic transmission or tinted glass we assume that the model which we want 'customised' or 'personalised' is basically sound. This cannot be assumed with the curriculum which was never designed with the whole range of customers in mind. If we customise our existing subject-based curriculum we're customising a basically defective model. We need a curricular model that puts the individual at the heart of learning (after Leadbetter, 2002). This is what the model presented in this chapter does: it assumes that all learners have more or less different needs but that they are all entitled to a curriculum that provides for the whole range of their present and future needs in the multiplicity of roles they will play in the various circumstances of their future lives, ie is comprehensive.

Diagram 1 A curriculum model derived from expressed aims: an abstract of the Regions of Application Model: Published as CSCS broadsheet number 78, June 2003

THE ELEMENTS OF A BROAD BALANCED CURRICULUM

(I) DEVELOPING KNOWLEDGE AND CONCEPTUAL UNDERSTANDING

1 Essential knowledge for basic competence (including economic, financial, political, technological, scientific, moral 'literacy')

2 Knowledge of problems issues and value conflicts

3 Knowledge of opportunities

4 Further useful knowledge which will generate interest and excite curiosity

5 How to find out more

6 General concepts, models, theories and forms of knowledge, eg empirical and logic based approaches of academic disciplines

(II) DEVELOPING SKILLS AND GENERAL ABILITIES

for example

Learning skills: skills of receiving

ICT etc, visual spatial skills, numeracy

Thinking skills

Problem identification and problem solving, creativity design

Communication skills, oral skills, empathising/conflict, resolution, social skills

Teamwork skills

Physical/kinesthetic skills, including skills for personal health and fitness, practical and technical skills, planning

Entrepreneurial skills etc

(III) DEVELOPING PERSONAL QUALITIES AND ATTITUDES

for example

1 Sound judgement

2 Self-discipline

3 Perseverance, patience and tenacity

4 Drive and initiative, 'can do' attitude

5 Open-mindedness

6 Rationality, determination to be objective, logical and fair

7 Tolerance of those who hold different views

8 Thoughtfulness

9 Sensitivity and empathy

10 Compassion

11 Magnanimity

12 Integrity

13 Courage to stand up for what is right

14 Self-confidence

15 Leadership

etc

(IV) REGIONS OF APPLICATION: CONTEXTS IN WHICH

THE LEARNING IS TO BE APPLIED

a: at work, in occupation individuals are likely to engage – as they have to adapt flexibly to an ever changeable job market

b: as citizens of their local, national, European and wider communities

c: in home and family where critical financial, practical and aesthetic judgements will determine whether their resources

are used wisely and creatively and where as parents they will be responsible for the next generation

d: as individuals with their own independent lives of personal decisions, reflection, recreation and intellectual and spiritual growth

Table 2 A modified version of the Regions of Application Model in a traditional structure

Column 1	Column 2	Column 3	Column 4	Column 5
Core Curriculum Subject Titles	**KEY SKILLS** (see diagram for full list)	**REGIONS OF APPLICATION** (examples)	**Specialist extension studies** (examples)	**ATTITUDES AND PERSONAL QUALITIES** see diagram for full list

A   'SYSTEMATIC' SPECIALISMS (based on clusters of KEY SKILLS) See Column 2

Column 1	Column 2	Column 3	Column 4	Column 5
ENGLISH	Communication/ literacy Learning skills	a World of work b Citizenship including environment c Home and family d Self/individual fulfilment/interest	English Literature Linguistics Philosophy	Activities and experiences designed to develop the whole range of designed attitudes and personal qualities, each to be subject to assessment which will carry as much weight as assessment of knowledge and skills. **Key qualities: examples** 1. **Self-discipline** 2. **Perseverance**, tenacity, courage 3. **Responsibility**, reliability, dependability 4. **Initiative**, entrepreneurial spirit, adaptability, flexibility 5. **Open-mindedness** and spirit of enquiry 6. **Self-confidence** 7. **Thoughtfulness** kindness, tolerance etc see Column 3 of the model in C (4 and 5)
MATHEMATICS/NUMERACY	Application of number/numeracy Problem solving Learning skills	World of work Citizenship including environment Home and family	Philosophy Pure mathematics Applied mathematics Statistics Accountancy	
PHYSICAL SCIENCES	Application of number Problem solving Learning skills Graphicacy Practical/technological	World of work Citizenship including environment Home and family	Physics Chemistry Geology Physical Geography Physical Anthropology Biology Zoology Botany	
TECHNOLOGY, ICT and ENGINEERING	Information technology Problem solving Learning skills Graphicacy Creativity/inventiveness Practical/technological	World of work Citizenship including environment Home	Design studies Architecture Town planning Engineering (various branches, eg vehicle management) Food studies ICT programming	
ARTS	Working with others Communication Learning skills Creativity/inventiveness Practical/technological Personal planning Emotional intelligence	World of work Citizenship Home and family Self, individual fulfilment/interest	Aesthetics Art History of art Ceramics Textiles, fabric and furnishing Music Dance Drama Theatre studies Media studies	

B   INTEGRATED REGIONS OF APPLICATION FOUNDATION SUBJECTS
        THE KEY FOCAL SYNTHESISING STUDIES

Column 1	Column 2	Column 3	Column 4	Column 5
HEALTH AND PHYSICAL EDUCATION incorporating SPORT, SEX EDUCATION, DOMESTIC ECONOMICS , CHILDCARE, PERSONAL RELATIONS AND PSYCHOLOGY	All key skills All personal qualities	c Home and family d Self, individual fulfilment	Anatomy Medical science Sports science Psychology Child care Home economics Domestic science Dietetics	
SOCIAL SCIENCES/ INTEGRATED HUMANITIES including CITIZENSHIP, MORAL AND RELIGIOUS STUDIES	All key skills All personal qualities	b Citizenship c Home and family d Self, individual fulfilment	Human and economic geography History and futurology Sociology Psychology Religious studies Ethics and philosophy Social anthropology Archaeology Political science Law	
BUSINESS STUDIES, ECONOMICS AND FINANCE	All key skills All personal qualities	a World of work also b Citizenship c Home and family	Economics Business Studies Accountancy Home economics	

C   OPTIONS

Column 1	Column 2	Column 3	Column 4	Column 5
eg selected from Column 4- including foreign languages and/or other subjects chosen/created by the school	As appropriate	a World of work b Citizenship including environment c Home and family d Self	All core curriculum subjects to include introduction to each of the above areas of specialist study	

9: Pedagogy, qualifications and status

Inextricably interrelated with the curriculum are issues of pedagogy and assessment/qualifications. Some have been inclined to argue that 'it's not what you teach but how you teach that matters'. This is a misleading and potentially harmful notion. However well taught, it would be difficult to justify a grossly unbalanced curriculum though there should ideally be some room in the curriculum for choice, even for idiosyncrasy, certainly space for learners to pursue their interests in real depth. The essential point is that pedagogy (how) and curriculum (what) are **both** important.

Some argue – and I agree – that the problem lies in a discriminatory, status-ridden qualifications system. We have a veritable thicket of different qualification labels conferring arbitrarily different levels of status to different sorts of work. One principle should apply: **parity of esteem should be accorded on the basis of the quality and standard of the work done regardless of type or content**. In particular, there is nothing more damaging than the labelling of vocational and practical work as of inferior status.

Cartoon: with acknowledgements to Bill Stott.

Conclusion

A comprehensive curriculum must embrace the whole range of components (knowledge, skills etc) in such a way as to enable the comprehensive achievement of the aims the curriculum is designed to achieve. It must equally give maximum opportunity for releasing and developing the talents of all learners of every ability and inclination. We must move on from a curricular system never designed to meet these criteria and realise a new comprehensive curricular paradigm. As I write this in 2005, it is possible to identify some challenges to the old irrelevant order. The Tomlinson proposals and the Nuffield 14-19 Curriculum Review, which penetrates beneath the surface of superficial assumption and untested acceptance of past practice endeavour to examine fundamentally important issues. DfES documentation, eg February 2005 White Paper 14-19 Education, reflects some appreciation that the curriculum has some serious flaws – but it is tentative and conservative. If it wants to achieve the excellent aims it espouses - to make the UK a prosperous and civilised country, a world leader - it needs to be bolder.

Finally, how does this model of a comprehensive curriculum – using the term in its literal sense – relate to the narrower notion of comprehensive as referring to the whole ability range of students? The answer is it is designed equally to draw out the best from students of **all** abilities.

Currently (2005) we see schools struggling to make their curricula more relevant and meaningful to the less able (as defined by those failing to get five good GCSEs) by expanding vocational courses. In virtually all schools (comprehensive and selective) it is assumed that what we call the traditional academic curriculum is appropriate for the above average students. Such thinking exposes absence of thought not just about what might constitute a balanced, relevant, challenging curriculum for all but about the meaning of the term academic. Uncritical acceptance of the term academic hides the fact that the curriculum of so-called 'academic' subjects, mostly overlapping and repetitive in terms of skills and abilities required, bears no particular relevance to the development of skills and qualities, eg organised, systematic thought, analysis, synthesis, imagination and so on, required for quality academic work in higher education, business and the public services: no more relevance (in fact probably less) than in the intellectual challenge required in undertaking a host of practical projects.

In schools the term academic is associated with respectability and status encouraging the lazy assumption that it is educationally acceptable. The Regions of Application model as outlined in this chapter is designed to elicit the knowledge, understanding, concept formation and critical skills so often lacking in the so called academic curriculum. As explained in Section 7 and amplified in Diagram 1 Variant B the whole structure of the Regions of Application model is designed to develop academic understanding and insights more carefully and explicitly than in the current fragmented 'academic' curriculum; the reader might infer here that it is thus more appropriate to the able student; I would argue that the development of such academic understandings and critical skills can be elicited from young people across the spectrum of ability.

In exhorting the profession to think more carefully and critically about the meaning of curriculum and producing a model which considers all aspects of the educational process I am setting out a curriculum which is comprehensive in both the wider and the narrower meaning of the term. The QCA Futures initiative asks many of the right questions; the RSA Opening Minds Project is piloting constructive ways ahead. ASDAN opens up real possibilities. But we are far from our goal.

19 EDUCATION AND TRAINING 14-19: COMPREHENSIVE PROVISION

Richard Pring

Increasingly schools and colleges are required to think of a 14 to 19 phase of education. A recent White Paper (2005) was entitled *14-19 Education and Training*; it followed the Tomlinson Report; the Welsh Assembly Government, post devolution of powers, is developing its own distinctive *Learning Pathways* from 14 to 19. The implications of this for comprehensive schools and the comprehensive system are profound.

14-19 phase of education

Educational provision inevitably needs to be broken into phases. But this always involves a certain arbitrariness (and not a little bad theory) in the division between phases – and between tracks within these phases. According to the Hadow Report (1926), 'there is a tide which begins to rise in the veins of youth at the age of 11; they call it adolescence'. And so the age of 11 seemed an advisable time to split schooling between primary and secondary. (And that split remains even though the tide now rises earlier and faster.) According to the Norwood Report (1943), there are three types of children: those good at thinking; those good at applying practically that thinking; and those who are simply good. And that became a justification for a tripartite system of schooling which, post comprehensive, lingers on in a tripartite tracking system of academic, general vocational and occupationally-based studies.

In seeking a justification for a separate 14-19 phase, therefore, we must be wary. We must be prepared for a degree of arbitrariness – as *post-hoc* justification for what is already emerging in practice.

In practice, certain things are happening. It is the end of Key Stage 3 when all pupils have been measured in their performance in 'core subjects'. It is the beginning of the two year programme towards GCSE when options are selected (sometimes on the basis of relevance to the future). Several subjects of the National Curriculum (which originally constituted a coherent learning package from 11 to 16) can be dispensed with in favour of more 'vocational' options – modern languages and the humanities. Careers advice kicks into gear as decisions are increasingly made and deliberations engaged in with regard to the future after school. And, furthermore, many students (currently over 120,000) are relocated to the very different environment of a further education college for part or the whole of their studies. Indeed, all students are obliged to undertake work experience.

Therefore, in practice, bit by bit, with no master plan, there is a significant change taking place at the age of 14. And, as so often happens, the 'making sense' of that change tries to catch up with the change itself – an attempt to give it a rational basis, a justification. Perhaps the tide that began to rise in the veins of youth at 11 has now become a flood, and a more adult environment and set of attitudes are required. Or perhaps it is an age when 'relevance to the future' becomes a criterion for what is appropriate to study – a criterion in the eyes of both the learner and those who are estimating the needs (economic and social) of the wider society. The period, when education should remain general for everyone (rooted possibly in the logically different forms of knowledge and appraisal), gives way to a period which should be more focused on specific choices and needs.

Of course, aspects of that more general education remain, namely, the continued compulsory study of certain subjects: English (both language and literature), mathematics and science. But others are seen to be no longer relevant in the same way – history, geography, and the arts. A distinction is implicitly made between a *general* education rooted in 'the best that has been thought and said' and a *relevant* education, shaped by an estimation of practical needs.

To summarise, therefore: a 14-19 phase of education and training is now generally accepted as a distinct phase for purposes of policy and practice. Such a phase is characterised by choice of different routes, the opportunity for work based learning and vocational options, the possibility of spending all or some of the time in further education colleges, and a greater emphasis on relevance to subsequent careers and employment, requiring continuing careers advice and counselling. All this is happening at the very time when Middle Schools are being abolished. There is little joined up policy.

Justification for reform

The Tomlinson Working Party had been asked to make recommendations about the most appropriate framework of qualifications for this phase of education and training. Although age 16 is the end of compulsory schooling, the majority of young people remain in some form of education and training, and indeed increased participation and retention are encouraged. Yet many, for whom the experience of education had meant little more than failure and deselection, needed a different kind of educational experience, different kinds of pathways through which they could progress. There is seen to be little future for those who leave school without qualifications, either the academic kind which enables them to proceed into higher education or the more vocational kind which prepare them for the world of work.

At the same time it was not defensible to assume that all would benefit from exactly the same educational provision. Respect needed to be given to different aspirations and motivations, to different learning styles and career ambitions, to different abilities and aptitudes. Different pathways needed to be provided. The danger needed to be avoided of stereotyping all young people (as the Norwood Report did, quoted above) into two or thee types. Hence, the need for different sorts of course and learning pathways, but with flexibility and choice built into the system. Work based learning should be compatible with academic studies. The Tomlinson Report (2004), therefore, recommended an integrated system of qualifications with progression through different levels, leading to an overarching diploma. It sought to achieve, thereby, greater equivalence in value between different kinds of learning, overcoming the low esteem which 'vocational' qualifications have. In the same way, the Welsh Assembly Government is pursuing a flexible system of learning pathways leading to the Welsh Baccalaureate.

However, in England, the government response, through the White Paper *14-19 Education and Training*, has been to maintain the 'academic' route through the current GCSE at 'Level 2' (or Key Stage 4) and the GCE A Levels (the 'cornerstone of the system'), and to create, from the age of 14 onwards, vocational diplomas in 20 vocational areas. In other words, there is being created from age of 14 a dual system – the academic and the vocational. Furthermore, those on the vocational route will follow their studies post 14 partly in the further education sector; post 16, those studies will take place almost entirely in the further education sector or in the work place. Selection, often hidden and unacknowledged, is gradually taking place at 14 and 16, creating in many areas a 'secondary modern system', albeit now in the further education colleges.

Aims and values

As the 14-19 phase of education and training develops into the dual system of awards, learning experience and institutions, it is important to examine the aims and values which are embodied within these developments and shape their direction. However, what is significant is the almost total absence of any attempt by government to articulate these aims – to indicate the overall purpose which underpins the gradual evolution in practice of the 14-19 phase as referred to above. The White Paper does indeed state that it is seeking to enable all young people to realise their potential (and indeed, the 2003 White Paper is entitled *Realising our Potential*). But it requires no sophisticated theological understanding of original sin to see that 'realising potential' as such cannot be an educational aim. Young people have as much 'potential' for doing bad things as they have for doing good. The second major aim set forth in the White Paper is for all young people to be stretched – indeed 'stretching' appears 63 times in one grammatical form or another. But again – stretched in what direction and with what consequences?

The failure to engage in any thoroughgoing analysis of and deliberations about educational aims has its consequences – mainly those of being trapped in an impoverished language through which educational purposes are spelt out. This is reflected particularly in the unquestioned distinction between the 'academic' and the 'vocational' – a distinction which is reflected practically in the different pathways to be maintained and developed. The distinction, however, is by no means clear. 'Academic' is often associated with certain sorts of subject, which do not have vocational relevance and which tend not to require too much 'hands on' experience. They are not seen to be practical; they involve a lot of reading and writing; they contain what is referred to as 'theory'. Such studies are often seen to be worth pursuing for their own sake, irrespective of their usefulness, because they constitute what it *means* to think, to reason, to understand. By contrast, the 'vocational' is shaped, not by reference to what is deemed to be intrinsically worthwhile, but to the skills relevant to a particular job.

But here we can so easily get into trouble. First, in this dichotomy, some very important activities get left out, especially in the arts (art, drama, dance). Are these academic or vocational? They can become 'academic' (talking about drama or studying the history of art), but then they lose their distinctively practical and aesthetic character. Second, the vocational comes to be confused with practical and experiential modes of learning, thereby undermining the practical and experiential for those who pursue the 'academic' pathways. In fact, the distinction between 'academic' and 'vocational', assumed to be self-evident in almost every report and document, is unintelligible upon further examination, yet is coming to shape the learning experiences of everyone.

Those with long memories will see similarities to the late 1960s when the extension of the school leaving age was being planned. A strong lobby argued that vocational relevance and skills training could make the extension viable for a potentially alienated group. But those with a wider vision of relevance argued otherwise; the 'Humanities Curriculum Project', 'Geography for the Young School Leaver' and 'History 13-16' were magnificent efforts to demonstrate the relevance of the humanities to the formation of young people as they prepared for the future (see Stenhouse, 1975). The themes of Shakespeare – love, oppression, injustice, relations between the sexes, authority, violence, jealousy, ambition – were seen to be the very stuff of conversations behind the bicycle shed. At stake were the meaning of education and the relevance of the values it embodied to everyone, irrespective of age, ability or social class.

An *educational* activity, therefore, is one that contributes to a broader perspective, to an understanding which, for whatever reason, is cherished, and to a form of life which is considered valuable. 'Education' is attributed to those activities and attainments which are judged to lead to an improvement of the person in terms of knowledge acquired, understanding achieved, skills mastered, values developed. Therefore, the establishment of the aims of education – what counts as an educated person in our society – is part of a much bigger moral debate. Vocational training can be conducted in an educational manner – that is, in such a way that implicit values are challenged, underlying principles understood and the wider social context appreciated. One can be educated *through* vocational training – it depends on the manner in which the training is conducted.

Reform of the 14-19 phase of education and training, therefore, needs to begin with the question: 'What counts as an educated 19 year old in this day and age?'

The answer will depend on the kinds of qualities and achievements which constitute the kind of life thought to be worth living, and the kind of society thought to be worth creating. Hence, there is a need for a constant appraisal of the values which are embedded in educational practice, which shape the learning experiences of young people, and which should reflect the changes in society and the wider environment.

In particular
- What knowledge and understanding (in different degrees depending on ability and interests) should all young people be helped to develop?
- What are the qualities and virtues which should be nurtured?
- What social competencies should be taught in preparation for adult life?
- What interests should young people be enabled to develop to enrich their lives (in, for example, the arts and sports)?
- What skills, knowledge and guidance do all young people need in order to choose a career which will be fulfilling and make them economically viable?
- What ideals of achievement and commitment should they be invited to respond to?

There are several implications of these considerations for the development of comprehensive schooling and the comprehensive system, two being a revision of the curriculum and a reform of the institutional framework.

Curriculum principles

Dividing the learning experience into the 'academic' and the 'vocational' from the age of 14 (with little consideration of how the 'vocational' might be an *educational* experience) distorts or ignores the questions raised above which are relevant to all young people and which are neither 'academic' nor 'vocational'. They are relevant across categories of ability, social background, religion and ethnicity. They evoke the principles which shape the development of the curriculum in a genuinely inclusive and comprehensive setting.

Such principles would include

Listening and responding to the voice of the learners in the shaping of the curriculum, including an attempt to understand the cultural environment which shapes their perceptions and values. There is ample research evidence to show how disengagement from education arises so often from the disconnection of the curriculum from the interests and concerns which animate young people. As targets are relentlessly pursued, so there is less room for the deliberation and discussion of issues of deep personal concern, even though such issues are at the core of the humanities (in literature, drama, history and the arts).

Introducing the concepts and skills through which young people might understand the physical, social and personal worlds they inhabit. That is precisely what the subjects of the traditional curriculum are supposed to be doing, but, as is admitted by subject specialists and professional associations, the connections between subject knowledge and the experiences and concerns of young people too often are not made. But there are currently interesting developments where subject associations, teachers, charitable foundations and examination boards are reclaiming the curriculum, relating it more closely to the interests and concerns of young people who do not aim to pursue those subjects in any academic depth. The University of York, supported by the Nuffield Foundation and cooperating with the examination board, OCR, is developing a suite of science curricula relevant to the 21st century. Similar developments are occurring in the humanities and mathematics – curricula which are faithful to the logical demands of the subject matter but maintaining relevance to the non-subject concerns and interests of the learner.

Focusing on pedagogy as much as on the curriculum content, especially valuing practical and experiential learning, emphasising co-operative learning and group goals and tasks, finding a place for the learners' personal and social experience, stressing the importance of evidence based discussion and using the retrieval methods of modern technology to support independent learning.

Providing opportunity for the exploration of values, especially through the arts and the humanities which focus upon what it means to be human and on an appreciation of human relations. So many of the 'big issues' which concern us all slip between the syllabuses of the different subjects – sustainability of the environment, global warming, racism in society at large or in our neighbourhoods.

Making available continuing personal support and guidance as young people require help in pursuing studies which will be personally fulfilling and which will ensure progression into higher education, further training or employment.

Such principles recognise the diversity of learners in terms of motivation, aspiration, prior experience and abilities. They recognise the educability of all young people – in different ways and at different levels – not just an academic few. They reflect, too, the importance of community – the sharing of the exploration of those issues and values which concern us all.

Assessment and qualifications

One barrier to learning across the relevant cohort of students is the demands of an assessment regime which is determined more by accountability than by a support for learning. 'Assessment for learning' is now the currency, but it is difficult to reconcile this with the 'high stakes testing' which leads to league table positions and to public shaming and blaming. Furthermore, assessment as it is presently conceived determines the kind of learning which is encouraged, rather than the other way around. If practical and experiential learning are important, it is necessary to find ways of assessing it without turning it into an academic exercise.

The Tomlinson Report was open to criticism, not so much for the quality of its work (it responded to its brief admirably in proposing an integrated framework of qualifications) but rather in the task it was set in the first place. A framework of qualifications requires prior decisions about the kind of learning to be encouraged and the appropriate ways in which that learning might be assessed. The structure of qualifications is not where reform should begin. Hence, there is a danger that the new vocational diplomas which are to be taught from 2008 onwards will be developed without proper analysis of the kind of learning which is desirable at key stage 4 – in what might be referred to as the prevocational education prior to selecting options which relate to occupational standards. There is a confusion between the 'prevocational' – more practically based general education with a vocational orientation – and vocational which teaches or trains in these skills which meet national occupational standards.

Institutional framework

However, such an extension of the principles which shaped comprehensive schools from the onset – namely, recognition of the potential for learning of all young people, albeit in different ways and to different degrees, inclusiveness in the recognition of all young people within the same learning community, opportunities to progress in different ways according to talent and aspiration, respect for each person irrespective of background or type of achievement – requires a revision of the institutional framework. It is not possible for such a variety of experiences and opportunities to be made available within the traditional school. There are neither the resources nor the expertise.

Therefore, the government speaks often of the need for collaboration and partnership between providers and with other institutions whose main job is not to provide formal education as such – voluntary bodies such as Changemakers, private training providers, employers, centres of the arts, museums. Indeed, schools would be increasingly seen as 'learning organisations', ensuring that each young person is able to benefit from the resources and expertise which are scattered around a wide range of providers.

Already this is happening to a greater extent than is generally known. Under the Increased Flexibility Programme many schools are co-operating with further education, using their facilities and teaching staff. Schools are, in many areas, 'clustered' together for the sharing of resources and teaching staff, possibly with a joint centre for vocational and practical learning. In such clusters there may be common timetables to facilitate the sharing of facilities – some schools taking the A Level physics from the neighbourhood, the others taking the A Level French, yet another specialising in Business Studies. Indeed, such clusters are now entering into 'federations' with a common governing body.

All this is changing the landscape of education and training – and the very meaning of a comprehensive system. Such a system would no longer mean a collection of autonomous and competing comprehensive schools, but a formally co-operating group of schools and colleges which, between them, provide flexibly for a wide range of interests, aspirations and talents.

However, although such a collaborative system is advocated and although many schools and colleges struggle bravely to achieve it, so much militates against it, undermining the very principles of comprehensive education. Collaboration sits uncomfortably with the competitive spirit which is shaped by league tables and examination results. The creation of Academies with different funding and admissions arrangements militates against collaboration. Colleges are funded on a different basis from schools for doing the same kind of work. 11-16 schools are encouraged to develop 6th forms even where there are adequate places in local colleges and where collaboration between providers would make more sense. The quality of work based learning requires much closer partnership between providers and employers. Collaboration costs money in coordination and transport, and too often that money is not forthcoming.